Two Years in Kurdistan

Also from Westphalia Press
westphaliapress.org

Two Years in Kurdistan
Experiences of a Political Officer, 1918-1920

by W. R. Hay

Introduction by Paul Rich

WESTPHALIA PRESS
An imprint of Policy Studies Organization

Westphalia Press
An imprint of Policy Studies Organization
1527 New Hampshire Ave., NW
Washington, D.C. 20036
info@ipsonet.org

ISBN-13: 978-1-63391-363-9
ISBN-10: 1-63391-363-5

Cover design by Jeffrey Barnes:
jbarnesdesign.com

Daniel Gutierrez-Sandoval, Executive Director
PSO and Westphalia Press

Updated material and comments on this edition
can be found at the Westphalia Press website:
www.westphaliapress.org

INTRODUCTION
by Paul Rich

Although Kurdistan is divided among five nations [Turkey, Iran, Iraq, Syria, the Soviet Union], and recognized by none, its people are united by blood, language, and sentiment – a sentiment often manifested in violent rebellion, which even the most brutal suppression has failed to stamp out. – Archie Roosevelt, *For Lust of Knowing*, 1988.

Britain put together three dissimilar provinces of the former Ottoman Empire, Mosul, Baghdad and Basra, with disparate populations of Shiites, Sunnis, Assyrians, and Kurds, and created the country of Iraq. Like Jordan, Iraq (name taken from the ancient Assyrian city of Uraq) was a country that was not a nation. – *Bet-Nahrain*, Assyrian exile journal, November 1990.

Kurdistan does not exist, which is why it is so important. It does not exist as a sovereign political unit; it does most certainly exist as a nation. This anomalous situation has long been part of the Middle East conundrum. Many nationalities of far smaller size have their own states. Few of such numbers and antiquity lack a sovereign homeland. None have exhibited more tenacity in seeking autonomy.

To understand Kurdistan's suffering it is necessary to understand something about Arab intransigence towards Kurdish aspirations and also something about recondite machinations by the foreign intelligence services involved through the years in Kurdish affairs. The Kurdish 'problem', like the Palestinian 'problem', has long served the purposes of all but those who are most affected. If ever *oxymoronic* could be applied to a political situation as well as to a phrase, the Kurdish struggle deserves the term.

Saladin was a Kurd, but there have been few Kurdish successes since his time. This really suited everyone but Kurds: Americans trying to thwart Russians, Iranians undermining Iraq, Gulf shaikhs stirring up trouble for both Iraq and Iran, and a baker's dozen of other plotters and intriguers. They all found Kurdish troubles to be a useful camouflage for their own priorities. Nor have the Kurds themselves been united: tribalism has been a curse since time immemorial for them. Spasmodically courted and more frequently shunned, they were demanding their day in court well before the author of *Two Years in Kurdistan*, William Rupert Hay, administered the largely Kurdish region of Arbil in Iraq for the Indian Political Service (IPS) in 1918–20.

For most people, at least until 1991 when the Kurdish calamity in the aftermath of the 'Hundred-Hour War' demanded the media's attention. Iraq has been an Arab country, pure and simple. In actual fact it is not and it never has been – not even going back to before the days of Nebuchadnezzar in the sixth century BC. If history is a matter of squatters' rights, there is more reason to think of Iraq as Kurdish rather than as Arab. The Arab refusal to own up to Iraq's multiculturalism, and the bitter confrontation between the various races in Iraq, is not a new phenomenon; pogroms have been depressingly regular.

The unwillingness of the Iraqi Arabs to accept the historical reality that they live in a diverse society and that they share the area known as Iraq with other national groups, some of whom had been on the scene long before any Arabs arrived, has frustrated all efforts for a peaceful solution to the country's continual civil warfare. The same contumacious refusal to acknowledge the rights of fellow countrymen and the existence of a pluralistic culture is a paramount problem of the majority of Arab and Islamic states, states whose governments today constitute the majority of the world's remaining totalitarian regimes.

Described by Arnold Toynbee in *A Study of History* as 'highlanders', Kurds cherish an identity which predates Islam by many centuries. Possessed of a rich folklore and music, they have always fought efforts to 'Arabize' their culture. They were forcefully incorporated in the Ottoman Empire by Sultan Selim the Stern and Inflexible in 1514. Although repressive, in respects and in retrospect the Turkish yoke through the centuries was considerably lighter than the impositions introduced by the Iraq state created after the First World War.[1] Despite the Muslim conquest of their homeland, Kurds have jealously preserved their identity. Racially they are Indo-European and have a recorded past going back to the time of the Assyrian Empire in the seventh century BC. A strength has been their highly expressive language, endowed with a considerable literature and one which has made a contribution to Arabic – a tongue which owes far more to other languages such as Hebrew, Assyrian and Kurdish than its speakers like to admit.

Nomadic herdsmen devoted to flocks of sheep and no respecters of Ottoman boundaries – let alone twentieth-century borders conjured up by distant bureaucracies – the Kurds have been notoriously contemptuous of any sort of impositions from Baghdad. That has been the case whether the authority was British or Bathist. An observer in 1943 warned that 'whatever may be thought of the Iraq state, its difficulties seem larger the better you get to know them'. The Kurds not only had a strong sense of community but were 'extremely jealous of their own freedom and local independence', and their affinities were with other Kurds across the Turkish and Persian frontiers rather than with the Kurds of the plains: 'The dislike of the Kurds for the Iraqis has been compared with that of the eighteenth-century Scottish Highlanders for the English, and the analogy is a helpful one.'[2]

The comparison of the Kurds to stubborn Scottish highlanders recurs too often to be entirely without substance. A. M. Hamilton, a road engineer in the late 1920s and early 1930s in the area that Hay had administered, made the same comparison with the Scots, finding that the Kurds were: 'a "dour" lot of people, so like are they in their reserve and taciturnity to the hillmen of Scotland. They have not the graceful manners of the Arabs, nor the same flattering eloquence to an unknown guest: yet I was to find that they had many more solid qualities.' A race 'poor yet proud' was Hamilton's summary.[3]

Hamilton's *Road Through Kurdistan* not only ruminates on the Kurdish character but mentions some of the same individuals that are prominent in Hay's book, including Nuri Bahil and Ismail Beg: the feud which Hay started between Bahil and Beg by appointing Ismail the Governor of Rawanduz ended in Hamilton's time with Bahil murdering Beg. Hay himself had become something of a legend when Hamilton arrived, and he was shown 'historic' spots where the Captain's various exploits had occurred.

The fierce Kurdish pride was well known to T. E. Lawrence (Lawrence of Arabia), who had first encountered Kurds while on an archaeological dig at Karkamis in Syria in 1911 and who had learned Kurdish. His experiences led him to support the idea of a Kurdish buffer state between Iraq and Turkey, but he was overruled at the Cairo Conference of 1922 which settled the boundaries of the post-war Middle East. Anyone such as Lawrence with a knowledge of the situation has doubts about the viability of Iraq as a country. For example, E. S. Stevens, a journalist who contributed to the *Baghdad Times* and *Times of Mesopotamia* in the 1920s, wrote in 1923 about the intractable nature of Iraq's ethnic-sectarian rivalries:

To leave Iraq to the Iraqi sounds excellent as a phrase, but what does it mean? To begin with, the Iraqi is not exclusively Arab or exclusively Moslem. Iraq contains several nations and several vestiges of nations, several creeds and many sects; in fact, the great land of two rivers, in which the Tower of Babel was built, is still a land of many tongues, many peoples and many creeds, between whom there is, in varying degrees, deadly hatred and intolerance. There are nearly a million Sunnis, a million and a quarter Shiahs, a quarter of a million Kurds, nearly as many Jews and Christians, besides Yazidis or devil worshippers, Sabaeans and others. To whom should power be given? [4]

Thus to the historically informed there is nothing surprising about the way Saddam Hussain has treated the Kurds. He is part of a dreary tradition of periodic reprisals against

Kurdish national aspirations launched by whoever ruled in Baghdad. Genocidal attacks on the Kurds and other Iraqi ethnic groups are not novel and neither are double- and triple-crosses in which high hopes stirred by outside forces are eventually dashed. The few occasions when reconciliation has ben attempted by Iraqi authorities themselves have ended in frustration. When the then prime minister of Iraq, Nuri al-Said, attempted to defuse the issue in 1944 by including Kurdish studies in the schools and a single Kurdish minister in the cabinet, he was soundly defeated by his fellow ministers.

For every such reasonable effort as Nuri al-Said's at a compromise, there have been a depressing number of violent attempts at solution.[5] Much has been made of Saddam Hussain's poison-gas attacks on Kurdish villages in 1988, but far more Kurds died in the 1960s and 1970s when the Bathist ruling party prosecuted a merciless campaign against them, highlighted by the massacre at Dakan (8 August 1969) when the village's women and children were burnt alive in a cave where they were hiding. The Kurds then were, as they so often have been, pawns in the international power game. The CIA in 1968–69 was peddling a fabricated story which the *New York Times, Newsweek*, the *Daily Mail* and *Le Monde* innocently picked up: the Russians were arming the leftish Kurds in order to destabilize democratic Iraq. A leading Kurdish nationalist, Mustapha Al Barazani, was dubbed the Red Mulla. However, the investigative reporter Sefton Delmer, a psychological warfare expert, disclosed that the arms actually were being furnished to the Kurds by the CIA, which was supplying Russian arms that had been captured by the Israelis in the 1967 Six-Day War.[6]

In the spring of 1974 the towns of Qualaat Diza and Zakho were napalmed and then razed, Kurdish students at Baghdad University were executed simply for being Kurds, and the town fathers of Erbil were all hanged. An estimated five thousand Kurds died in trying to escape from these horrors to Turkey. At least 100,000 Kurds sought asylum in Iran.[7] Of course, none of these incidents received a small fraction of the publicity that the recent débâcle did.

Hay and his fiefdom

Hay provides a thorough discussion of Kurdish society; he was not the only IPS agent to display such literary talent. The biographies of IPS officers who served in the Middle East which are contained in my *The Invasions of the Gulf* (Allborough, 1991) include the particulars of the volumes that the officers produced and which constitute an amazing library of first-hand observations about the Middle East. Sir Arnold Wilson wrote a shelf of books about the region and other Gulf contemporaries of Hay such as Harold Dickson (*The Arab of the Desert*) and Trenchard Fowle (*Travels in the Middle East*) have left equally important contributions. One of the purposes of *The Invasions of the Gulf* is to provide an introduction to the literature produced by the IPS.

Hay's book was published by Sidgwick & Jackson in 1921 at a time when the Paris Peace Conference of 1919 and the Treaty of Sèvres of 1920 had made Kurdish freedom seem a certainty. The Conference of San Remo earlier in 1920 had established the Great Power mandates in the Middle East, and the liquidation of the Ottoman Empire at Sèvres seemed only a housekeeping chore. Armenia was to get its independence; Kurdistan was to get at least autonomy. This reckoned without the success of Atatürk, who by restoring Turkish morale and by a spirited military campaign was able to force the concessions of the Treaty of Lausanne (1923), an accommodation with the Turks which conveniently omitted any reference to a Kurdish state.

None of this transpired with much knowledge or understanding of the peoples being shunted about. The area then, as Hay remarks, was *terra incognita* to Westerners. Nor has much changed in that respect, although the maps of Hay's fiefdom have names such as Mosul, Sharqat and Kirkuk that have been made a little more familiar following the Turkish tragedy of 1991. Misfortune is not new in those cities, which have sheltered not only Kurds but other hounded minorities, including Assyrians and Jews.[8] Recent Assyrian complaints about what has befallen them are similar to Kurdish ones: 'The Assyrians, who were promised their national rights by the Allies and fought side by side with the Allied Powers, were used as a "political football" to get Mosul from Turkey. France accepted the British plan, drawn by Mr Lloyd George, which left Mosul out of the French zone in exchange for a promise of 25% of Iraq's oil.[9] Armenians and Assyrians have endured as much as Kurds: homelessness and destitution are the least of what the region's minorities have faced throughout the years.

Two Years in Kurdistan gives a succinct account of the desperate efforts to create a civil administration in Iraq after the Armistice of November 1918, and details a grim picture of conditions in northern Iraq after the collapse of Ottoman rule. As the British penetrated deep into Iraq, anarchy spread. The Mesopotamian confusion provided a new playing-field for the IPS, which furnished the Political Resident and Political Agents who ran the Gulf shaikhdoms. Sir Arnold Wilson, sometime Gulf Political Resident and subsequently Civil Commissioner for Iraq, personally selected many of the new officers. Wilson was obliged to go outside the IPS and Indian Civil Service (ICS) in order to obtain enough staff, recruiting young British and Indian Army subalterns (page 19). A number of officers who would serve in the Gulf shaikhdoms in the era after the First World War, such as Hay, were originally chosen for Mesopotamia and only later joined the IPS. They were in their twenties and recent products of English public schools; they found themselves prefects absolutely in charge of areas as large as, or larger than, Wales or Yorkshire. These were swashbuckling days for the Imperial services, and some of the individuals that Hay recounts meeting were extraordinary. The Kurdish leaders were larger than life – Hama Agha, the ruler of the district around Koi, claimed to be 130 and perhaps was 95, smoked a two-foot-long pipe and produced a son when 90 (page 119).

Hay's story, for all its romance, is ultimately a story of failure. There were high hopes not only among Kurds but among Christians and other minorities that the British were going to bring a new beginning to an area that had been in constant turmoil. Certainly the portents were there. Much could be expected of the IPS, which often exercised more than the usual supervisory responsibilities in the affairs of the native Indian states and of the Gulf shaikhdoms – sometimes engaging in highly extracurricular activities. Hay's account

illustrates, as in his story of the abduction and death of
Yousuf Beg (pages 186ff.), that the British had little trepida-
tion about the means justifying the ends. There was no lack
of talent. The Mosul division to which Hay was posted was
under the direction of Gerard Leachman:

> Lieutenant Gerard Evelyn Leachman was a one-man band;
> all the heroes of Rider Haggard, *Boy's Own Paper* and the
> North-West Frontier rolled into a single frame; lithe, fear-
> less and belligerent . . . He set himself a single, uncompli-
> cated task in life, the defence of the Empire, and he often
> behaved as though he carried the entire burden of that
> struggle on his shoulders.[10]

For all this experience, self-confidence, and aplomb, the
IPS was no more able to straighten out the Kurdish situation
than anyone else. The scenes of desolation and despair following the American attack on Iraq in 1991 have their counter-
parts in the period Hay was writing about. However, the IPS
agents have not been the sole *agents provocateurs* to be involved in Kurdish issues. Political and intelligence officers of
several countries, sharing a strikingly similar old-boy *élan*,[11]
have enjoyed playing cat-and-mouse with the Kurds, whose
unhappy geographical dispersal over five countries means
that encouraging national aspirations has usually been useful to someone in squaring accounts with someone else. This
has been with scant regard for the subsequent fate of the
Kurds themselves. American temporizing after the defeat of
Iraq in the Hundred-Hour War of February 1991 was in respects a dismal replay of what the British did to Kurdish
hopes in the aftermath of the First and Second World Wars.

Competing powers in the Middle East have long manipu-
lated Kurdish aspirations for their own highly Machiavellian
purposes. As one consequence, an enormous amount of sub-
sidized printed material with murky origins circulates within
the expatriate Kurdish communities in the Middle East, a
bibliographer's nightmare. At the Doha Club in Qatar in the
Gulf I was once shown by a Kurdish exile a professionally
printed version in Kurdish of the infamous CIA assassination

manual.[12] Was this a canard promoted by a rival agency, or
mischief-making by an overly enthusiastic local American
operative? In its naïvety it would seem to be deliberate misin-
formation promoted by a competitor. There are in addition
many Arab translations of alleged CIA documents in circulation in the Gulf. Clandestine radio broadcasts have been
another source of disinformation, an instance being those
urging the Kurds to rebel against Saddam Hussain. The
making of such appeals to the Kurds to rise up became a
strong moral argument for further American intervention in
Iraq when Saddam Hussain beat the insurgents down.[13]

A familiar pattern

Thus from the time of Rupert Hay until now, there is a pat-
tern of Western involvement with the Kurds as with the
other Middle Eastern minorities: encouraging them and
egging them on, and then abandoning them. The crocodile
tears are quickly dried when other concerns press. Although
thanks partly to Saddam Hussain it appears that the Kurds
finally have paid enough of a price to get the world's attention, past solutions have been only temporary. In the mean-
time there has been a diaspora that has taken them near and
far. Anyone who has spent time in the Arabian Gulf will have
met Kurds, and there are lots of them in the shaikhdoms –
managing a local national's business, farming, teaching,
nursing – often concealing their origins, and each with a
story of flight by themselves or by their parents or by their
grandparents during the purges of the last seventy years.
When I lived in Qatar, a Kurdish gentleman used to joke to
me with gallows humour: 'Kurds are not in exile. I am plan-
ning to be in exile but first I have to get a country from which
to be in exile.' Genocide would not be too harsh a word for
what has been their lot. Concern for their welfare comes
rather late.

More common than any concern for their welfare has been
concern about their usefulness. As *Two Years in Kurdistan*
makes clear, the Kurds were a client of the British officers
struggling to administer Iraq in the uncertain days after the
invasion of Iraq during the First World War and in the dis-

turbances which followed that invasion. It is important to
bear in mind that Hay's book is written by someone serving
under and very much admiring Sir Arnold Wilson. The use of
Wilson's photograph as a frontispiece is an indication of this
admiration that many of the young 'Politicals' had for him
(see pages 16 and 318). Hay writes as a 'true believer' in Wilson's gospel.

Wilson was second-in-command to the 'Uncrowned King' of
the Gulf, Sir Percy Cox. Wilson and Cox were not content
with their suzerainty over the Gulf states. Their ambitions
included adding Iraq to the British Empire. The loyalty and
affection that Hay and the others working under them display gives some idea of the charisma of those two leaders.
Using their positions as Political Residents in the Gulf, they
made a bid to create nothing less than a second Indian Empire, an Arab Empire.

In some ways they came much closer to achieving their
dream than did their rival, T. E. Lawrence – Hay was writing
his account of Kurdistan at the same time that Lawrence was
writing his much more celebrated account of his own adventures. Hay urges that there be forceful and direct British intervention, one of the reasons being that otherwise the
various minorities will be 'consumed' (page 316). Following
the general uprising of 1920, into which Hay gives an insight,
the decision was rather for a halfway house. A monarchy was
created and the British were shadowy advisers. As with the
Gulf shaikhdoms, this proved a frustrating and unsatisfactory solution.

The old-boy mind

Two Years in Kurdistan is an example of how much the history of the Gulf depends on the administrations of the IPS
Residents and Agents. Hay begins with an acknowledgement
of Arnold Wilson's encouragement and a nod to E. B. Sloane's
noteworthy *To Mesopotamia and Kurdistan in Disguise*
(1912) and to my distant relative C. J. Rich's *Residence in
Koordistan* (1836). The tradition of British administration (or
interference) was already firmly established when Hay was
writing. Describing the appointment in 1909 as Kuwait's

Political Agent of Captain William Shakespear, then Cox's First Assistant at the Gulf Residency in Bushire, H. V. F. Winstone remarks: 'The newly appointed Political Agent adhered firmly to the edict of Britain's finest Consul in the East, Claudius Rich, who exerted a dominating influence over the Baghdad Residency in the early days of the nineteenth century and who left for his successors a rule for dealing with Oriental despots: "Nothing but the most decisive conduct will do; any other will increase the insolence of his disposition." '[14] (Claudius by family tradition was a Freemason and may have played a part in propagating Masonry in the Middle East.)

Hay's career was protypical of the 'Gulfites', the IPS officers who spent considerable time in the shaikhdoms rather than India, and his views take on extra significance when it is realized that he would become the successor to Cox and Wilson as Political Resident in the Gulf in the years 1946–55. A predominant characteristic of the 'old-boy mind' was the way in which it fastened on to the rituals of rule and made constant use of ceremony and symbolism to enforce hegemony. This attention to minute detail occupied Hay when he was Gulf Resident. For example, he engaged in a lengthy correspondence with the Political Agent at Kuwait, G. N. Jackson, about the Kuwaiti shaikh's use of a crown – frowned upon because it was considered the prerogative of the British monarchy.

Hay followed the careful path which brought a young public-school boy to the glittering Imperial prizes. He was born in 1893, the son of a medical doctor, William A. E. Hay. At the age of 14 he went off to Bradfield College, where he spent the years 1907–13. Hay gave the name of Harold Costley-White, headmaster at Bradfield for his last three years there, as a reference when he applied to the IPS, giving as another reference the Viceroy, Lord Chelmsford.

School success was an important beginning for an Imperial life. Hay was a Foundation Scholar and spent five years in the Upper Sixth (1909–13). He won the Wilder Divinity Prize in 1911, 1912 and 1913, and the Denny English Prize in the same years. He was the Stevens Scholar in 1911 and 1913 and became the school's Head Prefect. Open-air Greek plays were a hallmark of Bradfield and Hay played Clytemnestra in the school's Greek production of 1913.

He was only briefly at University College, Oxford, in 1913–14, winning a Heron Exhibition. In 1914 he joined the Army. So when he arrived in Kurdistan, the major experience in his life had been his public school.

Relatively late marriage is another characteristic of the Gulfites. In 1925 Hay married Sybil Ethel, daughter of Sir Stewart Abram, the Mayor of Reading. After his stint in Iraq he started on the IPS ladder. He was Assistant Political Agent at Chitral in 1921–22 and then Assistant Commissioner in Bannu in 1922–23. A year as Superintendent of the gaol in Bannu in 1923 was followed by being Political Officer in Moradabad in 1923–24. He was Assistant Commissioner in Tank in 1924, Political Agent in Wana in 1924–25, and Political Agent in South Waziristan in 1925–28. After being Deputy Commissioner in Peshawar in 1930–31, he became Special Magistrate for sentencing arising out of the D. I. Khan riots of 1931. A more senior appointment followed as Political Agent in Swat in 1931–32.

Having amassed seniority and not blotted his copybook, Hay became Chief Secretary for the North-West Frontier in 1932–33. Then he was Counsellor at the Kabul legation in 1933–36. He became Deputy Secretary of the Foreign Department of the Government of India in 1936, which changed its name to the External Affairs Department and which he continued to serve as Deputy Secretary in 1937–40. A short time as Temporary Resident in Waziristan in 1940–41 was followed by being sent back to the Gulf as Officiating Gulf Resident in 1941–42.

He was now at the top of the IPS ladder and was Resident in Baluchistan in 1942–46. Then he became the Gulf Resident for the important transitional period of 1946–47, retiring in 1948 on an IPS pension but continuing as the Gulf Resident under Commonwealth and then Foreign Office auspices until 1955. For these accomplishments he was made a Companion of the Order of the Indian Empire in 1932, a Companion of the Order of the Star of India in 1943, a Knight Commander of the Order of the Indian Empire in 1947, and a Knight Commander of the Order of St Michael and St George in 1952. He was elected a Fellow of the Royal Geographical

Society in 1924 and was a member of the East India Club. In short, he was one of the most important of the Gulf Residents.

The only thing Rupert Hay (which was what he preferred to be called) ever did that departed from the IPS career scenario was to be a Roman Catholic. He belonged to the Challoner Club in London, a gentlemen's club for Catholics which included high-ranking prelates. One of his sons went to Ampleforth and became a cleric, eventually being appointed head of the pontifical college in Rome for training English Catholics for the priesthood. Hay died on 3 April 1962, fortunately while the Gulf was still a British lake.

The mentality of the Gulfites was created in the English public schools. This was not altogether a bad preparation for ruling. The Gulfites were courageous: *Two Years in Kurdistan* surely proves that – witness the nonchalance with which Hay views attempts on his life. They exhibited a remarkable concern for the nuances of dress and decorum: Hay had a helmet with plumes, a home service helmet, a routine Indian helmet, and a cocked hat. They expected deference. But most important, their first concern was for the Empire, not for Kurds or Arabs or Assyrians.

The legacy

There are at least two ways to read *Two Years in Kurdistan.* It is an excellent source of information about the Kurds and there the matter can be left, or the reader can also consider the book as the product of a man who, twenty-five years later, would have a crucial say in the creation of the present Gulf. Here is evidence of the lasting influence on the Middle East of the protégés of George Curzon, Percy Cox and Arnold Wilson. Hay was staunchly a 'Wilson man' in the Gulf in the period following the First World War; when he was his own man in the Gulf following another war, he still displayed this affection.

The trials of Sir Percy Cox, KCIE, the tribulations of Sir Arnold Wilson, KCIE, and much later the frustrations of Sir Rupert Hay, KCIE, as British Political Residents in the Gulf illustrate the old-boy syndrome's not always salutary effects.

If Arnold Wilson was Imperialism's Gulf acolyte in the Ed-
wardian era, then Percy Cox was its high priest, and Rupert
Hay became the altar-boy and one of the successors.

The continuities in the style of the British IPS officers
during the time between Victoria and Elizabeth II are extraordinary. Cox himself was the chosen of Lord Curzon and
his career was the familiar one of an IPS recruit. At Harrow
from 1878 to 1882, he served in the Indian Army before entering the IPS in 1890. His chance meeting with Curzon
while serving in his first posting in Somalia (then a posting
for the IPS) was the beginning of a lifelong friendship that
aided in his promotion to Gulf Resident. The subsequently in-
tertwined careers of Cox and Wilson and then the involvement of Hay with both of these senior men help suggest how
the Imperial creed was passed along in the Gulf.

During the furore surrounding the Iraqi invasion of
Kuwait and the subsequent events, there has been only
muddled and slight mention of the circumstances at the
beginning of the century which produced the present Middle
Eastern quagmire. The exaltedness, and on occasion the
gross pomposity of the Resident in the Gulf, deserves much
more attention than it has received in accounts of what has
shaped the Gulf states. A fear of appearing too colonial in
outlook, too Western in viewpoint, too Imperialist in approach has distorted the work of a generation of Middle East
historians. The fact is that the Gulf was invaded with far
more permanent consequences by the British than it was by
Saddam Hussain or by the Americans. The uncrowned kings
of the Gulf were the Residents and Agents of the IPS. British
servicemen in the Middle East carried a card in Arabic stating that they were friends of 'Kakkus', the Arabian proconsul.
Yet he was, wrote another Gulf Resident, Sir Olaf Caroe, '. . .
forgotten by a later generation, to whom Cromer and
Lawrence are almost household words but who, seemingly,
have never heard of Sir Percy Cox, perhaps because he
possessed neither the Roman gravitas of the one nor the Re-
naissance flamboyance of the other'.[15]

The IPS claim to have a right to an involvement in Middle
Eastern affairs reaching beyond the Gulf into Mesopotamia
was enhanced by the fact that India was forced to provide the
matériel for the Middle Eastern campaigns. This was ex-

plained away and rationalized by claiming India's own security was involved. A quarter of a million Indian troops served
in the notoriously mismanaged Mesopotamian Command.
Like soldiers everywhere, they left a genetic legacy: Gulf
Arabs and Iraqis have Indian as well as African and Persian
blood, although few parts of the world of such heterogeneous
lineage proclaim more stridently a bogus racial homogeneity.

While homogeneity can be maintained as an ivory-tower
fiction, it cannot be maintained effectively in the bustle of
everyday affairs. Iraq has long floundered on that most vexa-
tious and poisonous of all the Middle East issues, the refusal
to accept a pluralistic and multicultural society. The minority
Sunnis in Iraq, as elsewhere in the region, insisted on carrying the mythology of an all-embracing Sunni Arabism into
the political arena, and the British aided this by a refusal to
provide political arrangements for the other sections of the
Iraqi population.

Chaos and anarchy ensued. The enlarged responsibilities
that Cox eagerly took on did not bring large rewards for the
British. Hay had a moment of introspection when he wrote
uncharacteristically on leaving Raqanduz, a town that he
especially appreciated: 'All the other inhabitants had fled, so
that the little of the town which was spared by the Russians
and the Turks is now desolate and falling into ruins. This,
then, was the fruit of all my efforts and hopes' (page 000).
Most of the time the IPS seemed so convinced that they were
bringing civilization to the Gulf that they were oblivious to
the real situation. Viewed with the perspective of subsequent
events, the paternalism and machinations of Rupert Hay will
seem small scale. He offered the book as a memorial to 'brave
spirits whose mortal remains lie scattered beneath the sands
of the Arabian deserts and the flowery turf of the little Kurdish valleys'. It is that, but it is also a sad reminder of how
often wars have been won and the peace has been lost.

NOTES

1. 'Parts of the mountain lands of Albania and Kurdistan, and
the desert of Arabia, though nominally under direct administration, were in very slight obedience; they retained their ancient
tribal organizations, under hereditary chieftains who were invested with Ottoman titles in return for military service, and

whose followers might or might not submit to taxation.' Albert Howe Lybyer, *The Government of the Ottoman Empire in the Time of Sulaiman the Magnificent*, Harvard Historical Studies, Vol. 18, Harvard University Press, Cambridge (Massachusetts), 1913, 173, qtd Zeine N. Zeine, *The Emergence of Arab Nationalism: With a Background Study of Arab–Turkish Relations in the Near East*, 3rd edn, Caravan Books, Delmar (New York), 1973, 22.

2. Richard Goold-Adams, *Middle East Journey*, John Murray, 1947, 96. Major Goold-Adams in his explorations of Kurdistan came across some Kurdish shepherd boys while swimming: 'While I was in the water one of the little Kurds pulled a reed flute out of his craggy clothing, and sitting well back on his haunches began to play. It was a wailing, plaintive air repeated again and again in a rhythm that seemed to speak for shepherds the world over. As he played the others sat still and quiet, and when he stopped we felt a sense of loss. Only the blue air and the far hills and the wide, bright water remained the same, ready to call again that tune which would surely be played till the end of time.' Ibid., 119.

3. A. M. Hamilton, *Road Through Kurdistan: The Narrative of an Engineer in Iraq*, Faber & Faber, London, 1958 [1937], 86.

4. E. S. Stevens, *By Tigris and Euphrates*, Hurst & Blackett, London, 1923, 17.

5. 'This stubborn refusal to recognize that Iraq could only achieve harmonious unity as a bi-national state has been responsible for much loss of life together with a weakening of Iraq in international affairs.' Edith and E. F. Penrose, *Iraq: International Relations and National Development*, Ernest Benn, London, 1978, 109.

6. Said K. Aburish, *Beirut Spy: The St George Hotel Bar*, Bloomsbury, 1990, 56–57 The St George was a haven for Kim Philby, Archie Roosevelt (cousin of Franklin D. Roosevelt and American spymaster) and – briefly and improbably – Dame Rebecca West.

7. See Samir al-Khalil, *Republic of Fear: Saddam's Iraq*, Hutchinson Radius, 1990 [1989], 23.

8. 'We believe that peace in the Middle East will be enhanced when the Assyrian people, one of the most ancient people in the world, are given their human and national rights in the geographical and political framework of the present-day Iraq. Granting the Assyrians their full administrative and cultural autonomous rights, based on the League of Nations' decision of December 20, 1925, in the region of Mosul (present-day Nineveh State), the original ancestral homeland of the Assyrian people, has been, and still

is, the national objective of the Assyrian National Congress.' *Bet-Nahrain*, Vol. XVII, No. 3, November 1990, 3. Bet-Nahrain (literally 'the land of two rivers') is one of several Assyrian exile organizations. Its motto, tired but appropriate, is 'If you are not a part of the Assyrian solution . . . you are a part of the Assyrian problem.'

9. 'The Mosul Controversy: A Homeland for the Assyrians', ibid., 8.

10. H. V. F. Winstone, The *Illicit Adventure: The Story of Political and Military Intelligence in the Middle East from 1898 to 1926*, Jonathan Cape, London, 1982, 30.

11. The production of this peculiar panache and pronounced style, and the lifelong love of secrecy and the covert, is discussed in my trilogy *English Public Schools and Ritualistic Imperialism: Elixir of Empire, Chains of Empire* and *Rituals of Empire*, Regency Press, London, 1991.

12. '. . . a manual for guerrillas that the CIA had distributed to the contras. Some of the instructions on how to conduct guerrilla warfare were offensive to many Americans. One section advocated 'neutralization of Nicaraguan civil officials, like judges and police . . . Here, then, the CIA had overstepped the bounds. It was rightly accused of being out of control.' Stanfield Turner, *Secrecy and Democracy: The CIA in Transition*, Houghton Mifflin, Boston, 1985, 171. Admiral Turner was Director of the CIA, 1977–81.

13. See ibid., 176.

14. Winstone, *Illicit Adventure*, 48.

15. Olaf Caroe, *Wells of Power*, De Cacaoo Press, New York, 1976 [1951], 54. See also Wendell Phillips, *Oman: A History*, Librarie du Liban, Beirut, 1971, 152.

TWO YEARS IN KURDISTAN

EXPERIENCES OF A POLITICAL OFFICER
1918–1920

by
W. R. Hay

Captain, attached to 24th Punjabis,
Political Dept., Government of India

TO THE MEMORY OF

THE BRITISH OFFICERS AND NON-GAZETTED OFFICIALS OF

THE CIVIL ADMINISTRATION OF MESOPOTAMIA

WHO IN THE YEARS 1919 AND 1920

IN THE SERVICE OF THEIR COUNTRY AND OF THE

PEOPLE COMMITTED TO THEIR CARE

LAID DOWN THEIR LIVES

THIS BOOK IS

DEDICATED

'I have always made a rule of conforming to the native customs, so far as my conscience and the honour of my country would admit.'

– C. J. RICH, *Residence in Koordistan*

SIR A. T WILSON, K.C.I.E , C.S.I., C.M.G., D.S.O.

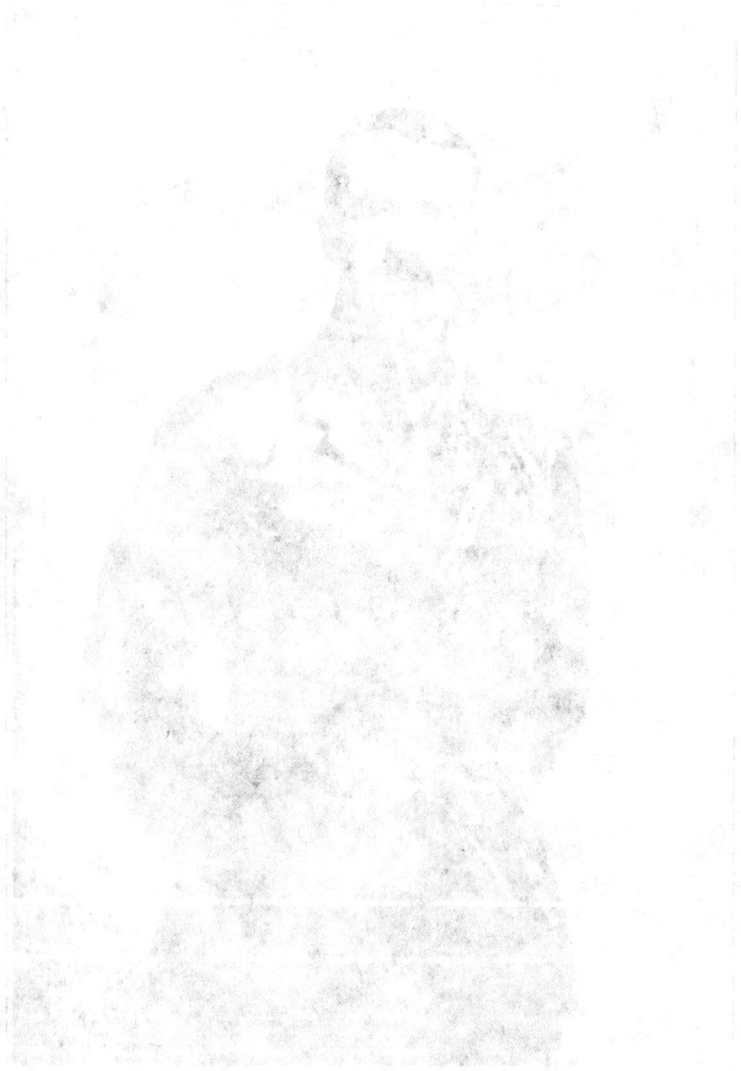

PREFACE

Wherever possible in the pages that follow the recognised method of transliteration for Arabic and Persian place-names has been followed. It has been necessary, however, to make some variation in the case of Turkish and Kurdish names. The spelling 'Koi' has been used throughout instead of the more usual 'Keui', as it is simpler and approximates more nearly to the actual pronunciation.

No Bibliography is given, and the only books other than ordinary works of reference which have been consulted are C. J. Rich's *Residence in Koordistan*, 1836, and Major E. B. Soane's *To Mesopotamia and Kurdistan in Disguise*, 1912.

Two appendices will be found at the end of the volume, in one of which a brief account of the administrative system of the Turkish Empire is given, and in the other a summary of events in Mesopotamia from the Turkish armistice in October, 1918, to the end of 1920.

The author wishes to acknowledge the assistance rendered to him, firstly, by Sir A. T. Wilson, K.C.I.E., C.S.I., C.M.G., D.S.O., through whose encouragement chiefly this book came to be written; and secondly, to Captain C. A. G. Rundle, M.C., who amongst other things has kindly consented to correct the proofs.

To Captain F. C. de L. Kirk he owes a great debt for permission to reproduce his admirable views of the Rawanduz district. It is regretted that it is only possible to use a few of the magnificent photographs which he took in that neighbourhood. The contributions of Major E. Noel, C.I.E., and Captain J. A. H. Miller, R.A.M.C., are also gratefully acknowledged, especially the latter's portrait of Hama Agha. For a few of the illustrations the author is uncertain as to whom he is indebted, and would apologise for using them without the photographer's permission.

The author further wishes to express his gratitude to Miss Sybil Abram, of Reading, for typing his almost illegible manuscript, and to the publishers for the kind consideration they have shown towards him throughout his dealings with them.

CONTENTS

10 CONTENTS

LIST OF ILLUSTRATIONS

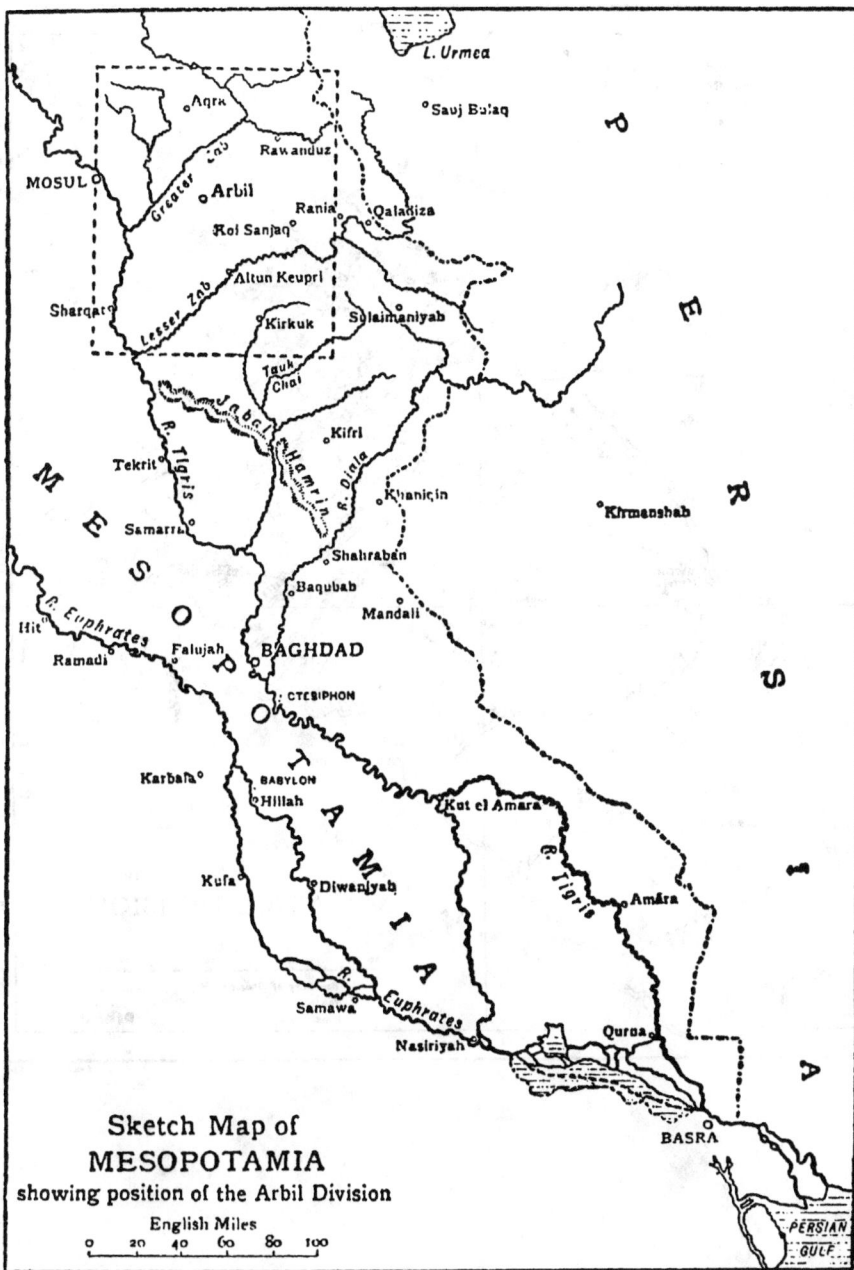

L. Urmca

Sauj Bulaq

P

Aqra

Rawanduz

MOSUL

Arbil

Greater Zab

Rania

Qaladiza

Rol Sanjaq

Altun Keupri

Sharqat

Lesser Zab

Kirkuk

Sulaimaniyah

E

Tauk Chai

Jabal Hamrin

R. Tigris

Kifri

Tekrit

R. Diala

M

Khaniqin

Kirmanshah

R

E

Samarra

S

Shahraban

O

Baqubah

C. Euphrates

Mandali

Hit

P

Ramadi

Falujah

O

BAGHDAD

CTESIPHON

T

Karbala

BABYLON

A

Hillah

Kut el Amara

M

Kufa

Diwaniyah

A

R. Tigris

Amara

I

R. Euphrates

A

Samawa

Qurna

Nasiriyah

A

Sketch Map of
MESOPOTAMIA
showing position of the Arbil Division

English Miles

0   20   40   60   80   100

BASRA

PERSIAN
GULF

Emery Walker Ltd. sc

The dotted lines indicate the area shown in the MAP OF THE
ARBIL DIVISION, which will be found overleaf.

Sketch Map of the ARBIL DIVISION

CHAPTER I

INTRODUCTORY

'Travelling, in the Younger Sort, is a part of Education; in the Elder, a part of Experience.' – Bacon: *Essays*.

DURING RECENT GENERATIONS to comparatively few has come the chance of exploring unmapped wilds and living on terms of close intimacy with strange and unrecorded tribes. Despite the attractions and influence of modern life many of us in England still feel the promptings of the Elizabethan spirit – the call of the uncharted sea, the fascination of what is new and mysterious. And those who have had the glorious opportunity of treading the untrod, and seeing the unseen, must be pardoned if, bursting with their experiences, they endeavour to describe them for the delectation of their fellows, and put their hands to the pen, be they never such unready writers.

Such, then, is the author's apology for writing this book – a book which contains no erudition, no traces of midnight oil, no deep thinking – but an egotistical record of things seen and done. During the last three years it has been the writer's fortune to serve in the Civil Administration of Mesopotamia, always in more or less remote parts of the country. Mesopotamia, though by no means unmapped, was before the war to most people *terra incognita*. Baghdad was the capital of the land of fairy tales, the Arabs we pictured spurring fiery steeds over the trackless desert, while the Kurd we had never heard of, or heard of only as the wildest of brigands.

As the army advanced from Basra into the interior, political officers were sent to all the important centres to serve as intermediaries between the military authorities and the people. With the Armistice military considerations assumed less importance; administration and the maintenance of law and order amongst the tribes became our chief aims in Meso-

potamia. The Political Department, which had formerly occupied a very subordinate position, began almost to rival
G.H.Q., and absorbed in quick succession other departments,
such as Irrigation, Posts, Telegraphs, and Railways. Until Sir
Percy Cox arrived in September, 1920, however, the Com-
mander-in-Chief was supreme, and Mesopotamia after the
Armistice remained, and still remains, in a state of war.

Many attacks have been made during the last year on the
Civil Administration of Mesopotamia but it is not proposed to
comment on them. It is one of the writer's chief objects in this
book to avoid all controversial matter. As to whether these attacks were justified or not, he does not proffer an opinion.
Neither will he endeavour in any detail to trace the causes of
the recent disturbances; and above all he will refrain from re-
cording his callow convictions as to the best policy for the future. All he desires is to carry his reader for a moment to a
remote land, where he may share with him his delight at
seeing strange things and talking to strange men, and may
live with him through such adventures and hours of danger
as it was his fortune to experience.

It is fitting here to make mention of Sir Arnold Wilson
who acted as head of the Civil Administration in Mesopotamia from March, 1918, to September, 1920, through the
period of its greatest expansion and up to and including the
time of its greatest troubles. To the writer and most of us in
'The Political', Sir Arnold Wilson besides being our 'chief' was
a personal friend, and the author and begetter of our efforts
and ambitions. There must be few men who can exact so
much willing work from their subordinates, and it is doubtful
if there is any man who could have borne such a burden of
work and responsibility as he did, or have faced so many difficulties in the spirit of the motto on the wall of his office,'aequam memento rebus in arduis servare mentem'.

Subsequently to the Armistice, Mesopotamia or 'Iraq,
which is its local name, was divided for the purposes of administration into thirteen divisions, each under a Political
Officer directly responsible to the Civil Commissioner at
Baghdad. Each division contained two or more districts
under Assistant Political Officers responsible to the Political
Officer at the headquarters of the division. In newly occupied
districts the A.P.O. was usually allowed considerable inde-

pendence. It was only when the routine began to crystallise that it became the P.O.'s duty to exercise control. The division normally corresponded to the old Turkish 'liwa' and the district to the 'qaza'. The population of a division averaged from 100,000 to 200,000, and its area from 2,000 to 6,000 square miles. In all divisional and in some district headquarters British officers were appointed to look after the local levies and gendarmerie. They were responsible partly to the Inspecting Officer of Levies at Baghdad, and partly to the Political Officer. In all divisional headquarters there was also a Civil Surgeon to attend to the health of the local population. Educational, judicial, and agricultural officers and other specialists were stationed in a few of the large towns. Troops were present in all but one or two divisional headquarters; A.P.O.s, however, were often called upon to live solitary lives in remote places with possibly only one white clerk as a companion.

The duties of the A.P.O. were many and various. His main tasks were as follows: Firstly, to establish and maintain law and order. This he did with the help of the gendarmes. Secondly, to obtain a thorough knowledge of the geography of his district, and of the nature, composition, and customs of the tribes who inhabited it. This meant extensive touring. Thirdly, to dispense impartial justice, a difficult task for an amateur in a land with a strange legal system, though most A.P.O.s managed pretty well with the code of their own common sense. Fourthly, to collect revenue. Almost the entire revenue of the country being derived from the produce of the soil, this necessitated taking an interest in and making a study of local agricultural practice. Fifthly, to collect municipal taxes and attend to sanitation and municipal improvements. Latterly these duties were partly taken over by municipal councils. Minor obligations also fell upon his shoulders, it being his duty to take an interest in whatever concerned the welfare of the population in his charge. Where troops were stationed it was also incumbent upon the A.P.O. to give the military authorities all possible assistance, especially in the purchase of local produce and the provision of labour. In the smaller divisions the P.O., in addition to supervising the work of the A.P.O.s in the outside districts, usually acted as A.P.O. of his own headquarters district.

Before the Armistice, when military considerations rendered it inadvisable to delegate much power to the local authorities, the A.P.O. was practically the sole local civil authority. After the Armistice, especially in Kurdistan, every effort was made to teach the people to rule themselves; but in the first warm welcome that was given to the British authorities, he was still regarded as a ruler hedged with divinity, a 'deus ex machina', who would provide a solution for all problems. His judicial powers, though limited to the infliction of two years rigorous imprisonment or Rs.2,000 fine, were sufficient for nearly every case with which he had to deal, and could be extended with the Civil Commissioner's permission under special circumstances. The peoples of the East, and above all wild races like the Kurds, are not by nature adapted to modern democratic forms of government, and strange as it may seem to some, it is nevertheless true that the more direct an A.P.O.'s rule, the more popular he was with the people at large, and with the more reasonably minded of the local gentry. It was only those hereditary chiefs who had been used to purchase justice in Turkish times that resented his presence.

The A.P.O. was normally assisted in his duties by one British clerk and one Indian accountant. The rest of his staff, comprising revenue and judicial officials, vernacular clerks, etc., was recruited locally. The British clerks were originally borrowed from the military, and after demobilisation were granted a civil contract for a period of from one to three years. They were usually men who took an interest in the people of the country, and knew at least one local language. They were of the very greatest assistance to the officers with whom they served. The Indian members of the staff were mostly recruited in India. They quickly acquired a knowledge of the local languages, and nearly always showed great tact in their dealings with the people. They were universally admired for their honesty and intelligence, and I rarely heard a complaint against them. Sometimes during the absence of the A.P.O. they had to assume positions of great responsibility; and in many cases they stuck to their posts in the face of the gravest danger.

In the early days of the occupation but few officers were required to organise the administration of the country, and

they were mostly members of the Political Department of the
Government of India or of the Indian Civil Service. The number of men available from these two services was naturally
limited, and after the occupation of Baghdad in March, 1917,
when the territory under British administration began to expand so rapidly, it became necessary to borrow officers from
the military authorities. These officers were in the majority
of cases selected personally by Sir A. T. Wilson, then Captain
Wilson, for their linguistic or other abilities. They naturally
had no previous administrative experience, but were usually
attached for a period to some older member of the Political in
order to learn their duties. Subsequently the Political Department of the Government of India, the Indian Civil and
similar services, owing to their own acute needs, were compelled to recall most of their officers from Mesopotamia. Thus
it came about that by 1920 nearly all the officers of the Civil
Administration of the country were military officers borrowed temporarily from their regiments or departments.
They were engaged on contracts for one or three years' service, on terms that were certainly good, but no more than reasonable when the conditions under which they undertook to
serve are considered.

For the life of an A.P.O. was by no means an easy one. He
was called upon to live in out-stations from which the ameni-
ties and comforts of civilisation were in most cases entirely
absent. Though a fairly capacious house could usually be
found for him, the furniture was of the simplest and the sanitary arrangements were, to say the least of it, primitive. The
food, though wholesome, lacked variety, usually consisting of
mutton or goat and rice, eked out with a limited selection of
vegetables. The climate was tolerably healthy, but trying; intense heat in the summer with, by comparison, intense cold
in the winter, accompanied by rain that turned the whole
country into a quagmire. The A.P.O. normally had to work
eight hours a day in his office, where the majority of his business was of a judicial character; when he was not in his office
he was touring his district, riding over a shelterless country
in a heat that was hell-like.

In addition to all this, his life was often dangerous in the
extreme. Despite the hardships there were few A.P.O.s that
were not deeply in love with their work. Each man took an

intense pride in his district, and would boast how his own
particular shaikhs were the most faithful and law-abiding in
the country; and it must be difficult for anyone to compre-
hend the extreme personal grief which such a man felt when
he saw his friends turn traitor and the work to which he had
devoted the utmost of his energies overthrown and trodden
under foot. Possibly those are happier who escaped this grief
by themselves perishing in the ruin.

Though a promise has been given not to analyse the
causes of the troubles in Mesopotamia, it is necessary to indicate briefly the manner in which events shaped themselves.
As the British advanced into the country they were everywhere received with open arms. Townships many miles distant from the route followed by the troops sent deputies to
tender their submission, and beg for the appointment of
A.P.O.s to govern them. As officers became available they
were duly sent out. Thus it came about that large areas, the
most notable of which is that of the Middle Euphrates, including the towns of Hillah, Kerbela, Nejef, Kufa, and
Tuwarij, accepted our administration without seeing a single
British soldier. In the north, in Kurdistan, it was much the
same. People said that they had known for years that the
British were coming, and mullas declared that long ago,
prophecies had been discovered in their books indicating that
the British Government would one day take over the country.
Everybody believed that the Golden Age had come, and a
period of great prosperity was expected. Agricultural machinery would be provided and the land would yield tenfold its
former produce; railways and canals would be built and trade
would flourish. It will probably be agreed by those who know
that everything possible was done to meet these expectations.
But the Oriental is always an idealist – he plans his beautiful castle but does not count the cost. Thus it came about that
'the dweller in Mesopotamia' was not only bitterly disappointed to find that the Age was not suddenly made Golden
as if by a magician's wand, but was also deeply chagrined to
find that he was losing some of his personal liberty. Highway
robbery with violence – a popular pastime in former times –
became a crime punishable with death. The great game of defrauding the Government of its revenue could no longer be
played. It was necessary to pay taxes punctually and in full,

though on a lower scale than in Turkish times. Hence a great
reaction sprang up, followed – thanks to propaganda from
Syria and Turkey, and to other causes into which we need not
enter – by rebellion.

On the whole religion counted for very little in Mesopotamia. It was some time before the tribesmen realised that
the British Government was a Christian Government. It is
related that one day an Arab shaikh was abusing Christians
to an A.P.O. when the latter remarked, 'Don't you know that I
am a Christian?' The Arab replied, 'No, you are not a Christian; you are an Englishman.' The only Christians that existed in the tribesman's mind were the degenerate but much
enduring sects of which small scattered communities still
survive in the country. It is doubtful if the recent movement
against the British in Mesopotamia could ever be styled a religious one – or for that matter a national one.

Having thus by way of preface outlined briefly the position
occupied by Political Officers in Mesopotamia and the duties
they were called upon to perform, the writer will endeavour
to give an account of himself and to indicate the lines upon
which his story is constructed.

When war broke out I had just completed one year at Oxford. In October, 1914, I sailed with the 1/4th Dorsets (T.F.)
for India. In December, 1915, I proceeded to Mesopotamia
and was in the neighbourhood of Shaikh Sa'ad and the Han-
nah position during the fighting in the first months of 1916.
In April of that year I received a slight wound and was sent
back to India; I did not return to Mesopotamia till a year
later, when I came out with the re-formed 24th Punjabis. We
were in Basra till June, and after that proceeded to the Euphrates. In October I passed an Arabic examination, and in
December was selected to serve in the Civil Administration.

I was posted as A.P.O. Mandali, a small town famous for
its dates, situated on the Persian border, about 100 miles due
east of Baghdad, and remained there till November 1st, 1918.
For the greater part of the time I was the only British officer
in the place, and was without any troops. Mandali was then
about the pleasantest spot under our occupation, and I was
thoroughly happy. The Government was popular, and there

was plenty of experience to be gained. Frontier questions and
occasional raids by brigands, who had taken refuge across
the border with the Wali of Pusht-i-Kuh, relieved the mono-
tony. Though I spent much energy in grappling with what, in
my inexperience, I considered matters of the gravest importance, I was never confronted by any really serious problem
or involved in any real anxiety or danger.

Mandali in fact was an ideal training ground. Four languages were current in the district, and most of the townsmen could speak all four. As children they learnt their
mother tongue, Turkish, from their parents, and the local
Kurdo-Lurish dialect from their nurses and the people of the
hills, whither they were sent for the hot weather. Subsequently they acquired Arabic from the men who tended
their date-gardens, and Persian from the merchants who visited their town and became guests in their houses. In the district there were both Arab and Kurdish tribes. In the town
there were Turks (not Ottomans), Persians, Kurds, and Lurs.
The Sunni and Shiah Muhammadan sects were both well represented, while there were also to be found a considerable
number of Ali Ilahis, so-called because they are said to regard
Ali, the son-in-law of Muhammad, as an incarnation of the
Deity, and a few Jews.

I had learnt some Persian in India and Arabic on the Euphrates. I was able to make considerable progress with both
these languages at Mandali, and I also started to learn
Turkish, and could understand and be understood in this language before I was transferred to Altun Keupri at the beginning of November, 1910. Subsequently while at Koi and Arbil
I improved my Turkish and learnt to speak Kurdish with
moderate fluency.

I arrived in Altun Keupri on November 3rd. On the 10th I
was sent with two troops of cavalry to take over Arbil from
the Turks in the name of the British Government: I remained
there only two days, after which I was relieved by Captain
(now Major) S. G. Murray, C.I.E., and returned to Altun
Keupri. On December 15th I handed over the Altun Keupri
district to the A.P.O. Kirkuk, Captain (now Major) S. H. Longrigg, and proceeded to Koi Sanjaq to re-establish law and
order there. I subsequently visited Rania and Qala Diza, but

Koi remained my headquarters until February 21st, 1919, when, owing to family affairs, I proceeded home on leave.

I returned to Mesopotamia at the end of June, and was posted to Arbil, which then constituted a district of the Mosul Division under the late Lieut.-Colonel Leachman, C.I.E., D.S.O. On November 1st a new Arbil Division was formed, consisting of the original Arbil district, less a small portion inhabited by Arabs which remained under Mosul, and the Koi and Rawanduz districts. I was appointed P.O. Arbil, with Captain C. A. G. Rundle, M.C., as A.P.O. at Koi, and Captain F. C. de L. Kirk in the same capacity in the Rawanduz district. Captain J. R. L. Bradshaw assisted me at Arbil. At the beginning of December Captain Kirk was transferred elsewhere, and no A.P.O. was subsequently appointed in his place. From this time onwards, therefore, in addition to being P.O. of the division, I was in direct charge of both the Arbil and Rawanduz districts.

In the summer of 1920 I was appointed a probationer in the Political Department of the Government of India, and services were demanded by the end of the year. In October, therefore, I handed over my duties as P.O. Arbil to Major C. C. Marshall, D.S.O., and proceeded to England to enjoy a few months' leave before returning to India. I left Mesopotamia with many regrets, and hope it may still be my fortune to revisit the country, especially the Arbil Division, and to shake hands again with Ahmad Effendi and the Kurdish chiefs who served me so loyally there.

In this narrative I shall deal only with my experiences in Mesopotamia since the Turkish armistice (October 31st, 1918), and with the country that lies between the Lesser and Greater Zabs, consisting of the Arbil Division, the Rania district, which is part of the Sulaimaniyah Division, and the town of Altun Keupri which is now under Kirkuk.

In the next five chapters I shall treat of the geography of this area, with the nature of its inhabitants, and their customs, with their agricultural methods and the system of land tenure in vogue, and with the products of the country and its trade. Of these subjects I shall write but briefly, and any reader who considers them dull is invited to skip them. I shall then pass to the narrative of my experiences, starting with Altun Keupri, my first visit to Arbil, and my residence at Koi, with which I shall not deal at great length. I shall devote more space to events during my second long stay at Arbil, describing in detail my series of adventures in the Rawanduz district and the final troubles at Arbil, which so nearly proved a débâcle. I shall conclude with a brief tribute to my fellows in the Civil Administration, especially those who have fallen.

CHAPTER II

GEOGRAPHICAL: FAUNA AND FLORA

ON PAGE 13 WILL BE found a small map which will illustrate the relation which the Arbil Division bears to the rest of 'Iraq, and on page 14 a more detailed map of the Arbil Division itself is provided. It is recommended that the latter be carefully studied in connection with the present chapter in order that it may not be necessary to make frequent reference to it when the tale begins to unfold itself.

The chief thing that it is necessary to remember in connection with the geographical features of Mesopotamia is that everything runs south-east and north-west. The country is an oblong lying in these directions with the Persian and Kurdish mountains forming the long side on the north-east, and the Euphrates and the desert-cliff (from which the name 'Iraq or cliff is said by some to be derived) making the parallel boundary on the south-west. The Tigris meanders down the centre.

Under the Turks 'Iraq was divided into three vilayets or provinces, those of Basra, Baghdad, and Mosul. Excluding their extreme eastern fringe the vilayets of Basra and Baghdad are dead flat, absolutely stoneless, and treeless, save for the date-palm. Their population is composed almost entirely of Arabs.

Upper Mesopotamia or the vilayet of Mosul is entirely different in character. It is separated from Lower Mesopotamia by the Jabal Hamrin or the 'Red Hills', a range which originates somewhere near Ahwaz and runs north-west with hardly a break for 50 miles till it fades away in the desert west of the Tigris not far from Mosul. This bare serrated ridge of red sandstone, which never rises 1000 feet above the surrounding country, appeared almost as high as the Himalayas to the troops who had marched so many hundred miles over the dead flat of the Tigris–Euphrates delta, but compared to the mountains which were eventually reached it is a mere ugly excrescence. Beyond this range the country begins to undulate; the ground becomes stony, but trees are still rare. A series of bare ridges, similar in character to the Jabal Hamrin, are next encountered with undulating plains between. These ridges are like lock-gates on a canal, each one successively raising the general level of the country; until at length a few miles east of Kirkuk, Altun Keupri, and Arbil, the great plains cease and the traveller meets first the tangled foothills like foaming surf, and then the great crested mountains, billow on billow culminating in the vast range which overlooks the Persian plateau.

From the Gulf to the Diyalah River the Persian frontier runs along the foothills. When it reaches this stream it turns up, and eventually climbs to the top of the watershed, which it follows till it meets the Russian frontier at Mt. Ararat. East of the Tigris, therefore, the Mosul vilayet contains a considerable area of extremely mountainous country.

West of the Tigris, except for the Jabal Sinjar, the home of the Yazidi tribe known as devil-worshippers, all is indefinite desert, and no tributaries join the main stream. The hills to the east, on the other hand, are drained by several large rivers. The Khabur meets the Tigris at Zakho in the extreme north of the occupied territories; 24 miles below Mosul the Greater Zab adds its contribution to the main flood, while the Lesser Zab flows in just above the gorge by which the waters pierce the Jabal Hamrin. In the Baghdad vilayet the Diyalah helps to swell the stream.

In this work we shall chiefly be concerned with the piece of country, roughly a parallelogram in shape, which is contained between the two Zabs, the Tigris and the Persian frontier. Its long sides measure approximately 100 miles and its ends 50. If the Greater Zab is followed upwards on the map it will be seen that it makes a bend to the north-west before it reaches the frontier; to complete our figure, therefore, it is necessary to make an imaginary prolongation of its course. It will be noticed that this area runs south-west and north-east, that is athwart the general lie of the country, so that every variety of scenery and climate can be obtained from the torrid Qaraj desert to the snow-capped Zagros mountains.

ON THE PERSIAN ROAD

(Showing Kola Dagh)

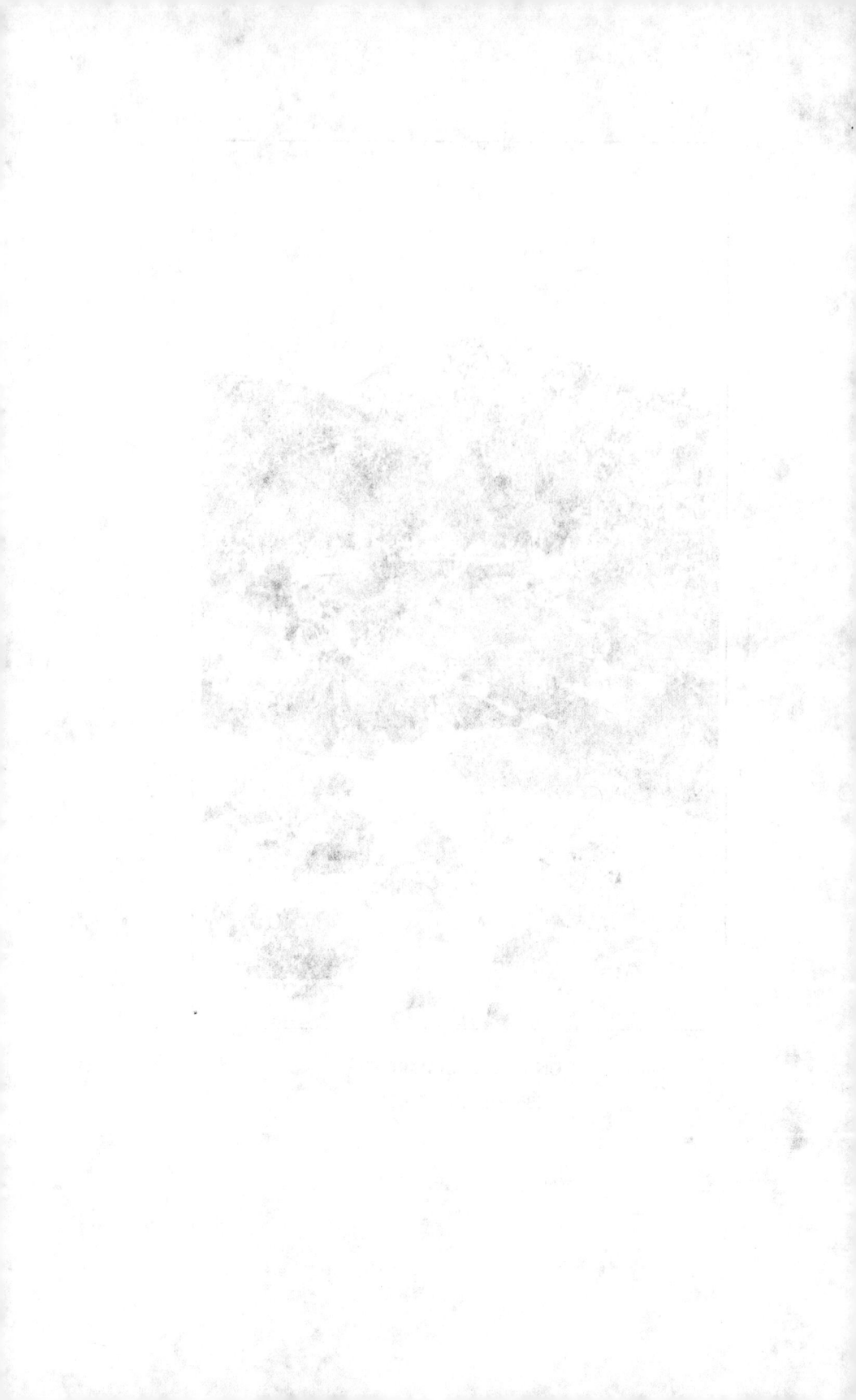

The word Zab or Ze is a generic term for river in Southern Kurdistan, and it is frequently used by the Kurds when speaking of the Tigris and the Rawanduz Chai. The Greater and Lesser Zabs are the rivers *par excellence* of Southern Kurdistan.

The Lesser Zab rises south of Lake Urmia, and is in most respects an inferior replica of its sister river. Its course, too, runs across the general lie of the country, and its waters are practically useless, at present, for irrigation purposes, though traces of large ancient canals exist on both banks below Altun Keupri. One of these flows right across the southern end of the Qaraj desert, and would place a large area of waste country under cultivation if re-excavated. Commercially this river is much more important than the Greater Zab, as rafts can be floated down it from just below Darband i Ramakan.

The Lesser Zab is liable to sudden and violent floods, hence its alternative name of Majnun or Mad River. It is shallow when the floods subside, and can easily be forded in many places in the summer and autumn.

The section of the Tigris which forms the western end of the parallelogram is not important. Its bank is lined with Arab villages, the inhabitants of which irrigate a small strip of land by means of lifts.

I will now endeavour to survey the country contained in our parallelogram, starting from its lowest point on the Tigris and travelling in a north-easterly direction until the frontier is reached.

From a point on the Lesser Zab, about 30 miles above its junction with the Tigris, a gaunt black range known as the Qara Choq Dagh runs in a north-easterly direction, and eventually dwindles away as it approaches the Greater Zab just below Quwair. The waterless area enclosed by these hills, the Lesser Zab, and the Tigris, is known as the Qara Choq desert or the Qaraj, and is famous for its fertility; it is said that in a year of plentiful rain it will give a return of as much as 100 to 1 for seed sown. Unfortunately, however, such an event is of rare occurrence, and it often happens that there is practically no rain at all in this region.

The Qara Choq desert approximates more nearly than any other portion of the Arbil Division to the plains of Lower

Mesopotamia. Though as a matter of fact it undulates slightly, and especially along its upper edge is intersected by numerous watercourses, it is in general appearance a dead flat, for the greater part of the year brown and bare, save for a few characteristic desert weeds. Wells are scarce and the water they contain is brackish. In summer the air is hot and scorching, and the traveller experiences the sensation of being in vast parched spaces where every living thing has been baked out of existence and the sun's fiery rays are all-pervading.

In a year of good rain, suddenly, about the beginning of March, the whole of this desert breaks into flower. It is as though a many-hued carpet of intricate design were suddenly laid upon its face. Then all the Kurds from the Arbil plain drive down their flocks to pasture, and pitch their great black tents where they will. The pools left by the rain provide them with water. The younger men, who are finely mounted, show off their prowess in the saddle, or chase the hare and gazelle. The old chiefs sit in richly furnished guest-tents, ready to receive visitors. For a month or six weeks the desert is a health resort. But towards the end of April the sun begins to exert his authority, and within a week or two all the grass and flowers have withered away.

The population of the Qara Choq desert varies with the rainfall. When there have been two or three fat years the upper end, i.e. the portion nearer the hills, is thickly covered with villages; a lean year comes and the population fade away, leaving only a few houses in favoured spots at the foot of the Dagh, while the rest of the desert is scattered here and there with collections of ruined mud walls, like empty shells on a dry beach.

The Qara Choq Dagh rises to a height of 2,800 ft. above the sea-level. It is divided by the pass of Hussein-i-Ghazi into two big masses, the more southerly of which is the larger. The face of the hill on both sides is very rough, worn and scored by the rains of centuries. This range is of little use to man, being waterless, except for a small sulphurous stream, and treeless. It is reported that less than a century ago trees and shrubs were plentiful on its slopes; when the Kurds came, however, they were quickly taken for firewood, and no trace of them now remains. Grass grows to a good length in

the spring: at the end of April it dries up, and remains standing providing pasture during the summer, autumn, and
winter for numerous flocks.

The country beyond the Qara Choq Dagh is divided into
two parts by an almost imperceptible watershed. The northern part, which drains into the Greater Zab, is known as
Shamamik, the southern half as Kandinawah. Both are separated from the Arbil plain by low gravelly hills.

The district of Shamamik is roughly semicircular in
shape, and lies along the left bank of the Greater Zab. It is
the most consistently fertile part of the Arbil Division, and is
thickly populated. The country is slightly undulating; wells
are frequent and sweet, and two perennial streams provide a
modicum of water for irrigation. Crops here ripen almost a
fortnight later than in the Qara Choq area. At the beginning
of May everything is still green, and sweet-scented flowers
abound; across the hills within a distance of 4 miles summer
has begun and the world is brown. The difference is chiefly
due to the greater rainfall on the northern side of the Qara
Choq Dagh.

Kandinawah is a strip of country, averaging 15 miles in
width, and about 30 miles long, lying between the Qara Choq
Dagh and the Zurga Zirau. 'Kanda' in Kurdish is the same as
'nala' in Hindustani, i.e. a narrow watercourse with steep
banks, and the district derives its name from a particularly
big kanda which runs down its centre. This is joined by
smaller kandas from either side at every mile or two of its
course, so that the whole country is intersected by them and
is difficult to cross in a car. The soil is as fertile as that of
Shamamik, but the crops are not as sure; the rainfall is
sometimes insufficient, and locusts often cause a great deal
of damage. The district is thickly populated at its northern
end; the southern extremity is more hilly and less fertile.
Water is derived from a few exiguous springs and wells; it is
mostly brackish.

The Zurga Zirau, a low serrated range of hills (for which
Zurga is a generic name in Kurdish), divides Kandinawah
from the famous Dasht i Haulair or Arbil Plain. This great
expanse stretches about 50 miles from the Greater to the
Lesser Zab, with a width of some 25 miles from the Zurga
Zirau to the foothills proper. The northern end by the Greater

Zab is very undulating and rather stony; but the main portion of the plain between the Arbil–Kirkuk road and the
Zurga Zirau presents only a gentle swell and is consistently
fertile. It has probably given a yearly yield of 10 for 1 for centuries. In spring the traveller may stand on one of the ancient mounds which dot its surface and, except for the white
roads, as far as he can see the whole country is under cultivation, either green with the standing crops or ploughed ready
for the autumn sowing. The population is dense, and this
plain has been the headquarters of the powerful Dizai tribe
for the last three centuries. East of the Kirkuk road the
country undulates more and more, and becomes very stony. It
was thickly populated before the war, but in 1918 many perished, and a large proportion of the survivors migrated to
other lands.

The Arbil Plain is chiefly watered by 'Karizes', which will
be described later. Wells are frequent, and water, which is invariably sweet, can always be found within 30 or 40 ft. of the
surface.

We have now reached the foothills. The Arbil Plain is
bounded along its north-eastern side by the Bastura Chai
and the Dardawan Dagh. The Bastura Chai is a broad watercourse running into the Greater Zab and containing a torrent
in spring, a small stream in summer and winter, and no
water at all in autumn. It marks the south-western border of
the Rawanduz district, and according to the people of Arbil it
is the boundary between 'Iraq and Kurdistan.

The Dardawan Dagh is a range as high as the Qara Choq,
but it does not stand out so prominently from the plain. Its
crest is the boundary between the Arbil and Koi districts.

The Koi district is divided into two portions, the Koi sub-
district and the Shaqlawah sub-district. The former is an in-
extricable mass of low sandstone hills and watercourses.
Trees are scarce and cultivation is only possible on occasional
small plateaus among the hills. Water is obtained from small
springs. This area is bounded on the south by the Lesser Zab,
and on the east by the hills proper.

The boundary between Koi and Rania is the Haib us Sultan Dagh, which reaches a height of 3,800 ft., and is a portion
of a range which stretches almost unbroken from the Persian
Gulf to Mardin. The northern continuation of the Haib us

Sultan rises to nearly 7,000 ft., and is called the Safin Dagh
or Ark Mountain because, according to Muhammadan tradition, the Ark grazed here before it finally rested on Mt. Judi,
near Jezirah. Practically speaking the Safin Dagh with its
slopes and outcrops forms the Shaqlawah sub-district. It is
well wooded with scrub-oak and small shrubs, and contains
many large springs. There is very little space available for
the cultivation of the normal crops, wheat and barley, but the
hillsides are covered with vineyards. The Safin Dagh is a
magnificent mountain, and dominates the landscape for
miles around. The traveller must proceed a day's journey up
country before he can find another range to equal it.

The Rania district, which contains also a portion of the
old Turkish district of Qala Diza, is bounded on the south, as
far as we are concerned, by the Lesser Zab, and consists
chiefly of two remarkable plains divided by a thin ridge,
known as the Kewa Resh or Black Comb, and a hinterland of
vast mountains. The first of these plains, Bituin, is roughly
circular in shape and is 150 square miles in extent. It is
watered by numerous streams and springs, many of the latter being hot, but is extremely unhealthy, Rania lying lower
than Arbil. It would be fertile if properly cultivated, but
nature here luxuriates with her flowers and grasses, and is
difficult to eradicate.

The second plain, usually known as the Pizhder plain, is
smaller than Bituin and much more undulating. It is intersected by frequent streams from the hills, but as they rush
down deep courses they are of little use for irrigation. East of
this plain is the Persian frontier where the mountains rise to
12,000 ft., while to the north, between it and Rawanduz, lies
a tangled mass of hills, some of them over 10,000 ft., the
general direction of which seems to run at right angles to the
main ranges. Amongst them are many thickly wooded valleys
inhabited by the wildest type of Kurd.

The boundary between Shaqlawah and Rawanduz is
tribal, and I will not tire the reader by attempting to define it
geographically. It is sufficient to remember that the Rawanduz district is roughly a leg of mutton in shape. Its narrow
end is at the Bastura Chai, and it broadens rapidly after the
Safin Dagh is passed. From the Bastura Chai eastwards we
have a succession of low ranges which gradually increase in

height for about 20 miles until we suddenly come to the
Dasht or Plain of Harir. This is an expanse of country some
20 miles long and averaging 8 miles in width. It is plentifully
watered with springs and streams, and is very fertile compared to the rest of the Rawanduz district. Beyond this we
have the Harir Dagh, a straight bare-looking ridge, and then
a tangled mass of peaks, ridges, spurs, and ravines, which it
is impossible to describe in detail, until the main watershed
and the Persian frontier is reached. Amongst these mountains springs are frequent, but the area of cultivable ground
is small.

The one main feature which it is necessary to notice is the
Rawanduz Chai. This stream rises on the Persian frontier
near the Garwa Shaikh or Pass of the Shaikh, where the
general level of the frontier range drops some 5,000 ft. and
allows an easy crossing into Persia, and flows down a deep
valley roughly east and west until at Rawanduz it starts to
pierce the heart of the mountains, and after passing through
a magnificent gorge 10 miles long finds its way to the Greater
Zab.

The geological formations in the Arbil Division vary from
Jurassic to Recent. A great variety of rocks are present, none
of them igneous. The mountains are almost entirely made up
of Cretaceous and Eocene rocks, in which shales and limestone predominate. The Arbil Plain is composed of Pliocene
beds, and consists chiefly of conglomerates and sandy shales.
In the Zurga Zirau and Qara Choq ranges beds of the Lower
Fars are exposed which contain large quantities of gypsum.

The country is poor mineralogically, possessing no known
veins of valuable ore. Oil oozes out in one place on the banks
of the Greater Zab, but the wells are not properly worked.
Gypsum, which is plentiful, is valuable for building purposes;
borax is also found. In a few places the gypsum has hardened
into a coarse marble.

The geological structure of the Arbil Plain is roughly
basin-shaped, which fact, in conjunction with the nature of
the beds beneath, suggests that the conditions suitable for
artesian water are fulfilled. Much of the heavy rainfall of the
hills must percolate the previous strata which are found
there, and it appears probable that by boring into the lower
beds large supplies of water would be tapped, and rise to the

surface under their own pressure. The value of such water would be inestimable.

There are no canals, in the proper sense of the term, at present in use in the Arbil Division, though traces of ancient ones exist. Channels are dug to lead water from springs and streams to the ground it is desired to irrigate, and lifts are used by the Arabs in the big rivers. The main feature of the Arbil District, however, in this connection is the Kariz, or Kahriz as it is spelt in Persian. A Kariz is a succession of wells of decreasing depth connected up by an underground channel which eventually brings the water out to the surface, and makes it available for irrigation by flow. The sketch on page 34 will serve to illustrate my meaning.

A–B is the surface of the ground. C is a supply of underground water. The Ds represent the well-heads. CEF is the water channel connecting the wells, E being the point where the water is conducted into the open, and E–F being a cutting which brings the water to a level with the surface. The amount of water so obtained is rarely more than two or three mill-power, which is the manner in which the Kurds express the volume of a current. Karizes can only be constructed in a sub-montane district where the ground possesses a considerable slope.

It is stated that in the time of the Abbasid Khalifs there were 365 Karizes on the Arbil Plain, and that the road from Arbil to Altun Keupri was lined with gardens so that a bird could hop from tree to tree the whole way. This tale of the bird, however, is told of many other treeless parts of Mesopotamia.

Undoubtedly a very large number of Karizes did exist, as the Arbil Plain is covered with rows of small circular mounds – the spoil from the excavated wells. About sixty Karizes are now in use, and several old ones are in the process of being re-excavated. There is one old man in Arbil called Usta Fatah, who is the Kariz expert, and who can tell by instinct and art where to dig and where not to dig, when an old Kariz is being re-opened, or an existing one prolonged. His family have been Kariz experts for generation after generation, and his son will succeed him when he dies. No one else in Arbil possesses the art. No attempt is ever made to open an entirely new Kariz; the science of divining is unknown, and I

think Usta Fatah only judges by the lie of the land and similar considerations which of the ancient wells it may be profi-
table to excavate. The digging of these Karizes is a dangerous
proceeding. The roof of the underground channel is in no way
supported and the unfortunate man who is burrowing is very
liable to be buried alive.

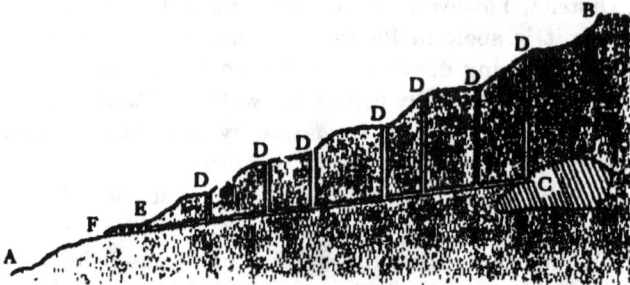

A KARIZ

The climate varies in different parts of the division, but
on the whole is equable. In Arbil itself there is rarely more
than a month's very hot weather, when the thermometer in
the shade rises to 110 degrees or over. It may rain any time
from November to May inclusive. The average rainfall for the
Arbil Plain is from 12 to 14 ins. It is considerably less in the
Qara Choq desert, and much more in the hills. January is the
wettest month. The winter is, on the whole, mild, though a
sharp cold snap is often experienced. It snowed on eleven
days in February, 1920, the first time snow had been seen in
Arbil for about seven years. In 1911 the whole country was
under snow for forty days, and the rivers were frozen over.
This is known to the Kurds as the year of snow, and is widely
used for dating events.

The weather begins to grow warm in March, and until the
end of May is everything that could be wished. Occasional
showers keep the air fresh, and the country gay with flowers.
June, with the first half of July, is hot, but not unpleasantly
so; the nights are delightfully cool. From the middle of July
to the middle of August intensely hot weather is usually experienced with scorching east winds. In the latter half of
August the weather suddenly cools down, and September and
October are temperate. Everything is dry and dusty; flies

swarm, and one longs for the rain to come and wash away the filth that has accumulated during the hot weather.

The Division is extremely healthy except in the rice-growing areas, where malaria is rampant. Whilst I was in Arbil I do not remember a single case of cholera, smallpox, or typhoid. Whooping cough was the worst epidemic we experienced, though in 1918, just before I arrived, Spanish influenza, locally known as 'Ispaniol', had carried off large numbers of the population, being worst, curiously enough, in some of the remote Kurdish villages, especially Shaqlawah, where in one of the leading men's houses every man, woman, and child died. The drinking water, especially in the Arbil Plain, is excellent, and may largely account for the absence of epidemics.

The chief towns in the area with which we are concerned are Arbil (pop. 14,000), situated towards the northern end of the Arbil Plain; Koi (pop. 5,000), at the edge of the Koi district under the Haib us Sultan Dagh; Altun Keupri (pop. 2,000), mostly built on an island in the Lesser Zab; Rawanduz (pop. 1,500), at the upper end of the gorge of the Rawanduz Chai; Shaqlawah (pop. 3,000), on the northern slopes of the Safin Dagh; and Makhmur (pop. 1,000), on the upper edge of the Qara Choq desert. I will deal with these places as I come to them in the narrative.

The total population of the Arbil Division, which includes Koi and Rawanduz, but not Altun Keupri or the Rania district, is estimated at about 105,000.

The most important road in the area is that which connects Mosul, Arbil, Altun Keupri, and Kirkuk with the railhead near Kifri. This can be used by cars throughout. There are bridges over the two branches of the Lower Zab at Altun Keupri. Before the war much trade from the hills flowed down this road, and it was a safer route from Mosul to Baghdad than the shorter way along the Tigris. The country along the road is fertile and thickly populated, and must have been a highway for thousands of years.

The Greater Zab may be crossed in two places, either at Kellek or at Quwair. The Kellek road is rough and not fit for cars, but it is 15 miles shorter than the Quwair road. The river is crossed by a ferry. There is a magnificent bridge built by the Turks, but it is deficient of the essential portion across

the main current of the stream. It was intended to complete
it by a suspension bridge, but as one of the columns on which
it would have rested has collapsed, it may be inferred that
the foundations of the whole structure are unsatisfactory.
Many similar monuments of Turkish inefficiency exist; the
money necessary to complete the scheme was undoubtedly
provided, but found its way into the pockets of greedy and
underpaid officials. The other route, which presents no difficulties, is via Quwair, where the river is crossed by a ferry
which can ply at any time except for a few days during the
highest floods. A direct road exists from Altun Keupri to
Quwair. It passes through Dibaka, and was the main Turkish
line of communication between Mosul and Kirkuk during the
war.

Another important road is that from Arbil to the rail-head
at Shargat, via Makhmur. The direct route is not passable for
cars, and at present a big detour has to be made. The Tigris
is crossed by a ferry. This road has greatly increased in importance since the coming of the railway to Shargat.

Nearly every village in the Arbil district can be reached by
car, but in the hills communications are very bad, and many
of the paths are not even fit for animals. Several roads exist
between Arbil and Koi – all of them very bad.

Two main roads from Persia pass through our area. The
more northerly of these comes from Saujbulaq, and crossing
the frontier at Garwa Shaikh passes down the valley of the
Rawanduz Chai, through Rawanduz itself and the Gorge,
across the Dasht-i-Harir and so to Arbil. This route was used
by the Russians when they occupied Rawanduz, and extensive efforts have been made to improve it. A couple of cars
even were brought down it, and the remains of one of them
are still to be seen at the bottom of the Gorge. Carts passed
along it regularly in Turkish times. Its value as a trade route
depends on the political situation on both sides of the border.
Tracks from Ushnu and Urmia join the main road at Rawanduz, and a track also leads out of it before Dera is reached,
providing a direct route for caravans to Mosul via the ferry at
Girdmamik.

The more southerly route crosses the frontier by the
Wazna Pass and proceeds over the Pizhder Plain and Bituin
to Koi. The track over the Haib us Sultan Dagh is very rough.

From Koi caravans proceed to Taqtaq on the Lesser Zab, where either passengers and goods are placed on rafts and floated down to Altun Keupri and Baghdad, or else the river is crossed in a ferry and the journey continued to Kirkuk.

The list of fauna is not a large one. Domestic animals I will leave to a later chapter. Of mammals, on the plains the commonest are the Persian gazelle, the grey wolf, the jackal, a fox with a tawny coat which turns grey at the tips in the winter, the hare, the wild pig, the jerboa, the common rodents, and the hedgehog. Large herds of gazelle are found, especially in the Qara Choq desert; their flesh is excellent, and they are often kept as pets. Wolves are alleged to carry off a large number of sheep; but I think these are more often human than not, for the shepherd finds in them an excellent excuse whereby to defraud his master. The hare provides plenty of sport for the Kurdish chiefs – also the wild pig, which does much damage to the crops, especially on Bituin. The peasant Kurd has little scruple in eating the flesh of the wild pig, and even of the fox, provided that no one of importance is watching. There was a plague of rats in 1919, and they did a great deal of damage to millet crops on the great rivers. The houses swarm with mice, of an unusually impudent variety. The jerboa, with its long hind legs, its tufted tail, and its enormous eyes, is a most fascinating creature, and can easily be tamed.

In the hills are found ibex in profusion, an animal called the 'Shur' which I think must be a musk-deer, the lynx, with squirrels, stone-martens, and smaller animals. The fox above-mentioned, and the wild pig, are also very common. The Kurd is fond of stalking the ibex, largely for the meat which it provides. Leopards are rare, and the skins are greatly in demand for saddle coverings. I have not seen the full-grown bear, but the cubs are often caught and kept as pets. I think they usually die; in any case, when they grow up they become unmanageable. The stone-marten is valuable on account of its fur; one skin would fetch about 14 rupees in Arbil in 1920. Large numbers of fox skins are also brought in. They sell at about Rs.2.8 each.

Reptiles, except for frogs and lizards, are not common. A few small snakes may be seen in the spring, and I believe that they are mostly harmless. The Kurds are extremely frightened of them, but I never heard of anybody dying of snake-bite, except one old woman, and that was under the most suspicious circumstances. In the hills a large snake, which may be a python, is sometimes found.

Fish abound in all the rivers. Those of the Greater Zab are excellent, but the product of the Lesser Zab is considered of a very inferior quality. They are usually netted or drugged with medicated bait by the local people. In the Greater Zab they are only caught in the winter and spring, when the water is turbid and the weather is cool enough to allow of their being transported and sold in Arbil. Some of them are very big, one often forming a whole donkey-load. The hill streams abound with fish, and excellent sport may be had.

The common birds are mostly similar to those found in England; the gaudy and noisy varieties of India are entirely absent. Sparrows, larks, and goldfinches abound, also many small birds which I cannot name. A fly-catcher of the most brilliant blue is often seen in the plains, also the hoopoe and a little bronze bee-eater. In the hills are found the jay, and a black-and-white bird with a very long tail and an ungainly flight. The black crow is seen everywhere, also various sorts of kites and hawks; majestic eagles soar among the mountain goats. The art of hawking is remembered but not practised. In the spring of 1920 a brood of hawks was captured and distributed amongst two or three Kurdish chiefs, who announced their intention of training them.

Of game birds there is a considerable variety. The Greater Bustard is common on the Arbil Plain and the Qara Choq desert. The Lesser Bustard I have only seen once in this area. The black partridge is plentiful along the Greater Zab, while the Indian sisi or small partridge may be found in the low hills. The bigger hills abound in chikhor, a large red-legged partridge. Enormous flocks of sand-grouse cover the plains from April to October, after which they fly off south. Of water birds the snipe and teal are common in the winter, together with several varieties of goose and duck. A large blue crane, the Qulun, is plentiful and its flesh is edible. The plover with its cry 'Oh, did you do it?' and the pigeon may be met everywhere on the plains.

But of all the birds the most remarkable is the common stork, and he deserves a paragraph to himself. He arrives about February with his wife and proceeds to make his nest on the house-top. He usually selects an old nest, which is probably already nearly a foot in height, and proceeds to add to it. When he is not collecting food or material, he may be seen standing on his nest clacking his beak, and in his ecstasy gradually raising his head until he brings it right over and touches his back. Then he returns to his first position, and starts all over again. From the noise that he makes, and from the fact that he is supposed to perform the pilgrimage to Mecca when he migrates in August, he is known as the Hajji Laqlaq. He is very much respected, and nobody would think of interfering with him or his nest, possibly because he would give them short shrift if they did. One or two couples may be seen on every house during the nesting season.

Insects are the greatest pest in Kurdistan. First and foremost comes the flea, of which more hereafter. Next comes the house fly, with whom is associated another fly exactly similar in appearance, but possessing a sharp proboscis, with which he can cause considerable pain. A tiny red ant which is very fond of biscuits is a great nuisance. Mosquitoes are a plague in the summer and autumn, wherever there is irrigation. The date fly, a large black-and-yellow hornet, eats the fruit in the summer, but is not nearly so dangerous as he looks. A funny animal with a slender waist and a high-pitched voice – I believe an ichneumon – builds houses for his progeny all over the walls of one's room, and proceeds to fill them with caterpillars. Scorpions are common, both the black and the more deadly yellow ones – also the jerrymandrum, a large yellowish spider, a specimen of which has been known to measure as much as six inches from knee to knee. He is quite harmless. Some people are fond of catching a scorpion and a jerrymandrum and putting them in a bowl together to see them fight. The latter always wins unless too bloated to move. He seizes the scorpion's tail just below the sting with his powerful mandibles, and saws it through. He then proceeds to feast on his victim.

Brilliant bronze and green beetles may be seen flying from flower to flower in the spring. When the summer comes the country is loud with the chirp of cicalas and grasshoppers, of which a hundred varieties must exist. Sometimes locusts arrive in swarms and do great damage to the crops. But

few butterflies are found, and those mostly similar to the
common English varieties. Bees are kept in the hill villages
and produce excellent honey.

Of the vegetable world I will not speak at great length.
Above 3,000 ft. the hills are covered with scrub oak, wild
pear, sumach, hawthorn, and other shrubs, up to the height
of 7,000 ft., after which they are bare. By the streams may be
found chinar, i.e. the plane tree, ash, the walnut tree, poplars, mulberries, and willows. I have seen juniper in one spot
only, and conifers are entirely absent. The bramble is common. Oleanders grow along the streams among the foothills,
and flower beautifully throughout the hot weather. On the
plains few trees grow wild; only an occasional mulberry may
be seen near water. The characteristic plants are the thistle
and camel-thorn. Liquorice is found in abundance near water,
especially on the banks of the Greater Zab. Several varieties
of fruit and timber trees are cultivated – these will be dealt
with later.

In the spring the whole country breaks into flower. One
day I counted thirty different varieties growing within
twenty yards of my house. The most noticeable to which I can
give a name, that are found on the plains, are the anemone in
mauve, white, and crimson, the scarlet and yellow ranunculus, several sorts of iris, the grape hyacinth, hollyhocks in
two colours, mullein, and poppy. In addition to these there
are many magnificent blossoms the identity of which I do not
know, including a delicate flower of the brightest blue like a
Canterbury bell, and a tall spire of white blossoms with black
centres, both of which grow among the green corn beside the
poppy and the hollyhock, and a pale pink flower growing in
bunches on a tall stem, which in April literally covers the
little valleys among the sandstone hills of the Koi district.
Amongst the grass glitter myriad minute blossoms in white,
yellow, and blue. Higher up in the hills you find narcissus in
acres, violets, squills, buttercups, fritillaries, orchids, great
scarlet tulips, roses, and tiger lilies. Every fortnight the
hillsides put on a different coloured garment; until the rains
cease and they return to their dull brown, which is often
turned to black by the fires that rage in the summer heat.

CHAPTER III

THE KURDS

EXCEPT FOR THE INHABITANTS of Arbil town, a few Christians in Ainkawa, Shaqlawah, and Koi, and scattered Arab villages in Shamamik and Qara Choq, the Arbil Division is entirely populated by Kurds.

Despite the fact that the Kurds are one of the most virile races in existence, that they occupy a very large portion of the Middle East, and that they are of the same Aryan stock as ourselves, the public at home know practically nothing about them, and there must be many who before the war had never even heard their name.

'Well,' the reader will ask, 'in what country does this wonderful race live, and why has it not made its power more felt in Eastern politics?' The name Kurdistan, which means 'the country of the Kurds', may be seen written large across maps of the Middle East; but if one looks for boundaries, there are none. For the term includes a large portion of northern Mesopotamia at present under British control, a broad strip along the western border of Persia, a solid lump of country under Turkish control round the towns of Van, Ezerum, Bitlis, Kharput, and Diabekr, and even a portion of the territory within the French sphere of influence to the north of Aleppo. This then explains why we hear so little of the Kurds. As a race they are not a political entity. They are a collection of tribes without any cohesion, and showing little desire for cohesion. They prefer to live in their mountain fastnesses and pay homage to whatever Government may be in power, as long as it exercises little more than a nominal authority. The day that the Kurds awake to a national consciousness and combine, the Turkish, Persian, and Arab states will crumble to dust before them. That day is yet far off.

The Kurds are an Aryan race, and are supposed to be identical with the ancient Medes. They are referred to in

Xenophon as the Carduchi.[1] The most famous Kurd in history is Saladin or Silah ud Din who once made Arbil his capital. Prominent chiefs have often established independent states, notably at Bayazid in the sixteenth century, and at Rawanduz and Sulaimaniyah in more recent times, but such states usually fell to pieces within a few years of their founder's death.

The Kurdish language is extremely interesting and is quite easy to learn for one who knows Persian and has plenty of opportunity of conversing with the people. Kurdish, though it is supposed to be the purer language, is like a rough dialect of Persian, and appears to one who is not a philological expert to bear much the same relation to that language as a broad Yorkshire dialect does to orthodox English. It possesses no alphabet of its own, and when it is written, the Arabic letters are used. As many sounds, especially vowel sounds, occur which do not exist in Arabic this arrangement is extremely awkward, and may account for the fact that the language is very rarely written. In the Arbil Division Persian is the sole medium of correspondence between Kurdish chiefs, in the Mosul Division Arabic is used. In Sulaimaniyah Major E. B. Soane, C.B.E., worked hard to persuade the people to use their own language, and Kurdish is employed for all official correspondence. A newspaper is issued in the same tongue. A suggestion has been made that the Roman alphabet should be adopted, as it fits the language so much better than the Arabic. The Turks, obsessed with Pan-Turanianism, did their best to suppress the Kurdish tongue, and few or no grammars or educational books exist in that language. Major Soane has written two English–Kurdish grammars.

As is inevitable with a widely scattered race possessing no written language, Kurdish is a tongue of many dialects; these are divided into two groups, the northern and the southern. The Arbil Division is on the border line. In the Arbil and Koi districts the dialect is distinctly southern, while the tribes to the north of Rawanduz, especially the migratory tribes who come down to the plains in the winter, speak a northern dialect. Each tribe has its own peculiarities, and there is a small community called the Darbandlis, living in a few villages

1 Probably the *Kudraha* of the cuneiform inscriptions.

round Taqtaq on the Lesser Zab, whose language is quite un-intelligible to their immediate neighbours. In Koi they tell a story of a mad Englishman who came to them asking what word they used for 'girl'. On learning that the Darbandlis used the word 'daut' (cf. daughter), he immediately rushed off to one of the villages and spent several days there studying their strange tongue. Old Abdulla Pasha, a Kurd of Rawan-duz, when appointed by the Turkish Government as Qaima-qam, or Governor of Amadia, found that he had to converse with the Kurdish population through the medium of Turkish, as they were mutually unintelligible in their own tongue.

A Kurdish literature exists, the best known author being Shaikh Riza, who wrote poetry in four languages. He was a native of Kirkuk, and belonged to the prominent Tālabāni family. His son was the Turkish Governor of Rania at the time of our occupation. Folk-songs are current, those used in the Arbil Division being mostly in the northern dialect. They deal with love and war.

The majority of the Kurdish race now belong to the Sunni or orthodox Muhammadan sect. With the exception of a few tribes, the Kurds adopted Muhammadanism at a very early date, but their faith sat lightly on them, and they were prac-tically heathen until the Turks, with considerable political acumen, saw that the sole means by which they could attach the race to themselves was through their religion, and did everything possible to promote Islam amongst them. The re-sult is that though traces of heathendom still exist in 'high places' upon the hilltops, and though the Kurdish peasant will neglect Ramazan and eat the flesh of the pig, the better-class Kurd is very strict in his devotions, and says his prayers regularly and at the proper time – but rather with the air of a small boy praying because he is told to by his bet-ters, and not because of any conviction of the efficacy or the necessity of prayer. I have often seen Kurds interrupt their devotions, without changing their positions, to add some re-mark to a conversation that interests them. Hence it follows that the Kurds are normally by no means fanatical, though they are powerfully influenced by their shaikhs and mullas in whom they place the most implicit trust.

The word 'shaikh' in Kurdistan does not mean a tribal chief as it does amongst the Arabs. It invariably refers to a man who is holy and venerated either on account of his descent from a sacred origin, or because of his pious life. Thus nearly all saiyids or descendants of the Prophet are in Kurdistan given the title of Shaikh. Some of the seshaikhs are really good men, others are fanatical intriguers. The influence of these holy men will be abundantly illustrated in the course of this book, and any traveller in Kurdistan will be well advised to pay them the greatest respect whenever he meets them.

There is a mulla in nearly every village. He always comes to the guest-room, and helps to entertain an honoured visitor, and is very useful as an interpreter if one is needed. These mullas advise many of the chiefs in everything they do, and nearly every good Kurdish chief I know has some good old mulla behind him, notably Babekr Agha of the Pizhder, who is the biggest chief in Kurdistan, and incidentally the most loyal, and who relies entirely on the advice of a local divine. The mullas, too, are the sole source of education in Kurdish villages.

Some of the Kurdish tribes in the north must have been Christians at one time. A remnant survives among the Nestorians. Other tribes covered their heathen practices with a veneer of Muhammadanism and became Qizilbashes and Kakais. In the extreme south several tribes are found which have come under Persian influence and adopted the Shiah faith. But in the Arbil Division all the Kurds are Sunnis except in two villages belonging to the Saralu tribe.

Roughly speaking, within Mesopotamia all the country east of the Tigris and northwards of a line drawn from Mandali to the junction of the Lesser Zab with that river, is inhabited by Kurds. The two most important centres south of the Lesser Zab are Kirkuk and Sulaimaniyah. The former town, like Arbil, possesses a Turkish population, the latter is entirely Kurdish. Each is the headquarters of a political division. The Kurds of this area are mostly settled folk, and except for the Jaf and Hamawand possess comparatively little tribal feeling. North of the Lesser Zab are found great tribal organisations, like the Dizai and Pizhder, and the wild clans of the Rawanduz mountains who are intensely tribal in feeling. Beyond the Greater Zab the chief centres are Aqra,

Amadia, and Zakho, round which dwell some of the most savage and uncivilised tribes of Kurdistan.

In this chapter it is my intention to describe briefly the appearance and manner of life of the Kurds who live between the two Zabs.

In the Arbil Division the Kurds belong to two main types, the 'dundok-khwar' or 'eater of wheat cakes' of the plain, and the 'doshab-khwar' or 'eater of grape-syrup' of the hills; though it must be remembered that the Kurds are all in origin a hill-people, and that the plain dwellers only left the hills two or three centuries ago, and still retain many of the characteristics of a hill people. In both types a wide divergence is nearly always found, both in appearance and manner of life, between the agha or chief and the peasant.

The Kurdish peasant is generally short, broad, and wiry. He is rarely over 5 ft. 6 ins. in height, except in the plains where bigger men are sometimes found. He allows his beard to grow, but normally shaves his head except for a small fringe. His face is typically Aryan, except in rare cases where the eyes have a narrow Mongolian appearance. The hair is normally black or dark brown, the eyes brown, and the complexion a light olive, as light or lighter than that of the Italian or Spaniard. It is not rare to find bright red hair, blue eyes, and a freckled face.

His dress normally consists of a white cotton shirt with long sleeves, baggy cotton trousers, and a black quilted coat which crosses in front over the stomach and is tucked into the trousers. Round his waist he winds a long piece of printed calico, interlacing it backwards and forwards. It is usually blue and black in colour, and may be anything from three to fifteen yards long. When laced up it often reaches from the waist to the armpits. In the winter he usually wears in addition trousers of homespun yarn, generally drab with blue stripes down the leg, and over his coat a ribbed sleeveless waistcoat of plain undyed felt. A rough felt overcoat is also worn in cold weather. It possesses short stiff sleeves, which, as the arms are rarely placed through them, stick out from the shoulders, giving the wearer a scarecrow-like appearance. His head-dress consists of a skull cap wound round loosely with two or three silk or cotton scarves. In the hills a conical cap with a tassel on it often takes the place of the

skull cap. During the harvest in the Arbil Plain a broad-
brimmed felt hat is worn, of the type usually associated with
Robinson Crusoe and Mexican bandits. A big tuft of goat's
hair on the top makes the wearer even more brigand like. It
can nearly always be ascertained whether a man is Muhammadan, Christian, or Jew, and if a Muhammadan from what
place or tribe he comes, by the way he ties his head-dress. In
the Rawanduz district the costume varies slightly. Bell-
mouthed trousers shaped like a sailor's and made of homespun yarn are worn, with a light coat of the same material
with or without a quilted coat underneath. These trousers
are typical of the northern Kurd; the southerner's trousers
are always baggy at the top and narrow at the ankle.

The Kurd's footwear consists of various kinds of slippers,
the most noticeable being the 'qaliq'. These are made of one
unstitched piece of buffalo hide shaped to the foot, and deco-
rated on top with coloured wool or silk. On either side of the
heel are holes, with the help of which the slipper is tied to
the foot by a thick woollen cord. These qaliqs are largely used
in the hill districts. Among the Rania tribes fine stockings of
white wool are worn reaching to the knee. Some of the young
Dizai aghas indulge in long riding boots.

In the bigger tribes the aghas, whose families for many
generations have been entirely disassociated from manual
labour, are of a far finer type than the peasants. They sometimes reach 6ft. in height, and usually possess handsome
aquiline features. I know one or two who are very stout, but
stoutness is a great rarity in Kurdistan. Their dress is similar to that of the peasants, except that the materials are
richer and more brightly coloured, and, in the plains especially, instead of the quilted coat a long dress of brilliant silk
material reaching to the ground is the rule. This comes from
the Arabs. Over it is placed a short jacket of blue, brown, or
grey cloth, shaped not unlike an Eton jacket, and sometimes
embroidered with gold. On state occasions the Arab 'abah
mantle is also worn. An old man is sometimes seen in a long
quilted silk jacket of bright yellow or pink reaching below the
knees. In the remotest hill tribes the dress and appearance of
the agha differs very little from that of his tribesman.

A word must be said about the long white sleeve which
every Kurd wears. The Arab often wears them, too, but not in

such an exaggerated form. I have several times asked the reason for their length, and am usually told that the object is to enable the wearer to tie the ends behind his neck, thereby pulling up his coat sleeve as far as his elbow, and keeping his arms free for working, eating, washing, or fighting as may be necessary. When not tied together behind the neck these sleeves are normally wound round the arm above the wrist. They are loosened while praying.

Women when they appear in public are always dressed in an ample dark blue gown caught in at the waist. On their heads they wear a small turban of the same colour. They are the only women in the East to wear this type of head-dress. Except for the chief's wives, they never go veiled. Very small children are usually loaded with ornaments and dressed in bright colours, until the age of seven or eight, when they are clad in the same fashion as their elders.

The Kurds treat their womenfolk with much more respect than do most Muhammadan races. Only the chiefs keep their wives in seclusion, and this practice has quite recently sprung up, being due to Turkish influence. All other women move about much as the men, and I have even known the wife of a village headman come into the guest-house. It is commonly considered dishonourable for women to speak to Europeans, but they are quite free with strangers of their own race. Most chiefs are to a greater or less extent under the thumb of their womenfolk, who, I think, exercise a great deal of influence for good and do much to prevent their husbands from making fools of themselves. A chief will normally refer to his wife as So-and-so's mother, naming the eldest son she has borne him. Women always prepare the food, wash the clothes, and draw the water. They perform the arduous duties of the house, while their husbands are in the fields, or if they are of high rank, while they sit in the guest-house and smoke.

It sometimes happens that a woman may become the head of a village, or even the chief of a tribe, especially when she has an infant son for whom she holds her husband's former property in trust. It is rare, however, for her to occupy such a position, and it generally leads to trouble when she does.

Children live with the womenfolk till the age of seven, after which the boys join their fathers. The latter are usually present in the guest-house when strangers arrive, and kiss the hand of those of high rank. They also serve the coffee, and make themselves generally useful.

Infant mortality is very great. Old Ibrahim Agha of the Dizai was the father of seventeen sons in all. Of these fourteen died in infancy. Incidentally during his lifetime of seventy odd years he had nineteen wives.

The laws that govern marriage and divorce are those that are universal amongst Muhammadans, though several strange customs exist in relation to tribal law; some of these will be noted later. A man is allowed four wives. A chief if he can afford it generally avails himself of the full number; the peasant is nearly always monogamous. Divorce is ridiculously easy, as according to the local interpretation of the law it is only necessary for a man to say to his wife, 'I divorce you' three times, and the union is dissolved. The husband is responsible for the maintenance of his former wife for three months after the divorce, or longer if she is pregnant. The better-class woman is also insured against divorce by a settlement which the husband makes at the time of the marriage. By this he settles a sum, of say £100, on his wife to be paid on divorce, or in the event of his predeceasing her.

By Muhammadan law a man can only bequeath a small portion of his estate; the rest must be divided in fixed proportions amongst his relations including his wives. In Kurdistan, when a man dies his brothers, if he has any, will usually marry his wives to prevent any portion of the property leaving the family.

A wife in Kurdistan has to be bought. A chief may have to pay as much as £500 for a lady of high birth, and in addition will give her father a pony and some costly changes of raiment. The price will, of course, vary with the rank of the lady and the suitor. The latter is usually allowed to see his intended once before the bargain is closed. The nearest male relation, either father, brother, or uncle, receives the money.

The wedding takes place amid much rejoicing and merrymaking, and is a long proceeding. Men and women join together in a dance, forming a ring and jogging up and down to the music of drums and the zurnai, an instrument with a note not unlike that of a bagpipe.

KURDS OF THE RAWANDUZ DISTRICT

KURDISH WOMEN

AND CHILDREN

If a girl is left without any near male relation she becomes anybody's property. She usually throws herself on the mercy of the nearest chief, who keeps her as a servant, or gives her as a wife to one of his retainers.

By tribal law a cousin has first refusal of a lady's hand. A most gruesome murder occurred whilst I was in Arbil, owing to the refusal of this right. The details will be related in the next chapter.

Except for two or three nomadic tribes who spend their summer on the Persian hills, and winter on the Arbil Plain, the Kurds of the Arbil Division are all sedentary or only semi-nomadic, and live for the greater part of the year in settled villages. These consist entirely of mud houses, of which the only valurble portion is the beams which support the roof. If a Kurd does not like the site of his village he simply pulls off his roof, loads the wood on his donkeys and moves elsewhere. Deserted villages may often be seen on the roadside, but if the traveller looks round he will probably see a brand new settlement a mile or so away. The former village was too near the path of the Turkish soldiery to be pleasant, so the inhabitants moved elsewhere.

These mud houses are extremely simple in design. For the poorer class of peasant they may consist of only one room, in which he, his wife, and children, his ox and his poultry sleep, in which his store of firewood, butter and cheese is kept, and in which all his meals are cooked. In spite of this, except for very smoky walls and roof, everything will be spotlessly clean. The better-class peasant will probably possess a house containing two or three rooms with a yard attached for his animals; while a chief or headman of a village, in addition to a fine building for his womenfolk, will keep a separate establishment or guest-house for the entertainment of his friends and the passing wayfarer. The guest-house is the centre round which life in Kurdistan revolves.

Before I proceed to describe this important institution I must just mention that the Kurd does not pass the whole year in his village. With the advent of spring he brings out his black tent, and proceeds with his household and flocks to the nearest pasture, where he spends the two pleasantest months of the year. Whether it is the hot blood pulsing in his veins with the oncoming of spring and filling him with a longing for movement and fresh air, or whether it is a sense of beauty calling him to come and view nature in her brightest garments, that drives him to his migration I know not: all I know is that when I asked an old Kurdish farmer for the reason, he replied that he was induced to go into camp firstly by the fleas, and secondly on account of the mess the cows made of the village after eating the new grass.

There are few more beautiful sights in this world than a camp of black Kurdish tents amongst the luxuriant grasses and flowers, with a group of hot-blooded young Kurdish aghas in their fine clothes standing outside, or galloping up and down on their full-fed, high-spirited horses.

In May the Kurd of the Arbil plain returns to his village, and builds a booth of branches on the top of his house for his womenfolk to sleep in. In the Koi district and the lower parts of the Rawanduz district the people build entirely new villages out of branches and reeds, in which they live until the summer heat abates. Whatever breeze there is blows cool through these reed huts, and can be made cooler still by frequently saturating the windward wall with water. In Shaqlawah booths are erected in the fruit gardens.

The most important tribes in the Rania district and some of the small communities in the Rawanduz area migrate to the hills in summer, leaving only a few men behind to look after the crops and houses.

There is this big difference between the Kurd and the Arab, that whereas in the majority of cases the Arab is nomadic by choice and cannot be persuaded to settle, the Kurd, a pastoral race, is nomadic from necessity or by force of habit, and will readily settle when he sees it will pay him to do so.

I must now ask the reader's patience while I describe the guest-house or 'diwan-khana' at some length. I must have spent several hundreds of hours in the guest-houses of various chiefs and village headmen during my stay in Kurdistan, and it was in these that I learnt all the little I know of the Kurds and their language, and in which I transacted most of my important business. It is on his guest-house that a chief's reputation largely depends. The more lavish his hospitality the greater his claim to be called a 'piao' or 'man'. The guest-house is built in the most prominent part of the

village – in the Arbil plain usually on top of one of the many
old Assyrian mounds. It may consist of from one to three
rooms, according to the wealth and standing of the chief to
whom it belongs. I will take as an example the guest-house of
Ahmed Pasha, the richest but by no means the most lavish of
the Dizai chiefs. It is built so as to form three sides of a
square on the top of a large mound. The opening faces north.
The eastern wing consists of one large room about 45 ft. by
15, which is used in the winter. During the summer the
guests are entertained in the central portion, which is in the
form of a verandah. The closed side to the south is pierced by
small windows to create a draught; these can be stopped up if
a dusty south wind is blowing. The western wing consists of
small rooms where the tea-things and bedding are kept, and
where the servants sit and chat. A small door here gives
access to the women's quarters, which are built as an exten-
sion to the western wing. The accompanying sketch will
make my meaning clearer.

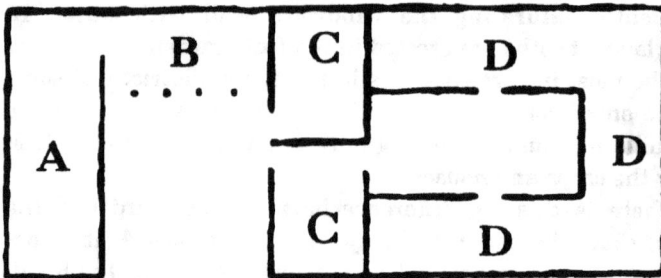

A is the winter room. B is the verandah. The Cs and Ds represent the servants' rooms and women's quarters respectively.

A commoner form of guest-house consists of two rooms
with a small verandah between. For the summer a raised
dais is constructed outside from 'laban' (mud and straw). This
can only be used when the sun has gone down, unless wood is
plentiful when a 'chardaq' is built. This consists of a roof of
light branches, with the leaves still on, supported by four
wooden poles. It is often constructed over a stone water tank
through which a stream is allowed to run. In such case it
provides a delightfully cool retreat on a hot summer's day.

Nearly all guest-houses have a small mosque attached to them, and in many villages the guest-house itself is used as and called the mosque. No objection is made to a European lodging there, and when the people assemble for prayers there will be no necessity for him to disturb himself.

In winter the main room is heated by an open fireplace in the centre; the smoke passes out (or does not, as the case may be) by a hole in the middle of the roof. Many a time have I wept bitterly, but the Kurds seem to be little affected. You can always tell the age of the building by the blackness of the roof and walls. The fuel used is generally the dried dung of sheep and goats, which burns very slowly, with sticks or logs of wood. When it is necessary to warm a room quickly large bundles of dead thistles or brushwood are burnt.

The guest-house is built by free labour; for this is one of the duties which the villagers owe to their chief or headman. Also if the chief is either a poor or a mean man, when a guest arrives he will send to Umr and Zaid (the Kurdish equivalent of Tom, Dick, and Harry) for a pound of butter, a couple of fowls, and two pounds of rice. In reality the guest-house in most places is more of a village club than the private property of the headman. In it the village elders assemble every evening to smoke and discuss the weather, the crops, and the latest scandals. With the bigger chiefs the diwan-khana is a living-room in which they sit all day with their own friends and relations making plans to kill their enemies and defraud the Government.

Hospitality is one of the finest features in the Kurd's character. It is, it is true, enjoined by their religion, and the same custom prevails amongst other Muhammadan races. But the Kurd has carried it to a fine art. A chief will consider it a great insult if you pass his house by without stopping for a cup of tea, and many is the time I have been constrained to come in against my will. The Arab is just as pressing, and is a much better conversationalist, but he does not make his guest nearly so comfortable.

In order to explain the routine I will take my reader on a visit to Ibrahim Agha, the chief of the Dizaiat Makhmur. We have arrived unexpectedly. Old Ibrahim Agha comes out with a loud 'Khair hati', which literally translated means 'Welcome'. We reply 'Salamat bi', 'Peace be on you', and inquire after his health and that of his relations. Meanwhile he gives hurried orders to his servants to fetch mattresses and cushions, and leads us into his main guest room. The floor is bare and spotlessly clean. While we are waiting he produces some cigarettes.

The Kurdish cigarette is an inch or more longer than ours, the extra length consisting chiefly of a mouthpiece. The tobacco is dry and powdery, and if it is of the best Kurdish variety is very good. These cigarettes will be served out to us at frequent intervals during the rest of the day. The Kurd rarely stops smoking except when he is eating. He always carries a bag of tobacco attached to his waistbelt and a packet of cigarette-papers. Some of the older peasants still possess flints and tinder for lighting purposes, but most of them use a patent cigarette lighter which I suspect comes from Japan. A short clay pipe is often smoked by the old farmer type, while some of the elderly aghas indulge in a wooden pipe with a very long stem. Old Hama Agha of Koi had a pipe two feet long. The hubble-bubble has practically gone out of use in Kurdistan; for some reason or other they seem to consider it immoral. I have often offered cigars to Kurdish chiefs. They profess to be delighted with them, but I notice that when I present them with a whole box they nearly always reserve them for European visitors. Our tobacco they consider too mild for a pipe.

Cushions and rugs are quickly brought, and placed along the sides and tops of the room. Special mattresses are placed for us at the top. We take off our shoes and sit down with our legs crossed. There are three rules to remember when visiting a Kurdish chief, never stretch your legs out, in any case in the direction of another person, never convey food to your mouth with your left hand, and never fondle a dog. Provided these rules are observed and we behave otherwise with due courtesy we shall run no risk of offending our host.

After the cushions have been placed the floor will be sprinkled with water to keep the room clean and cool. The floor will be constantly kept moist if the weather is at all hot.

It is now about noon. The first thing we must do is to warn our host that we do not want a large meal, otherwise we shall not get anything to eat till 3 p.m. I have often been caught in this way. I have arrived in a village, and without

my knowing it the chief has immediately given orders for a
sheep to be killed. After half an hour I have asked leave to
depart, and my host has replied, 'You can't possibly go; I have
already killed a sheep and incurred all sorts of expense. You
can't let it all be wasted.' In which case I have had to sit and
wait for another two or three hours while the meal is being
prepared. Ibrahim Agha will protest at great length, but if we
promise him to stay for the evening meal will consent to
order a light lunch.

By this time if we had been in the guest-house of a smaller chief all the village elders would have come in and would
be sitting round the walls listening to what we had got to say.
They are terribly dour and taciturn, and have no idea of making conversation. I normally had little to talk to them about,
and used to pass long hours in asking them questions about
their language, customs, and past history. Meanwhile crowds
of little boys would be staring at us through the windows.

With Ibrahim Agha, however, this will not be the case. Except for one or two young relations standing at a respectful
distance, watching us, and ready to pounce on us with fresh
cigarettes, lit in their own mouths, before we have quite
finished what we are already smoking, and some servants
busy making coffee and tea at the other end of the room,
nobody will be present. Our host, who is a delightful and
well-educated old man, will entertain us with conversation
until coffee is served. It will be the sweet Turkish coffee in
little cups and saucers, and the relation in attendance will
take the cups in turn from the tray which the servants hold
behind him, and hand them to us in his right hand, holding
the left hand over his heart in token of submission. Personally I prefer the bitter Arab coffee which you more often
find among the Kurds. A very small quantity of this,
flavoured sometimes with cardamom, is served at the bottom
of a little handleless cup. You are allowed one or two refills.
This coffee comes as a great relief after the quantities of
sweet tea one is made to drink.

The duties of qahwachi, or the man who makes the coffee,
are usually performed by one of the agha's most trusted retainers. He holds a privileged position, and receives a small
proportion of his master's crops.

By the time we have finished our coffee, tea will be ready. The Kurd is a great tea drinker, and the samovar and chest of cups, or rather glasses, are always produced as soon as a visitor arrives, and are usually taken on a long journey. The samovar is a sort of urn, manufactured in Russia and Persia. Through the centre from top to bottom runs a cylindrical hole, in which red-hot pieces of wood or charcoal are placed. A chimney is then fixed on top to draw out the heat while the chaichi or tea-man blows hard at the ashes from below. When the water is hot he washes the teapot and the glasses thoroughly, and when it boils he makes the tea very strong in the teapot, which he places on top of the urn, having removed the chimney. The glasses are about 3 ins. in height, and just over an inch in diameter at the top and base. They narrow in the centre. They are served on little saucers with a small tin spoon. In each glass the chaichi places the equivalent of two lumps of sugar: he then pours in a small quantity of tea, and fills them up with water. No milk is added. The tea is practically stewed, and lies heavy on the stomach. It is undrinkable without the sugar. We shall have to drink two or three glasses, and each time the glass will be thoroughly washed before it is refilled.

When we have finished our tea lunch will be brought. It will probably consist of very thin slabs of unleavened bread, some thicker slabs fried in butter, a dish of lumps of fried meat (mutton), a dish of mast, whatever fruit is in season, and a bowl of 'mastao'. No knives and forks are provided, only spoons for those who cannot eat with their hands. The best way to eat the meat and the mast is to pick it up with pieces of thin bread.

This brings me to the question of mast or curds, one of the delicacies of Kurdistan. The fresh milk of the sheep, goat, cow, or buffalo is heated up to a certain temperature and then curdled with sour milk. The result is mast, which is always sour, but delightfully creamy if fresh. Mast mixed with water produces 'mastao', the favourite drink of the Kurds. Nothing is more refreshing than the big bowl of this beverage, with a lump of snow floating in the middle, which usually greets the traveller when he arrives tired and thirsty at a Kurdish village in the hot weather. It is drunk from a large wooden spoon. The mast that is not consumed in its original

state is placed in a skin and suspended from a pole. The
women push it vigorously backwards and forwards, and butter and buttermilk are produced. The latter, which is known
as 'du', is also an excellent drink, but the better-class Kurd
does not normally offer it to an honoured guest. The butter is
not usually eaten in its fresh state, but is clarified by a series
of boilings and becomes 'rūn', which is the same as the Indian
'ghi'. It is used for cooking purposes.

Before we commence our meal a servant will bring a ewer,
basin, and towels, and pour water over our right hands. After
the meal he will bring the same articles with the addition of
soap, and we shall then wash both our hands. Ibrahim Agha
will not eat with us as he has had his meal previously.

During the afternoon we shall either sit in the guest-room
and talk business, in which case we shall have to drink large
numbers of cups of tea and coffee and smoke numerous cigarettes, or else sleep, and afterwards take a stroll through the
village. Shortly before sunset we shall return, and when the
call to prayer comes Ibrahim Agha will perform his ablutions
and, spreading out a mat, say his prayers close beside us.
When he has finished, the evening meal will be brought in.
An enormous tray almost five feet in diameter is placed on a
low stool, and round this we gather with old Ibrahim Agha
and any other important guest who may be present.

The first course consists of either a large dish containing
a meat pasty, or if it is in season a lamb roast whole, and
stuffed with rice, sultanas, and spices. This is followed by an
equally large dish of sweet pastry containing ground walnuts
soaked in honey. These are only preliminaries, and would not
be served in a smaller chief's house. The normal meal consists of one or two dishes of pilau, i.e. rice prepared with rūn,
with lumps of meat and sultanas on the top, and a number of
small dishes containing meat, vegetables, omelettes, sweet
cakes, mast, fruit, etc. These are now all placed on the tray
at the same time, and we take our choice. Ibrahim Agha will
probably pick out the best pieces of meat and place them on
our bread before us. The rice we eat with our hands. It is
quite easy. You pick up a handful, squeeze it into a sort of
ball, get your thumb behind it and gently push it into your
mouth. We will wash everything with 'mastao', a bowl of

which will be placed under the tray, as there will not be room on top.

After the meal we sit and smoke and drink tea and coffee till our host asks us if we are sleepy, when we prepare to go to bed. Fine silk quilts are brought for us, and if necessary blankets. We curl up on our mattresses and, as there are scarcely any fleas at Mukhmur, quickly fall asleep. Ibrahim Agha is a tactful old man, and will leave us to ourselves. In some guest-houses the chief and village elders would gather round the fire within a few feet of us and discuss us. This is most tantalising, as one can never quite hear what they are saying.

In the morning we shall wake up soon after dawn and when we are ready a meal will be brought to us, consisting of hot milk, tea, bread, mast, and cheese. The milk is served in large encrusted cups with 'Love Me' and 'Souvenir' on them, and 'Made in Germany' on the bottom. Presumably a market for them was found in Mesopotamia when the war broke out, and they could no longer be exported to England. Similarly in the most remote places I frequently came across ash-trays with portraits of our King and Queen, made to commemorate their Coronation.

Having broken our fast we ask our leave to depart, which our host, protesting that he is preparing a midday meal for us, reluctantly grants. To his 'Khair hati' we reply with the words 'Bdu'a', implying that we pray, or shall pray, for his health and prosperity.

The above is more or less what happens every time a Kurdish chief is visited.

The Kurdish meals are really only two in number, the midday meal shortly before noon, and the evening meal just before or after sunset. In addition the better-class Kurd will break his fast at sunrise with a cup of tea and some bread. The staple foods of the peasant are wheat-bread, raisins, which take the place of dates in Lower Mesopotamia, vegetables, mast, and 'burghul'. The latter is crushed wheat. It is served up in the same way as rice, and makes an excellent substitute for that article. Meat is little eaten, though it is always offered to an honoured guest. The Kurd is an artist in cooking vegetables. In the hills 'doshab' or grape-syrup and honey eke out the poor man's fare, while in the remote mountain districts acorns become a staple food. These are ground into a flour from which an exceedingly bitter black bread is baked.

Intoxicants are unknown, and the ordinary drinks are water, 'mastao', and buttermilk. Cordials are made from the grape-syrup. Amongst the Kurd's domestic animals first and foremost comes the horse. The tribes of the Arbil plain possess some remarkably fine mounts of Arab origin. In the hills the ponies are smaller and coarser in type, being more suited to the rough roads they have to traverse. One animal, especially a mare, may be the property of from two to four different persons. In the case of a mare each partner receives a foal in turn. Stallions are rarely gelded. A decent mount cannot be bought under £70, and a good pony will change hands at £200 or more. A chief's horse is well looked after, being fed liberally on barley and chopped straw and turned out to grass in the spring. The Kurds have little idea of grooming. In riding they never trot: a long journey will be performed at a walk averaging about 3½ miles an hour. A horse's walk is the standard of measurement for distance, which is always described by hours. The young aghas are very fond of showing off their equestrian prowess, but they are usually bad riders. The saddle is thickly padded, and curves sharply in front; I always found it most uncomfortable, and trotting is impossible. The stirrups are narrow, and have a large flat base that accommodates all the forepart of the foot. The bit is of the cruel type common throughout Mesopotamia.

The hill tribes, especially migratory tribes like the Herki, breed large numbers of small sturdy ponies that are used solely as beasts of burden.

The mule is of importance, and some remarkably fine types may be seen. On the Arbil plain it is the only animal that is in demand for ploughing purposes. It is also largely employed as a beast of burden. The finest type of mule is used for riding purposes. Dignified old townsmen much prefer this comparatively sedate animal to a frisky horse. For the hills, too, a mule is the more reliable animal. A good plough mule costs about £40.

The donkey is ubiquitous. Almost every peasant, however poor, possesses at least one. They are used as beasts of burden for every purpose, often taking the place of our wheelbar-

row, for treading out corn, and occasionally even for ploughing. The lawsuits that arise over them are interminable.
Every day I used to receive two or three petitions running
somewhat as follows: 'Your respectful servant humbly begs to
state that a grey ass worth twenty pounds, with a black mark
on its back and a torn right ear, which was born and bred in
his house and disappeared five and a half years ago, has been
seen in the possession of Qadir, son of Nadir, of the Serai
quarter of Arbil, and he begs restitution of the same in accordance with the world-famed justice of the mighty British
Government. His be the command who has the right to command.' The case will be sent to the Qazi or judge, and if the
petitioner can establish the identity of the animal, which he
can recognise quite as easily as one of his own children, it
will be returned to him. The aforesaid Qadir, son of Nadir,
will then bring a suit against Ahmed, son of Hamad, from
whom he bought the donkey, to recover its price, and so on,
and so on, until the whole history of the animal for the last
five and a half years has been unfolded. A donkey will fetch
from £5 to £10, or more if it be of the large white variety so
much in demand as riding animals for ladies.

I would remark here that the Kurd proper does not ill-
treat his animals in the way that the Persian Kurd does. You
rarely see a donkey with a bad back, whereas on the Baghdad–Kermanshah road it is the practice to produce festering
sores on the haunches, which may be prodded to make the
unfortunate animal go quicker. The Kurd if left to himself
does not overwork his animals, but when there is no grass
and the owner is poor and grain dear they are sometimes
miserably underfed. However, they pick up again when
spring comes along, and the animals that tread out the corn
are never muzzled.

The Kurd cannot manage a camel; a chief sometimes owns
a few, but always keeps a tame Arab to look after them.

The Kurds are in origin a pastoral race, and sheep and
goats play a most important part in their lives. The sheep
possess great fat tails, almost a foot square, while the goats
are of the variety familiar to us at home, and not like the
misshapen creatures seen in India. The Angora goat is often
kept in the hills. The sheep and goat together provide the
Kurd with milk and its products, viz: 'mast', butter, butter-

milk, and cheese, all of which are necessaries and form part of his staple diet. They supply meat for the table when he requires it, wool for his clothes, felt overcoats, waistcoats, and hats, and hair for the black tents, which once were his only dwelling-place. The skins are used for carrying water and the making of butter, also as floats for the rafts that travel down the river. Finally, the dung is used as fuel, and for manuring tobacco plots. A good sheep before the war could be purchased for about 5s.; the same sized sheep will now cost 30s. The flocks have been much depleted during the war. They are a source of revenue to the Government, 8 annas per animal being collected yearly. At the count carried out early in 1920 there were 200,000 sheep and goats in the Arbil district alone.

Large numbers of cattle are kept, and serve many purposes. They are rarely slaughtered for meat till they are on the point of death, when, of course, only the poorer people will buy. The cow yields milk, but not nearly to the extent she does at home, and sheep and goat's milk holds the premier place. The oxen are used as beasts of burden, for ploughing purposes, and for treading out the corn. They are practically the only plough animals employed in the hills; and the poorer class of peasant also uses them on the plains. The hides are valuable for leather. A good animal of local breed for ploughing purposes will cost about £12. A large number of Indian bullocks were introduced into Kurdistan as plough animals, and proved a great success. Buffaloes are kept where there is water, notably on the Bituin plain. These yield milk from which a cream is made known as 'qaimaq'. The cow will not give her milk unless her calf is present, and in the event of the calf dying it is necessary to stuff its skin and place it in the stable. The result, it is alleged, completely deceives the bereaved mother. These buffaloes are ungainly, hideously ugly animals. Their skins are most valuable for tanning purposes.

Dogs are considered unclean, but nearly every house possesses at least one, usually a large hairy beast and very fierce, especially in the hills, where enormous animals may be seen. They are most useful as sentries over the houses and flocks. Nearly every chief possesses one or more 'tazhis' or Persian greyhounds. These are similar in shape to the variety with which we are familiar, but have a longer coat of hair and most graceful ears. They are used for hunting purposes. They often lie in the corner of a guest-house, but are shooed away if they come near guests at meal-time. I have kept one as a pet, but they are not very affectionate animals. A small terrier may occasionally be found, which possesses the delightful name of 'boojy'.

Cats frequent the houses, but are always very wild; the only time I have ever met a friendly cat that sat by the fire and purred was in an Arab's tent in the Mandali district.

Chickens are kept in every village with sometimes geese and turkeys. The fowls are a good deal larger than the Indian type. There is one remarkable variety which possess no tail. Eggs are plentiful.

The Kurd, if he is permitted, goes about fully armed, with a dagger and one or two pistols in his belt, four bandoliers full of ammunition round his waist and shoulders, and a well-kept narrow-bore rifle. All the bigger tribes are well armed, usually with the .301 Turkish rifle, while the poorer communities possess considerable numbers of the old .450 Mausers. The dagger has a blade about a foot long, slightly curved at the end, a type common to Kurd and Arab.

The Kurd's occupations are principally agricultural and pastoral. A few indulge in trade, though many villages keep a tame Jew for this purpose, or serve as muleteers and donkey men on the main caravan routes. In times of scarcity large numbers will migrate to work on military roads and railways.

His pastimes are not many in number. First and foremost comes highway robbery. In Turkish times every young agha would maintain a body of 'Khubzas' or armed retainers, who lived in his house and fed at his table. When he was not engaged in fighting his neighbour (which I ought possibly to have included in my paragraph on occupations), he would send his men out to watch one of the main roads. They would pounce on the first respectable caravan that came along (poor people with only one or two donkeys were not usually molested) and carry off the spoil to their master, who would divide it up, keeping the lion's share for himself. If the owner of the caravan was fortunate enough to discover the identity of his assailants, he would pay a personal visit to their master, who, if he belonged to the class of good aghas, would

probably restore the goods, after deducting a percentage for
his pains. So it was only a game after all. One of the Dizai
aghas always refused to return property stolen in this way,
and obtained a most unenviable reputation in consequence.

Other pastimes are hunting with greyhounds, the game
being either hare or gazelle, and shooting – generally gazelle,
ibex, or pig. Very few possess shot-guns, and they are not experts. A game of touch-last is played on horseback, polo being
unknown except from Persian literature. I have seen children
play a sort of hockey with crooked sticks and a lump of wood
for a ball. Gambling is rare in the villages, though some
games of cards are popular, while the children play with
knuckle-bones, and also have a complicated game in which
they shift pebbles about in little holes in the ground. The
only amusement in which the adult peasant indulges is sitting down and smoking after a long day's work.

The Kurds do not seem very fond of music. They are
terrible Puritans, and I believe they consider it immoral. The
only instruments I have heard are drums, the zurnai, and a
small reed pipe. Some chiefs keep a special man to sing folk
songs, which are pitched very high, and usually entail a certain amount of yodelling.

As has been mentioned, education can only be obtained
from the village mullas, and consists chiefly of reading the
Quran and a few Persian works such as the 'Gulistan' of
Sadi. Most of the leading chiefs can read and write Persian.
The mullas themselves are often very well-read in Oriental
literature, and have usually studied under some leading
divine of the neighbourhood.

With regard to the Kurdish character, in an official report
I once divided the race into three classes, the good aghas, the
bad aghas, and the people. We will deal first with the people,
who are the finest type I have yet met in the East. They
possess almost a northern temperament, being exact counter-
parts to the volatile Arab and the decadent Persian. The
Kurd is in the first place exceptionally industrious, steady-
going, and thrifty. He prefers saving money to spending it.
Next, unless he is extremely poor, he is always clean. During
the daytime in the neighbourhood of every village a large
party of women will be seen washing clothes. Thirdly, he is
moral to the extent of being puritanical, vices which are com-

mon elsewhere in the East being unmentioned and almost unknown in the tribal areas of Kurdistan. He is normally extremely taciturn; when he speaks he is brief and to the point, and he calls a spade a spade. His brains are exceptionally dense, and his sense of humour, if he possesses one, is very slow. Above all he is a 'zahirbin', a man who only sees what is before him, and after due deliberations shapes his action accordingly. The peasant Kurd is unswerving in his fidelity to his master, however much the latter oppresses him. He has not learnt the lessons of liberty, equality, and fraternity, and good birth counts for a great deal. All Kurds possess a violent temper, which can be roused most unexpectedly. It is said that once two Kurds travelling by night quarrelled so violently about the identity of a star that a combat ensued which was fatal to both. Rich also relates that a Khushnao chief became so enraged with a fly that would settle on his eyelid, that drawing his dagger he struck at his eye and blinded himself. The Kurd has few scruples at taking life, and goes mad at the smell of blood. A chance of obtaining loot will arouse all his avaricious passions. His honour is centred in his women-folk; and he is compelled by the strictest of codes to seek vengeance when once this has been touched. From the above it will be seen that the character of the average Kurd is partly that of a hard-working farmer, and partly that of an untamed savage. In the more remote of the hill tribes the latter element predominates.

The aghas as a class are much more highly developed. They possess better reasoning powers, and higher spirits. Their characteristics are broadly the same as those of the peasants, only the corners have been rubbed off by the more cultivated life they and their ancestors have led for generations. Every agha is consumed more or less by the passion of avarice. Those who keep it under control are the good aghas, while those who give it rein are the bad aghas.

The Kurd has a curious habit of disparaging himself and his brethren – probably inculcated by the Turks, who were bent on Ottomanising him, and stamping out all racial feeling. He will continually refer to himself as 'zahirbin', one who sees the exterior only, 'tamakar' or avaricious, and 'wahshi' (savage).

I always like to compare the Kurd to a schoolboy. He possesses the same half-developed nature, under most circumstances phlegmatic and steady-going, easily shocked, obedient only if his master has a cane, equally spoilt by too much severity or too much kindness, often thoughtlessly cruel and regardless of other people's feelings, possessing a very strict code of honour about sneaking, and game on occasions for a tremendous rag.

CHAPTER IV

THE TRIBE

A TRIBE IS A COMMUNITY or confederation of communities which exists for the protection of its members against external aggression, and for the maintenance of the old racial customs and standards of life. Some tribes have no recognised chief, some have many.

Almost every true Kurd, whether he lives in a town or a village, even though he is a member of no recognised tribe, will refer to himself as a tribesman, by which he means that he recognises tribal law and customs, and expects others to treat him as enjoying tribal rights. 'Ashiratam', 'I am a tribesman', is the equivalent of 'Civis Romanus sum', or 'I belong to a Trade Union' – a claim that must be respected.

The position of the chief varies greatly in different tribes. In the remoter mountains, though granted the most ungrudging obedience, he is distinctly one with the tribesmen, the leading member of a family which has won its headship through military prowess. Lower down he often belongs to an entirely separate caste, and comes from a different stock to the tribesmen. The large tribes are divided into sections, and in different tribes we find many sections with the same names. This points to the fact that the sections represent the original owners of the soil, while the present chiefs belong to powerful families who have invaded their domains and seized their lands. This is notably the case in the Dizai where nearly all the land belongs to one powerful family, against which a few old tribal aghas and headmen still maintain an unequal struggle. Here the chief is a landlord, and the system that prevails is feudal rather than tribal.

The Surchi tribe are a case in point. They live partly to the north of the Greater Zab in the Aqra district, and partly to the south in the Rawanduz district. In the north a family of shaikhs, the descendants of a holy man who obtained great influence in the tribe, have become possessors of the land and tribal chiefs. To the south the old sections still exist, and each village headman is independent though all recognise the common tribal bond.

Of tribal confederations the most noticeable are the Bilbas and the Khushnao. The Bilbas consist of seven or eight tribes, some in Persian territory and some in the Rania district, but each with its own boundary. The various members are often at war with each other, but would presumably unite against an external enemy. The titular head is one Agha, son of Baiz, who is overlord of only five or six villages. It is probable that his ancestors once commanded the allegiance of the whole confederation, but now his authority is in no wise recognised except that he is given the highest place at a meeting of tribal chiefs. He might possibly be called upon to lead if all the tribes were compelled to take common action.

The Khushnao is a confederation of three tribes, two of which are separated by no boundary, their villages being intermingled. Here the authority of the head of the confederation is recognised in a general way, though some of the minor chiefs like to pretend that they are completely independent.

Non-tribal Kurds are usually the tenants of some town agha who protects their rights in the same way as a tribal chief. If they are independent they will place themselves under the protection of the nearest powerful tribal agha in time of trouble.

The tribal chief has many obligations towards his tenants or tribesmen, the most important of which is that he will become their spokesman in all matters which concern the Government. In any litigation or criminal suit he will plead his tribesman's cause whether he is in the right or wrong. If a theft or murder is proved against a man he will take action to see that property is restored or blood-money paid, but he can hardly ever be persuaded to hand the culprit over to the authorities, or to take any punitive action, beyond the fact that he will probably exact some tribute for himself. He will plead for a reduction in a man's revenue demand, though if it is granted he will often seize a whole or part of the amount remitted for himself.

For these aghas are very oppressive to their tenants, more
especially where the Government is close at hand and can
exert its authority. In the mountain districts the tribesmen
are exceedingly poor, they have little to fear from the Government, and their chief finds it difficult to coerce them. A rival
chief would probably soon appear if he did. The average
tribal Kurd regards the Government as some strange unknown deity, speaking an unintelligible language. Rather
than appear before this monster he will allow his chief, whom
at any rate he understands, to fleece him unmercifully, trust-
ing in him to placate the aforesaid monster should occasion
arise. And should he appeal against his chief retribution will
swiftly follow. His enemies will rise up against him, steal his
animals, cut off his water, and interfere with his women-folk.
It is not every chief that oppresses his tenants; some of them
are the fathers of their people, and the objects of affection,
though there are few that are not avaricious. Even the worst
agha is respected on account of his birth and the protection
he affords his tribesmen from external enemies. In some
places Kurdish chiefs keep Christians and Jews practically as
slaves. There is great trouble, however, if anybody from outside interferes with them; to injure a man's Christian is as
bad as maiming his cow.

As landlord a chief is entitled to a tenth of the produce of
the soil; beyond this he has no legal right. It is, however, the
tribal custom to present the paramount chief with a pregnant
ewe from every considerable flock at the beginning of the
year. Further, on the occasions of the two 'Ids, the great
Muhammadan festivals, it is usual for minor chiefs to visit
their superior and bring presents. In this way village headmen will acknowledge the authority of a chief who is not
their landlord. Similarly the minor chiefs will expect a visit
and presents from their subordinates.

Servants and tribesmen will readily and loyally support
their chiefs against an external enemy, and usually against
the Government, though there was an occasion when the
Dizai refused to assist their aghas in a struggle against the
authorities. The Dizai is one of the most advanced of Kurdish
tribes, and signs are not wanting that the people are beginning to dispute their overlord's authority. Tribal law is based
on the old law of retaliation. The tribal chief has no magis-

terial powers, unless they are given him by the Government; he can only act as arbitrator in a quarrel between his tribesmen, and that only when both sides appeal to him. In cases of flagrant injustice he may occasionally take the side of the wronged party, and persuade the aggressor to make amends. Tribal law allows for no judicial courts, and affixes no definite penalty for crimes, except where a woman's honour is concerned. The offended party must take executive action himself to recover whatever is due to him.

Thus if a man wakes up in the morning to find that his donkey has been stolen, he will at once set out on its tracks, and will eventually discover to which village it has been taken. He then appeals to the headman of that village, who, if the theft has been committed without his knowledge, will probably cause the animal to be returned. If, however, he is at enmity with the claimant or the claimant's chief he will refuse. The injured man will then appeal to his agha, who will send his retainers to steal two donkeys from the other man's village. And so the good game goes on until it ends in bloodshed, or a third party is called in to arbitrate.

A really bad character who thieves for his own ends without his master's cognisance, will sooner or later be ejected from his village. He will then join the local police or gendarmes, the asylum of all scoundrels.

If the property of a traveller or stranger is stolen while he is staying in a village, the headman is responsible for either finding the property or paying up its value, provided that the stranger has notified him of his arrival in the village.

With regard to a woman's honour the law is most strict. A woman of any social standing who misconducts herself, or who is suspected on reasonable grounds of misconducting herself, must surely die; and the husband, brother, or whoever is responsible for her, who fails to put her out of the way, is considered to have lost his honour; and a Kurd's 'nāmūs' or honour is one of his most precious possessions. Many women must have been murdered in this way while I was at Arbil, but very few cases came to my ears, and then usually a long time after the event. I know of one fair lady who was tied up in a sack and thrown into the river. Even when I did get wind of such affairs it was out of the question to take any action, seeing that the entire tribal opinion supported the murderer, and it was impossible to obtain evidence. With regard to the man who is the cause of a woman's downfall the law is not so severe. In some cases he, too, is murdered, but more usually he escapes by paying the price of the woman's blood.

An interesting case where the man suffered more than the woman occurred in the Rania district during the summer of 1919. Mamand Agha, chief of the Ako, was married to the sister of Sawar Agha, chief of the Piran. The cousin of the former, one Sulaiman Agha, was suspected on good grounds of paying too much attention to the above-mentioned lady. So one day Mamand Agha, with a notorious villain whom we shall meet later, called Mamand, son of Sheikh Agha, accompanied him on a journey across Bituin; and while he was riding in front the second Mamand suddenly shot him through the back. The two then riddled his body with bullets, lighting a fire thereby, which blackened the face of half the plain, and consumed the unfortunate victim's remains. Returning to his house Mamand Agha sent back his wife to her brother, Sawar Agha, intimating to him that it was his duty to put her out of the way. He, however, for some reason or another refused to do so, much to Mamand Agha's chagrin. When the deed became known the murderers fled the country.

Woman is the cause of most of the trouble in Kurdistan, and many a Helen has brought woe to her country. The two rival parties of the Pizhder, the strongest tribe in southern Kurdistan, were nearly led through the question of a woman into a conflict that would have caused the Government the greatest embarrassment. Arrangements were being made for the fair lady to wed a member of the one party, when the other party, considering they had a prior claim, suddenly seized her from her home and carried her off. Negotiations ensued which lasted for several months, but just as things were coming to a climax, a third party from an entirely different tribe, the Mangur, came and snatched the damsel from their midst, leaving the rival factions gaping.

I have already mentioned that a cousin has first claim to a lady's hand. A refusal to grant this right had a ghastly sequel in July 1920, in a village called Kapanak Resh on the eastern slope of the Choq Dagh. The head of this village was one Khalbekr, and under his protection lived his widowed sister, Amina Khanum, and her beautiful daughter, Fatima. In a village the other side of the hill dwelt Fatima's cousins, Farhan the Lame and Rahman Agha. Farhan several times sent his brother to ask Khalbekr for his niece's hand in marriage – it would have been bad form for him to go himself – but each time met with a refusal. Finally, one of the three big Dizai chiefs, Hajji Pir Daoud Agha, secretly made overtures with a view to obtaining the lady for his son M'aruf. A big price was offered, and Khalbekr consented. Preparations were made for the marriage with the utmost secrecy; even the official consent of the Arbil Qazi or Muhammadan judge was obtained, so that no legal hitch should occur. However, all was in vain. One night Fatima was sleeping with her mother and maid in a booth of branches just outside their house, when suddenly two men appeared: the lady and her maid were stabbed to death, and the old mother narrowly escaped a similar fate. There can be little doubt that Rahman Agha was one of the murderers. The whole tribe was horrified. The correct thing to have done would have been to murder Hajji Pir Daoud's son, or carry off the maid by force: to kill her was quite out of order, seeing that she was merely a chattel in her guardian's hands. Hajji Pir Daoud, an arch-hypocrite, came to me and wept crocodile's tears in my office, complaining that his son – a miserable worm whom I loathed – was prostrated, and that his honour and prestige were gone. Rahman Agha was imprisoned. No proof against him could be found, and in the critical times that followed it became convenient to release him. The various parties concerned, in view of the situation, agreed to drop the matter, all being equally in the wrong.

Apart from matters where women are concerned murder is not common. One man will see another allowing sheep to stray into his crops, and fire at him and kill him in a fit of temper. More often murders occur over quarrels as to the possession of land or flocks. In such cases the victim's wife or mother would appear in my office with her dear one's bloodstained clothes crying, 'Dad, dad', 'Justice, justice'. At Mandali I remember an entire corpse was brought and laid at my door on Christmas morning, a most unseasonable gift. The gendarmes are sent out to apprehend the murderer, but always fail. For the murdered man's relations to take their revenge is quite in order, but an execution at the hands of that monster the Government is an entirely different matter. The culprit therefore is carefully concealed until he can make good his escape to the hills. To avoid further murders, for his relations may become the objects of revenge, permission is eventually given for 'fasl' to be made, and after the blood-money has been paid up with possibly a fine of equal amount, the murderer is allowed to return in peace to the bosom of his family.

'Fasl' means the settlement by tribal methods of any quarrel, but more especially of a blood feud. Such settlement may be made by a single person, either a chief or some prominent man agreed upon by the parties concerned, or it may be referred to a 'mejlis' or court of tribal chiefs, usually three or five. Such a court normally only arbitrates, though Government may insist upon its giving a decision which shall be binding. A blood feud is usually settled by the payment of blood-money; every condition of man or woman has his or her price, and even the parts of the body are catalogued. A Kurmanji or middle class Kurdish farmer is valued at £90, one of his women at £45, and his leg or arm at say £20. Such payment is often made in kind, some cattle or a horse, or so much wheat being handed over to the aggrieved party. It is very common for a girl to be given away in marriage in payment of blood-money. Thus, if £90 were owing, the price of the blood of one man, the debt might be paid by the delivery of one girl, three cows, and a donkey. If the feud has been a big one, and several people have lost their lives, they reckon up the number of men, women, and children on each side, calculate their prices, and the party which has won pays up the difference between the two amounts. Sometimes when the matter has been settled, to prevent trouble breaking out again, the antagonists will seal the peace by each giving the other a girl in marriage.

Fasl is usually effective where middle and lower class Kurds are concerned, because their chiefs will see that it is so. But the case is different where the chiefs themselves are affected. With them it takes many years to forget an injury, and though peace may be made under Government pressure, it will be broken as soon as that pressure is withdrawn.

When a murder has occurred the Political Officer's chief anxiety is to prevent it leading to a serious affair amongst the tribesmen. In Turkish times tribal wars were frequent.

They more often took place between two rival parties of the
same tribe than between two different tribes. A minute spark
would start a conflagration, but there were usually present
deeper and more significant causes, essentially in the plains,
where the desire for expansion and possession of land are the
chief motives in a Kurdish chief's life. Many tribal conflicts
have been recorded in songs which help to beguile the long
winter evenings.

During the last five or six years two big struggles have occurred between rival factions of the Dizai, the members of
which all spring from a common ancestor five generations
back. The first of these was caused by an attempt on the part
of one of the old peasant proprietors to sell his village.
Ahmad Pasha's party fought that of Ibrahim Agha as to
which should have the right of purchasing it. About sixty
men lost their lives. The second was in progress when our
forces reached Kirkuk in October, 1918. A dispute occurred
between the parties of Ibrahim Agha and Hajji Pir Daoud
over the possession of a well. One of the latter's relations was
shot at and killed as he came to draw water. Much sporadic
fighting took place, during which Ibrahim Agha's eldest son
fell a victim, and hostilities only ceased with the approach of
the British forces, when a hasty peace was patched up.

About twenty years ago a famous fight occurred on Bituin.
When the Piran, whose custom it was to go to the hills in the
summer, were about to descend again to their winter quarters, all their neighbours formed a league with the object of
preventing their return, and of sharing out their lands. The
Piran, only 120 horsemen strong, came through the defile by
which the Lesser Zab pierces the Kara Resh range and found
a force of 3,000 waiting for them. The opposing parties sat
down and watched each other for several days. The theft of a
favourite greyhound at length brought on a battle in which
the Piran, a tribe noted for their bravery, won a practically
bloodless victory.

Such conflicts are usually fought on recognised lines, each
party withdrawing to take its meals at the proper time, and
result in a great deal of noise and very little bloodshed. The
Kurd loves firing off ammunition, and thousands of rounds
may be expended without a single casualty. Tribal wars more

often than not consist of a series of raids on the enemy's property and rarely result in a pitched battle.

For the Kurd is a bad fighter, judged by our standards. During the war the Turks succeeded in enlisting very few of them, and they nearly all deserted. In the first place, a Kurd loves his home, which means his family; a chief of the Mangur informed me that he could not possibly be away from his home for more than ten days, and wondered how Europeans could endure life in strange lands and separation from their relations for such long periods. This characteristic explains the success of the Piran in their conflict on Bituin. They were fighting to protect their families and open a way to their villages; their opponents had been absent from their homes for several days, and therefore had no stomach for the battle. The Kurd is essentially a guerilla fighter, and excels in ambushes and the attacking of isolated outposts. If pressed by an equal or superior force he will fly without offering any resistance to his mountain fastnesses, which provide him with an impenetrable retreat. After a short struggle he is usually ready to make peace, and readier to renew the conflict when he has recovered his strength.

As regards civil suits, tribal law makes no special provisions. They are either referred to the chief as arbitrator, to the local mulla as interpreter of the 'shar'a' or Muhammadan law, or to the Civil Courts in the nearest centre of Government. The most common form of dispute is that concerning the possession of land, which often leads to bloodshed. Such a case can only be legally settled by the Government authorities, a lengthy proceeding, but the tribal chief will often step in and arrange a compromise between the parties concerned.

A common form of settlement for a dispute is by oath. If A has accused B of stealing his donkey, and cannot adduce sufficient proof to secure a conviction, he can call upon B to swear that he has not taken the animal. If B refuses to swear, he is the guilty party; if he takes the prescribed oath, the case is dropped. An arbitrator in a case may call upon either of the parties to take a similar oath.

There are several forms for an oath. The commonest practice is to swear by the Name of God, 'Wallahi, Billahi, Tillahi'. To make it more impressive this oath may be sworn on the Quran. The Kurd, however, is a trained liar, and will perjure himself several times in a day . One of them once said to me, 'As soon as a Kurd starts swearing, disbelieve him.' If a man says, 'By God and His Prophet, by the Holy Quran, by all my ancestors and the head of my father, I was not in the village the day the donkey was stolen', one may be pretty sure he was there the whole time. If, however, he plucks the left side of his coat with his right hand and shakes it saying, 'I have heard, but I am not sure, I wouldn't swear an oath to it, that Qadir sold his land to Rashid Agha ten days ago for fifty pounds', there is little doubt that he is speaking the truth.

The Kurd, therefore, being so ready to perjure himself, special forms of oath have to be invented for him. He is either made to travel to some distant tomb in the hills where dire punishments are supposed to overtake the false swearer, or he is required to take the oath by divorce. In the former case he often has an attack of nerves before he reaches the end of his journey and tells the truth; the latter form of oath he may manage to circumvent by a verbal quibble, but it usually defeats him. When an oath is taken by the divorce the swearer has to utter from three to twelve divorces according as his wives number from one to four. Then if he has sworn falsely, all his wives are automatically divorced from him, that is to say their relations may come and take them away, and that both they and he are dishonoured and subject to the relations' revenge if any intercourse takes place subsequent to the swearing of the oath. It is not easy to put the matter right by a re-marriage, for according to the law a divorced woman has to wed another man and be divorced again before she can re-marry her former husband.

I will conclude this chapter by briefly enumerating the principal Kurdish tribes living between the two Zabs.

More than half the Arbil district, consisting of the Qara Choq desert, Kandinawah, and the most fertile portion of the Arbil plain, is occupied by the Dizai tribe, who also supply much of the population of the so-called non-tribal villages in other parts of the district. They must number nearly 30,000 souls, and can produce 600 horsemen and 4,400 well armed infantry. They descended from the hills about three centuries ago, and occupied a few villages round Qush Tappah; for a considerable period they paid tribute to the Arabs. About sixty years ago they started to expand, and rapidly covered the whole country up to the Tigris, displacing the nomad Arabs who had previously roamed it at will.

In the neighbourhood of Arbil itself the villages, though Kurdish, are mostly non-tribal. In the north of the district the Girdi, a small but vigorous tribe, who have before now successfully resisted the Dizai, occupy fifteen villages. Another section of the same tribe is found in the Koi district, which outside the Shaqlawah sub-district is otherwise mainly non-tribal.

The Shaqlawah sub-district, except for the western extremity which belongs to a small tribe called the Kora, is occupied entirely by the Khushnao confederation. Their villages number nearly a hundred, the population of which must exceed 10,000 souls.

In the Rania district north of the Lesser Zab the chief tribes are the Piran, the Ako, and the Pizhder. The Piran belong to the Bilbas confederation, and are a small but powerful community. The Ako consist of several sections loosely knitted together. They inhabit the great mountains to the north of Rania and Qala Diza, and their villages number between forty and fifty. The tribesmen belong to one of the wildest types of Kurds, and are reported to be little more human than the bears which inhabit their rocky fastnesses. The Pizhder are the most powerful tribe in Southern Kurdistan. Their chief resides at Qala Diza, north of the Lesser Zab, but their villages extend eastward across the Persian border, and southwards nearly to Sulaimaniyah. Their numbers probably do not exceed those of the Dizai, but they are of much more warlike material.

The Rawanduz district is remarkable for the absence of large tribes and prominent tribal chiefs. North of the Bastura Chai dwell the Zarari, who possess about a dozen villages; beyond them come various sections of Surchi, who stretch along the bank of the Greater Zab to just north of the Rawanduz Chai. They own some forty villages, but probably do not number more than 2,500 souls. They suffered much during the war. Round Rawanduz itself we find separate communities owning some seven or eight villages inhabiting each mountain valley. Most of them are led by aghas who have sprung from one of the leading families of the town. The hills along the upper part of the valley of the Rawanduz Chai are in-

habited by the Balik tribe, who are of some importance, as
they command the main road from Persia. The people are
poor and inoffensive, but the aghas are numerous and find
little to amuse them except highway robbery. Their villages
number sixty odd, many of them well populated. The extreme
north of the Rawanduz district is in the hands of the Shirwan
and Baradost tribes. These are both split up into small sections, but the former is a definite entity, and recognises one
strong chief. The tribesmen are extremely wild, and their villages almost inaccessible. The two tribes together probably
do not number as much as 8,000 souls. They suffered heavily
in the war from the depredations of the Russians and from
famine.

There remain the migratory tribes which for practical
purposes are three in number: the Harki, the Khailani, and
the Boli. Of these the Harki are far the most important.
Their numbers must reach 20,000, of which some remain all
the year round in their home on the mountains of the Turco-
Persian frontier, while one party comes down to the Aqra district, and another, numbering about 8,000 souls, penetrates
the Rawanduz district and settles round Dera and the Bastura Chai. The Harki are noted for their bravery and their
men are armed with modern rifles. Their passage through
the country has been compared to the invasion of a flock of
locusts, and they are supposed to strip everything that they
encounter; but while I was at Arbil they were remarkably
well behaved. The portion of the tribe which visits the
Rawanduz district is usually led by three important chiefs. It
was the custom of the Turks to elect one each year as paramount, i.e. as spokesman to the Government for the whole
tribe.

The Khailani and Boli each consist of a number of small
sections without a common head. They are noted for their
thieving propensities. The former, who number about 1,000
souls, descend from the mountains to the north of the Balik,
and camp round Arbil town; while the latter, who are weaker
still, come from the southern part of the Balik country and
winter in the Koi district.

CHAPTER V

THE POPULATION OF THE TOWNS, AND OTHER RACES

STARTING WITH THE Nebi Yunis (the tomb of the Prophet Jonah) on the bank of the Tigris opposite Mosul, and running down through Arbil, Altun Keupri, Kirkuk, Kifri, and Qizil Robat to Mandali, we find a line of towns with Turkish-speaking inhabitants. It is practically the same line which divides predominantly Kurdish from predominantly Arab territory. Kirkuk is the main centre of this Turkish population, and before the war possessed 30,000 inhabitants. Several villages in its vicinity are also Turkish speaking, whereas the other towns are isolated communities surrounded by Kurds and Arabs.

The origin of this population, which sometimes refers to itself as Turcoman to show that it is not Ottoman, is wrapped in mystery, but it is generally inferred that it must be descended from a line of colonies settled by the Seljuks as the outposts of their rule. The Seljuks were a Turkish race, who, starting from their home in Central Asia, in the eleventh and twelfth centuries, overran Asia Minor and Mesopotamia and established their rule there. They eventually fell under the sway of the great descendants of Osman, the founder of the Osmanli or Ottoman Empire. The language of the Turks of Mesopotamia differs only from that of Constantinople in that it is generally harder, some of the gutturals which have been softened in the more highly developed tongue of the capital retaining their original values. Some people aver that Kirkuk[1] is an abbreviated form of Qala Seljuk (Fort Seljuk)!

---

1 Major E. B. Soane writes: 'The origin of the name Kirkuk is stated on fairly authoritative grounds to be Qalat d-Slūkid – the Castle of the Seleucids, a Chaldaeo-Syriac name dating from about the time of Christ.'

In Arbil a tradition is current that the inhabitants are descended from a camp of Persian soldiers (presumably from Turkish-speaking Azerbaijan), left there by Nadir Shah when he occupied the town in 1732. Certainly in grace and elegance some of the people of Arbil approximate more nearly to the Persians than any of the other races in Mesopotamia, but the fact that they are pure Sunnis in religion without any trace of Shiah tendencies militates against the above idea.

The only two places with a Turkish-speaking population which concern us closely are Arbil and Altun Keupri. The latter is situated on an island in the middle of the Lesser Zab, and is connected with the banks on either side by bridges. It owes its existence to these bridges, and to the 'kellek' trade; for the grain of the surrounding country, and raisins from the hills are here placed on 'kelleks' or rafts and floated down to Baghdad. The population are a poor and degenerate race, rough and dirty with ugly faces and dissolute habits. They are of the same type as the lower classes of Kirkuk, who provided the most corrupt and unscrupulous gendarmes that were to be found in the Turkish service.

The population of Arbil are very different, and must have been improved by a liberal infusion of Kurdish blood. One mahalla or quarter of the town is purely Kurdish, and in the rest the lower classes resemble the Kurds in appearance and dress. All can speak Kurdish fluently, but the language of their homes is Turkish. In the upper town, which contains 6,000 inhabitants, the purest Turkish element is found. Here nearly everyone is, comparatively speaking, rich, and the possessor of a house and lands. The men are dressed in a fashion resembling the Kurdish chiefs of the plains, with long silk or cotton gowns reaching to the feet, short surcoats, and gracefully flowing abas. In build they are usually tall and slight, with aquiline features and a narrower face than the Kurd's. They are elegant in their movements, and many possess remarkably delicate hands. Their head-dress is similar to the Kurds, but neater and smaller. The older men wear either a fez or a white head-dress with gold embroidery. Gentlemen of religious inclinations wear a white or pale blue, or, if they are descendants of the Prophet, a green scarf closely wound round the fez. Those of the women who appear out of doors are attired in a long dress of blue, paler than

that which the Kurdish women wear, and a hood of the same
colour over their heads. To the hood a black vizor, made of
some stiff material, with a yellow border, is attached. Containing no aperture for the eyes, it is normally bent upwards
in order that the lady may see where she is going, but is
quickly lowered if a European appears. For footwear the
women affect a sort of Wellington of yellow leather, reaching
halfway to the knee. The little girls up to the age of twelve or
fourteen appear abroad unveiled, with a jacket or dress of
brilliant colours and a cap surrounded by gold coins, and
often with a fine piece of gold work covering the crown.

In their houses, food, and manner of life the Turks of Arbil
resemble the Kurds of the surrounding country, except that
they are generally more advanced. The aghas possess magnificent guest-houses, built of bricks, some of them with marble
pavements and columns inside. Those that are situated on
the outside edge of the Fort have balconies, whence a view of
the country for miles around can be obtained. The rooms are
built round a courtyard, in which a few trees are usually
growing. In these guest-houses the aghas entertain visitors
from the town, and give a lodging to the Kurds who come in
from the country. Every chief is the client of one or other of
the town aghas. The connection has usually existed for
generations, and though he may be on bad terms with his
host, a chief will very rarely go to another man. The town
agha asks for no return for his hospitality, though it is the
custom to send him occasional presents from the villages
such as cheese or fruit; the client also is expected to look
after his patron's interests in the country in the event of any
tribal disturbances, while the latter will sometimes act as the
chief's representative in the town. Some of the aghas of Arbil
wear European dress, while the majority have adopted a
semi-European style at meals. They sit down on chairs at a
table, and use plates, knives, forks, and spoons. A clean plate
is brought for each course, but the other three articles are not
changed. Their dishes are more varied than those of the
Kurds.

Marriage customs in the towns differ from those in the
country. In particular, it is customary for the bride's relations
to provide a dowry for her, instead of the young man having

to collect a large sum of money in order to purchase her. The seclusion and veiling of women is much more strict.

The town aghas, who possess a considerable number of villages, usually lead a sedentary life. Most of them have country houses to which they occasionally retire in order to see how their crops are progressing, and take a really intelligent interest in agriculture. They are all eager to improve their minds, reading their newspapers regularly and discoursing freely on European and Oriental politics. One or two have money invested in Europe. Under more favourable conditions they would be active in introducing the latest agricultural improvements, and extending their commercial relations. The heads of families consider Government appointments rather beneath them, but they often start their young relatives upon an official career. Their main source of income is grain, and during the latter part of the war they amassed very large fortunes. They are not less avaricious than the Kurdish chiefs, and are always striving to add field to field.

Some of the young aghas are great swells, riding out into the country with their greyhounds, or strolling round the town in the evening with their heads erect, and their brightly coloured abas streaming behind them. Large numbers of the middle-class Turks of Kirkuk and Arbil who possess some land, but wish to augment their incomes, become 'effendis', i.e. they learn to read and write, wear European clothes, and undertake appointments in the Government service. 'Effendi' is a Turkish term which in speaking is equivalent to the English 'sir', being used in addressing any man who is 'respectable', and as a title corresponds to 'Esquire'. It is applied to all religious dignitaries in towns, to the lower grades of officer in the army, to the professional classes, and to the clerks and officials in Government service. Any man who relies upon his power of reading and writing to earn a living becomes an 'effendi'. All Turkish Government offices contained a swarm of effendis, most of them lazy and corrupt, to be seen any day hanging about the coffee shops with unclean faces, dirty collars, badly tied ties, and two or three trouser buttons undone. It is this type of man who has brought the term 'effendi' into disrepute. I know of one Political Officer who used forcibly to expel from his office anyone who in speaking to him called him 'effendi', although this is the normal mode of address. Kirkuk and Arbil, especially the former, provided large numbers of officials to the Turkish Government, who favoured them owing to their knowledge of the State language.

Next below the effendi class come the shopkeepers, of whom there are many, for Arbil possesses a large bazaar, and then those who are occupied in tanning, making felt, etc., and the Karwanchis or mule and donkey owners, who provide the only transport that is available for trade. Some of the women earn a livelihood by cotton-spinning, but the majority depend upon their menfolk for their daily bread. Of the very poor there are few, and casual labour is extremely hard to obtain.

The difference between the people of Arbil and the Kurds outside is mainly that which exists everywhere between town and country folk. The Arbilli looks down upon the Kurd as rough and uneducated, while the latter considers the townsman effeminate, immoral, and corrupt. Though drunkenness, gambling, and immorality do exist in Arbil, it is much better in these respects than most of the towns of Mesopotamia. None of the leading aghas touch alcohol, and the municipal council insists on the most puritanical regulations being enforced among the population. Most of the bad characters that are found here come to the town from elsewhere.

The town population of Koi, although entirely Kurdish, is similar to that of Arbil, but not so advanced. In particular the aghas much more resemble tribal chiefs than do those of Arbil. The few inhabitants that remain in Rawanduz are in civilisation a long way behind the villagers of the Arbil plain.

Communities of Jews are found in the towns of Arbil and Koi, and in the village of Raitwata, which is situated in the remotest part of the Khushnao country, and in Batas on the Dasht i Harir. Single families are met with in many Kurdish villages, where they keep miniature general stores.

The country between the Zabs is predominantly agricultural, and commerce is of secondary importance. The Jews therefore do not occupy a prominent position as in Baghdad, and there are none who are really wealthy. A few small merchants are found in Arbil, and some of the principal cloth shops are kept by Jews. The majority of the community are dyers or weavers. They have the monopoly of making "araq', a spirit distilled from raisins; for this occupation is unlawful to Muhammadans, though a certain number drink it when it is made.

The Jews are universally despised and are often maltreated in the villages, though I have never heard of anything approaching an organised persecution. Girls are sometimes carried off and made to change their religion. If a Kurd wishes to express his contempt for an official he will say, 'Even a Jew would be better than he'; or if he wishes to show how well behaved his tribe is he remarks, 'Even a Jew could keep us in order.'

The Jews speak and write their own tongue, and in the towns prefer to talk in Arabic rather than Kurdish or Turkish.

Two Chaldaean Christian villages exist, Ainkawa, three miles from Arbil, and Armuta, just outside Koi. There are also fairly large communities in Shaqlawah, and Koi itself. All four places have churches. The total number of Christians in the district is about 40,000, of whom 2,500 live in Ainkawa.

The Chaldaeans were originally the same in religion as the Nestorians, but during the sixteenth century were persuaded to acknowledge the authority of the Church of Rome. Large communities of them exist north of the Greater Zab in the Mosul Division, and it is said that two or three centuries ago a considerable district in the neighbourhood of Rawanduz was under their sway. The inhabitants of the last surviving village in this area fled after the withdrawal of the Russians in 1916. The plain to the north of the town is still known as the Dasht i Dian, the Christians' Plain. From the evidence of place-names and from tradition it is probable that previous to the rise of Muhammadanism the Christians owned the whole or the greater part of the undulating country that lies between the Tigris and the foothills to the east from Kirkuk upwards. They are Semitic by race, and the language of their Scriptures is Syriac. They speak a tongue of their own, but all know Kurdish.

A few have become 'Protestants', but they are found chiefly in Mosul. I remember a man from Ainkawa put in a petition one day asking me to make him 'English'. He had apparently quarrelled with the priests.

The priests are the curse of these communities. Ainkawa possesses about six, and the other places three or four each. The majority are ill-educated and bigoted. As far as I could make out they have very little idea of moral right and wrong, and use their position to batten upon their people. They act as the heads of their communities in matters both temporal and spiritual, and are generally the spokesmen with the Government. They wear big black cassocks, with a hat that consists of several bands of some stiff shiny black substance wound round a small cap. We always referred to them as 'black crows'.

The Mutran or Metropolitan of Kirkuk, Istefan by name, is a dear old man with a fine character, who realises well enough the defects of his clergy. He usually appears in a most imposing purple robe.

The Chaldaeans possess a complicated hierarchy, which includes a Patriarch, Metropolitans, Archbishops, and Bishops. Those offices, which entail celibacy, are usually hereditary, that is only members of certain families can hold them, and succession normally passes from uncle to nephew. The ordinary priests are not celibate.

The laymen are attired much in the same way as the Kurds. In Ainkawa they are especially fond of the long robe with the short jacket or 'salta' over it. The head-dress is smaller and tied more closely than that of the Kurds.

For centuries these Christians have lived in subjection to the surrounding Muhammadans. On this account they have lost their virility and become mean and cringing. They have suffered much, greedy aghas making continual attempts to seize their lands and flocks. But, on the whole, they are regarded with pity and a certain amount of respect, and public opinion does not now support aggression against them. Towards the end of the war the Turkish Government ordered a massacre in Ainkawa, but the people of Arbil refused to carry it out. In times of trouble the Christians will pay tribute to a Kurdish chief or town agha thereby buying his protection. They live, however, in a constant state of suspicion and terror, and are always maligning the Muhammadans, even when they have no grounds for doing so. This is their worst characteristic. If permitted, they will come to the Political Officer every day with long tales of intrigue and

CHRISTIAN WOMEN OF KOI

roguery, the majority of which are absolutely false. This is
not unnaturally the cause of considerable animosity amongst
the Muhammadans. The Christians of Shaqlawah in the
middle of tribal territory have always been comparatively
well treated; they recognise the ruling chief as overlord, and
are allowed to enjoy their possessions in peace, no one interfering with them.

In Shaqlawah and Koi the Christians are occupied in
weaving, and in the former place they possess large fruit gardens. It is they who chiefly make the homespun material
which the hill-Kurds use for their clothes. Weaving, like dy-
eing, is considered by the Muhammadans a degrading occupation, and it is probably on this account that the
Christians have survived in the hills. At Ainkawa and
Armuta they are tillers of the soil; in the former place they
possess a very wide acreage of the finest land in the Arbil district. In 1920 they produced 600 tons of barley, with the same
quantity of wheat, besides other crops. They are usually regarded, and with justice, as the best farmers in the neighbourhood. Though Ainkawa is overcrowded, and the land
does not suffice the population, Christians will not normally
become tenants of Kurdish landlords, except on property
within the boundaries of their own village.

Some of the bigger farmers in Ainkawa possess a considerable standing, in particular Khoja Sibi and Khoja Shabu.
Khoja is a title of respect given to an old man, and more especially to an old mulla. These two gentlemen are related by
marriage to some of the leading families in Arbil – for
Muhammadans may take Christian girls to wife, though they
may not give their daughters away to members of the other
religion. They possess very lovable characters, especially
Khoja Sibi, who is one of the dearest old men I met in the
East. Both the Turkish and British authorities employed
them whenever possible as estimators of crops for revenue
purposes, it being recognised by Government and people
alike that they were more honest than any Muhammadan
was likely to be. I have often toured with them when the
crops were ripe, and found that they were on terms of intimacy and affection with most of the Kurdish chiefs in the
Arbil plain.

Christians are in demand as servants in Muhammadan houses, and they are generally considered to be more honest and trustworthy than Muhammadan servants. My personal attendant while I was in Arbil was one Verdu, a native of Ainkawa. He was extraordinarily dense and lacked initiative; but he was willing, faithful, and honest, and not without a sense of humour.

These Christians, though they fawn and cringe, though more wife-beatings and family squabbles occur in Ainkawa than in all the other villages of the Division put together, though many of them are notorious as receivers of stolen goods, have in their general life a reputation for truth and honesty that is rare in the East. Their religion is a degraded form of Christianity full of gross superstitions and blind beliefs without understanding; but scrape off the dirt on the surface and you find below like a precious jewel the faith which, with untold courage and endurance, they have preserved intact in wild and isolated spots through twelve centuries of Muhammadan domination and persecution.

It is interesting to note that within the Division there are two or three old tombs which are said to mark the burial places of disciples of Christ, and to which the Muhammadans pay universal respect.

Scattered Arab villages, mostly belonging to the Tai tribe, are found in Shamamik and the Qara Choq desert, while the left bank of the Tigris between the two Zabs is solidly Arab, being occupied by the Jubur tribe.

The Tai are one of the most famous and ancient of all the Arab tribes. The name of one of their great chiefs, Hatim Tai, is still a byword for liberality and generosity through a large part of the East. A century ago this tribe roamed at will over Shamamik, Kandinawah, and Qara Choq, all of which were desert. The Dizai chiefs at Qush Tappeh paid tribute to them. Gradually the Kurds expanded, and as cultivation advanced its borders, the Tai withdrew, apparently without a struggle, and rejoined the headquarters of their tribe near Nisibin. Only a few settled down and endeavoured to build villages and cultivate like the Kurds. But the Arabs are lazy and indolent by nature; their only wish is to make just enough to enable themselves to live in a moderate degree of comfort, and they entirely lack the Kurd's persistent avarice and

desire to accumulate wealth. Consequently where Kurdish
and Arab villages adjoin, we find the former with their available acreage fully cultivated and asking for more, while the
Arabs have only scratched the soil in a few places and left the
rest of their village lands fallow. The result is that the Kurds
are continually expanding at their expense, and I have little
doubt that they will eventually squeeze them right out of the
district.

As may be imagined, the Kurds and Arabs have a considerable dislike for each other. The Arab is of an essentially
volatile disposition, alternately energetic and lazy, incon-
sistent and unreliable by nature, but generally extremely
cheerful and loquacious, with an immense sense of humour.
As regards ideas of cleanliness or morality he is but little removed from the animals. The slow-going, industrious, and respectable Kurd regards him as a being of a lower order, a
garrulous ape, or a dirty and shameless 'sansculotte', who is
always trying to intrude his presence where he is not wanted.
This only refers to the ordinary tribesman. An Arab chief is
treated with the greatest respect on account of his ancient
descent, and Shaikh Hanash of the Tai, a young man of no
ability or importance, will be offered a seat above the biggest
Dizai chiefs. Nearly every Kurdish agha boasts of Arab descent, and endeavours to connect himself with the Prophet or
one of his early adherents. The Arab regards the Kurd as an
incubus which weighs upon him and restricts his liberty of
action. He has a proverb which runs:

'Thalatha bad-dunya fasad
Al Kurdi al jurdi wa al jarrad.'
'There are three plagues in the world,
The Kurd, the rat, and the locust.'

The tribes who live on the Tigris belong to the lowest type
of Arab, and are little removed from chattering apes. They
are experts at 'lift' cultivation, by which they earn their livelihood, and live in tents, but rarely leave their village areas.
It was sometimes a relief after sitting for hours in a company
of taciturn and highly respectable Kurds, to go on to one of
the Jubur tents, when a dozen hands would drag me in, and
set me down in the circle round the fire where none was

highest or lowest, and twenty tongues would wag all at once to the accompaniment of the most infectious merriment and uncontrollable laughter. The Kurd is a convinced aristocrat, whereas the Arabs waver between democracy and anarchy.

Before concluding this chapter I must just refer to the Saralu tribe, who occupy two villages not far from Quwair on the left bank of the Greater Zab, and half a dozen or more villages on the opposite bank. In appearance they closely resemble the Kurds, wearing usually the long gown and short jacket. As farmers they almost rival the Christians of Ainkawa. But their religion is peculiar. It is said to be the same as that of the Kakais, who are found south of Kirkuk, and similar to that of the Ali Ilahis in the neighbourhood of Khaniqin and Mandali on the Persian frontier. The ordinary Muhammadans recognise them as 'People of the book', by which is meant those who acknowledge one of God's written Words, whether it be the Talmud, the Gospel, or the Quran. In fact, as they are supposed to recognise the Quran they are considered as a sect of the Muhammadans. What their real beliefs and practices are nobody except themselves knows, and strange and immoral rites are ascribed to them.

It is probable that the Saralu are a race who have covered some ancient heathen religion with a veneer of Muhammadanism in order to save themselves from persecution. It may be that they were originally Yazidis; for Yazidis are occupationally found amongst them, and they themselves sometimes wear the long locks that are characteristic of that sect.

CHAPTER VI

AGRICULTURE AND TRADE

AS FAR AS THE Arbil Division is concerned agricultural
lands may be divided into three classes; firstly, 'tapu' or regis-
tered property, which is held largely by the big landowners
under formal title deeds; secondly 'tahrir' or property by the
right of possession, which occurs chiefly in the remote hill
districts where registration has hitherto been impossible; and
thirdly 'sanniyah' or crown lands owned by the State. But the
whole system of land tenure throughout Mesopotamia is extremely complicated, especially in the case of tapu property,
where both the registers and the title-deeds have largely
been composed by corrupt and incapable officials, and are full
of errors which give rise to endless litigation.

The terms of tenancy and the amount of revenue due to
the Government vary on the different classes of land. On
tapu property the normal rule is for a tenth of the crops to be
paid to the Government and a tenth to the landlord, and the
same applies roughly in the hill districts. If, however, the
landlord advances seed or lends plough animals to the
tenant, the latter will have to pay two or three times as
much. The aghas employ farm labourers on properties which
they work themselves. These are usually paid in kind. In
Khidhran on the edge of Bituin, I inquired early in 1919 what
Hama Agha of Koi gave his men, and was told they were engaged for nine months (the period of ploughing), and were
either fed by him, or if they lived out were given monthly 88
pounds of grain, 4½ pounds of butter, and some salt. Before
the war, when living was much cheaper, they were also given
a small wage. At the end of the period of engagement every
man who had worked well received one felt coat, one outfit of
clothes, and possibly £1 in cash.

On Crown lands the Government collects 17½ per cent of
the crops. The chiefs or headmen of villages, if they are

powerful enough, exact the remaining 2½ per cent, and whatever the Government fails to collect through faulty estimation or the devices of the Kurds, who hide large quantities of their grain when the estimators are abroad. Everywhere the agha will extort as much as possible from the peasant, and will aid him in defrauding the Government so that his own share may be larger.

There are two sorts of crops, the winter and the summer. The former are sown in the autumn or winter and reaped in the spring. In northern Mesopotamia they usually do not require irrigation. Summer crops are sown in the early spring, and reaped in summer or autumn. They require frequent waterings.

The Kurds are excellent dry farmers, and the Arbil district is an ideal country for them. It is probably the finest wheat-producing area in Mesopotamia; Arbil is essentially a grain centre, and the population of the district is almost wholly agricultural. In the hills it is different. The cultivable area is small and water is plentiful; the hill people therefore rely more upon summer crops and fruit gardens for their livelihood.

Though a few pulses are also grown, some for human and some for animal consumption, the winter crops are for practical purposes confined to wheat and barley. Of wheat there are two main varieties, a hard one called 'Reshgul' or 'Black flower', which is used for making burghul or wheatmeal, one of the staple foods of the people, and a soft one called Kandahari which yields the best flour for bread making. Wheat from Arbil was exported to Europe before the war. The barley is always of the black variety. It is interesting to compare prices: before the war wheat and barley fell as low as Rs.40 and Rs.24 per ton respectively; in 1918 they rose to somewhere about Rs.1,500 and Rs.1,200; when I left Arbil in October, 1920, they were about Rs.350 and Rs.200. In Lower Mesopotamia double as much barley as wheat is grown; in the Arbil district the reverse is the case.

Ploughing for the autumn sowings normally begins in January or February, and may go on as long as the soil remains moist, say till the end of April. The plough consists merely of a sharp steel spike fixed on a pole, to which mules or oxen are attached by a yoke. The ground is ploughed twice, the first ploughing is known as 'shŭkhm', and the second, which is a cross-ploughing, as 'wărd'. By April around a prosperous village all the land will either be under crops from the previous autumn's sowing, or ploughed ready for the next autumn.

From May to August the fields are left to themselves, unless patches of melon and cucumber are sown. The melons so produced are small and sweet, while the cucumbers are short and fat. They ripen at the end of May, and flourish for about a month. They are not irrigated, but late May rains are required to make them grow.

The Kurd knows little about the rotation of crops, but his ignorance is supplemented by Nature, who in the hot weather covers his land with camel-thorn, or 'shauq', a leguminous plant with roots 20 ft. long. This draws up moisture to the surface, and when winter arrives enriches the soil with its leaves and pods. It provides fodder for the animals when grass is scarce, and fuel for the houses in the winter. In the year of famine (1918) the poor collected the pods and ground the seed into a flour, from which they made bread, unpalatable, it is true, and indigestible except for the hardiest, but sufficient to fend off starvation. This plant, as its name implies, is the fodder *par excellence* for camels.

In August, September, and October the prepared ground is sown. The traveller will see a bare-legged Kurd (for trousers are removed when working in the fields in hot weather) walking down the furrows scattering the seed while another follows closely behind with the plough, turning the soil over. Where water is available and the soil is strong, it is the custom to irrigate the land seven days before sowing. This serves to bring out the weeds, which are killed by the subsequent ploughing. Round Arbil crops so irrigated are known as 'răbās'. They mature earlier and give a bigger yield.

When the sowing has been completed there is nothing to do but sit down and wait for the rain. In normal years it may be expected about the middle of November. Small falls are of little use, and nothing begins to grow until what is known as 'pără' has fallen. This means rain sufficient to percolate the soil until the lower moisture is reached. When this has happened moisture is continuously sucked up to the surface until the summer heat arrives. About twenty-four hours' continuous rainfall is required. In the winter of 1919–20 this did not occur till the beginning of March, and the crops were only saved by a heavy snow-fall in February. South of the Lesser Zab, where the snow was less, they were a failure. During January and February but little rain is required, and there is usually plenty, for these are the wettest months of the year. March and April are the critical times, a heavy shower at least once in ten days is essential. After May 15th rain is apt to interfere with harvesting operations. One year a heavy storm occurred in June, and carried off large quantities of cut corn down the water-courses.

In November or December, when the first rain arrives that is sufficient to moisten the soil to a depth of 3 or 4 ins., the Kurd starts to plough and sow any land previously neglected through lack of plough animals. Such crops are known as 'tărăkāl'. In the winter of 1918–19 nearly all the crops were of this nature, as the disturbed conditions that prevailed in 1918, and more particularly the fact that they knew the Turks would seize all the crops if they remained in the country, prevented the Kurds from ploughing in the spring. The yield from such sowings is more than 20 per cent less than that from 'wărd' crops.

In January the Kurd will be busy again with the ploughings for the next autumn. If the crops he has already sown sprout early he will allow his animals to graze them down. Manure is rarely used on irrigated land except to force small patches of barley for fodder purposes, and the crops of melons and cucumbers which I have already mentioned. With the arrival of March there is nothing more to be done with the crops that are growing except pray for rain and the absence of pests. The chief of these are rust, the 'sunn', and the locust. Smut also occurs and did a good deal of damage in the foothills in 1920. Rust is a fungus growth which usually appears after a very wet winter, and does much harm to the wheat, especially the Kandahari variety. The Kurds know of no remedy for it. The sunn is a small bug which sometimes appears in large quantities and devours the grain in the ear. It is the most dreaded of all pests, and will often entirely ruin the crops over wide areas. Large quantities of locusts arrived from the west in 1920, luckily too late to do any damage to the wheat and barley. They have, however, laid their eggs all over the country, especially in out-of-the-way spots in the Qara Choq Dagh, and the foothills, and will probably make their presence felt in 1921. If the young locusts can be found when they have just hatched out it is possible to destroy them, otherwise there is little that can be done. They eat all the green off the crops, and do a great deal of damage, but they usually leave something for the unfortunate farmer.

The barley harvest begins early in May, and continues to the end of the month. The wheat harvest starts in June, and in 1920 when labour was scarce I saw crops still standing at the end of July. The reaping is entirely done by hand, and all and sundry, men, women, and children, take part in the operations. Large numbers of poor people from the hills, who have probably spent the winter on the plains, now find employment which will enable them to return to their homes with something in their pockets. These 'sapans', as they are called, receive about one-sixth of the crops on which they are engaged. Where the crops are poor, therefore, it is extremely difficult to find labour. During the harvest if any person of importance passes a field that is being reaped, one of the reapers will rush out towards him with a handful of the cut corn, as a sort of first fruits. He expects to be rewarded with some bakhshish. This is the only occasion on which the Kurd does anything approaching begging. The corn when reaped is left in small bundles, and gleaners will be seen busy collecting stray ears that have been left behind. The bundles are taken to a threshing floor on donkeys and other animals, special racks being used for carrying them.

The threshing floors are cleared spaces in the immediate vicinity of the villages. They are public property. Each farmer selects a spot for himself, and lays out his corn in circular heaps round a pole. When the pile is complete he yokes together from two to six miscellaneous draught animals, attaches them to the pole by a rope, and drives them round, thereby treading out the corn. The better-class farmer generally uses a small sleigh-like machine with a revolving axle to which a series of blunt blades are fixed. This is pulled round the heap by a pair of mules, and you will often see a couple of children aged five and six driving it. These threshing operations are carried out in the middle of the hot weather, and it is then that you meet the Kurds of the plains wearing their wonderful Robinson Crusoe hats.

For winnowing a favourable wind is necessary. The threshed corn is then thrown up into the air with a five-pronged wooden fork. The grain drops down and the chaff falls some way to leeward of it. When the whole pile has been disposed of the grain is sifted to remove pieces of stalk and dirt, gathered into neat heaps, and marked all over with the impress of the fork to prevent pilfering. The fork is then stuck head upwards in the centre of the heap as a triumphant sign that the long work of producing the corn is finished. In big villages threshing and winnowing are often carried on well into September. The best land in the Arbil district is expected to give a return for seed of from 10 to 15 for 1 for wărd sowings, and from 8 to 10 for tărăkāl. In the hills 8 for 1 is considered a good return for the former, while from the latter little more than 5 for 1 is usually forthcoming. In bumper years the Qara Choq desert may yield as much as 30 or 40 to 1.

The grain is next stored in some secure place, often under the ground. The chaff or 'Kah' (Indian 'bhoosa') is also gathered in to be used as fodder for the animals until the next spring, and to serve in the making of bricks.

Often just outside a village after the harvest you will see a line of boiling cauldrons with women attending them. They are making 'burghul'. The wheat is first boiled and then dried in the sun. It is next crushed by a heavy circular stone, which is made to revolve on its edge round a platform by means of a pony dragging a pole fixed through a hole in its centre and fastened to an upright in the middle of the platform. The softer wheat is taken to a water-mill to be made into flour, as required.

Having described at length the essential crops of wheat and barley I will deal more briefly with the summer crops. The first desideratum for these is water, which, except in the case of the great rivers, is usually privately owned. There are one or two state-owned springs or streams in the Arbil district, which are farmed yearly to the highest bidder. One quite small stream fetched Rs.12,000 (over £1,000 at the rate of exchange then current) for the year 1920, from which it may be seen that water well situated for irrigation purposes is extremely valuable. A landlord does not usually let out his irrigable land to the farmers, but works it himself with hired labour.

The chief summer crop grown in the plains and in some of the hill districts is rice. It is almost all of a variety called 'Girda', which I believe is peculiar to this part of the world. It yields a thick heavy grain which is very satisfying, and which I personally find more succulent than the commoner varieties. The much finer and lighter rices known as 'Ambar' and 'Sadri' are sometimes grown, but no market can be found for them in Arbil. The Kurdish agha considers they are not substantial enough to form a meal. It would be tedious to enter into all the details of rice cultivation. It is sown in March and harvested in October. On the Arbil plain a return for seed of over 300 to 1 is not abnormal, whereas in Bituin, where the methods of cultivation are more careless, 80 to 1 is as much as can be expected.

Other summer crops include mash and nuhkud, both pulses highly esteemed for human consumption, sesame, which is used as a flavouring for bread and cakes, and from which an oil is expressed much valued in Jewish quarters, maize, cotton, and various kinds of millet. A spring wheat is also seen which requires irrigation. In the Balik country, where the snow does not melt till late in March, most of the wheat grown is of this variety.

Many experiments with high grade cotton have been successfully carried out by the Agricultural Department, and the country is said to have a great future in this respect. The Kurdish cotton is of poor quality and is produced entirely to meet local needs.

Millet is grown by the Arabs on the Zabs and Tigris, and is nearly all of the 'white' variety, which attains to a height of 10 to 12 ft. It is irrigated by means of 'lifts' or Persian wheels. In the former case the water is raised from the river in a skin or leathern bucket attached to a draught animal by two ropes, which work over a system of pulleys. The animal is driven down a ramp sloping away from the river, thereby pulling up the skin which on reaching the top of the bank is automatically emptied into a channel. The creaking of the pulleys may be heard for miles. Two of these lifts usually work side by side, and are sufficient to irrigate a crop giving an average return of four tons of grain. The Persian wheel is worked in water-holes near the river bank. It consists of a chain of buckets which is made to revolve by a system of cogwheels. It is worked by a draught-animal attached by a pole to the main wheel at the top.

In the hills by far the most important irrigated crop is tobacco. Owing to the high price which prevails for this article the hill Kurds are using almost all their available water for its cultivation. Several varieties exist, but the Kurds will only grow the better qualities for their own use. The Arab is perfectly content with inferior stuff, and as the superior tobaccos require much care in their cultivation, it is unlikely that they will be grown in greater quantities until a demand for them makes itself felt. It is the opinion of experts that Kurdish tobacco could not be made suitable for general European consumption, as owing to the nature of the climate it cannot be cut. It has to be dried and crumbled, as a result of which it requires an unpleasantly thick cigarette paper. Some of the finer varieties are mild and possess a beautiful aroma, but the normal tobacco grown for export is strong and catches the throat.

Tobacco is sown early in the year in nurseries which are covered with branches to protect the young plants from snow and frost. In the spring it is planted out into plots of ground which have been carefully dug and manured. It is picked from June onwards. The leaves are strung together with pieces of stick and placed on the housetops to dry. In due course the sticks are removed and the leaves having been slightly damped are packed in sacks ready for the merchants to come and buy. In Turkish times tobacco was a Government monopoly. It pays a heavy duty and is a considerable source of revenue.

A large variety of vegetables are grown, mostly on irrigated ground, or in the beds of the rivers in summer near the water's edge. Summer vegetables include very fine sweet melons, cucumbers, pumpkins, tomatoes, onions, bamia or 'lady's fingers', and badinjan or the egg-plant. The bamia when cooked by the Kurd or Arab is one of the most delicious vegetables I know; as served by the normal Indian cook it is a slimy and revolting mess. It is often dried and threaded on strings. Chains of them may be seen hanging in every Kurd's house, and they keep good throughout the winter. It is the Kurd's favourite vegetable. In winter, turnips, radishes, beetroot, celery, cress, and spinach are grown. Artichokes are also found at Koi. The Arbil aghas are very keen on obtaining new varieties of vegetable, essentially potatoes, which are sometimes imported from Mosul. The Agricultural Department issued some sugar-beet seed. If this grows well and refineries can be set up, it should prove a source of considerable profit, as sugar is very expensive and has to be imported from India.

In the hills the vine is of great importance. The hillsides, especially in the Khushnao country, are covered with vineyards which require no irrigation. They yield small purple grapes which are in season from August to December. The fruit, however, is mostly gathered in October, spread out on the hillsides, and dried for raisins. The Christians make a wine which is not of very good quality. A few irrigated vineyards are found on the plains and in the hills; these produce white and purple dessert grapes.

Other fruits which grow plentifully round the hill villages, and occasionally on the plains, are peaches, nectarines, plums, apricots, apples, pears, pomegranates, and figs. Shaqlawah is noted for its fruit, but the trees are not carefully tended, and the produce does not nearly come up to the standard of the English varieties. The apples ripen in June, and are of poor quality; much finer autumn apples are found in the Balik country. The pomegranate is a great favourite; in addition to its qualities as a fruit it is supposed to be an excellent febrifuge, and its skin is largely used in tanning. Figs grow in large quantities, and are dried and threaded on strings. The mulberry tree is found in profusion in the hills, and here and there in the plains. The fruit is mostly of the white variety, though the Royal Mulberry which yields a large red fruit is sometimes met with. The mulberries are often dried and preserved for the winter. The timber of the tree is highly valued.

Walnut trees grow in abundance in the hill country, many of them reaching a large size. The nuts are of excellent quality, and I have seen them as large as hen's eggs. The timber is in great demand for ploughs and other articles which require a good hard wood. The pistachio nut grows in some gardens round Arbil.

The only tree which is found wild in profusion is the oak, and its timber is usually not large enough to be serviceable. The 'aspindar' which is a sort of silver poplar, is therefore cultivated to a considerable extent. It grows very rapidly, and a tree fifteen years old should attain to a diameter of 18 ins. at its base. This wood is used almost exclusively for roofing and building purposes. Plane trees are also cultivated for their timber, and plantations of willow and Euphrates poplar, a twisted tree very different from the slender aspindar, may be seen in various places along the two Zabs. One of the chief features of the plain is the lack of timber, and everything is being done to encourage the people to plant willows and other trees along their water channels.

There are one or two natural products of importance. The chief of these is gall-nuts, which are found on one of the varieties of scrub oak. They are gathered in large quantities and sent down to Baghdad, whence they are exported to Europe. They are used for tanning, and are a source of considerable revenue as the Government has the right to demand a tenth of anything the soil produces, whether with or without cultivation. Gum tragacanth is also collected from a small plant that grows in the hills.

The sumach yields a berry which is much valued as a flavouring for meat and other dishes, while liquorice, which grows in abundance in hill and plain, especially in the neighbourhood of water, was before the war much exploited by European or American companies. The Kurd has no use for it; in many places it chokes his crops and renders reaping almost impossible.

I am convinced that, given settled conditions, agriculture has a great future in the Arbil district. Geological experts have reported that the Arbil plain offers ideal conditions for obtaining artesian water; if wells were dug and abundant water struck, the rice and cotton of Arbil would become as important as her wheat. The soil is of excellent quality, and there is every reason why the best grades of cotton and also sugar-beet should flourish. Further, by introducing a good rust-resisting wheat and modern agricultural implements, especially an improved type of plough, the out-turn of grain should be more than doubled.

As may be gathered from the foregoing pages, the exports of the Arbil Division consist entirely of agricultural, pastoral and natural products such as grains, wood, tobacco, gall-nuts, gums, timber, cheese, honey, raisins, and other dried fruits. These are either sent by road to the railheads at Kifri and Sherqat, or else are floated down to Baghdad on rafts which are put together at Taqtaq and Altun Keupri. A fair amount of grain is also sold in Mosul, especially when it is necessary to raise cash for revenue purposes.

The chief imports are tea, sugar, coffee, and manufactured articles from Baghdad, and livestock from Persia. Two important trade routes between Mesopotamia and north-western Persia pass through the Arbil Division, and when peace reigns on both sides of the border the transit trade is important. As it is, a fair number of caravans proceed to Saujbulaq and Urmia, taking with them tea, sugar, coffee, and manufactured articles, especially piece goods, and bringing back rugs, silks, skins, furs, samovars, and livestock. The roads are closed by snow from December to March.

A considerable local trade also exists, the hill tribes exchanging their fruits and tobacco for the Dizai grain.

There are no banks in Arbil; the Kurds therefore are apt to hoard their money, though they would probably be ready enough to invest it if opportunity offered. The capitalists finance the smaller merchants giving them what is known as 'sarmaya', or capital, and going shares with them in the profit or loss that may accrue. Usury, though forbidden by the Muhammadan law, is common; Ahmad Pasha is said to have over £50,000 out at an interest of 33⅓ per cent per annum. It is usually the peasants who borrow, requiring the wherewithal to purchase plough animals or seed; if the resultant crop is not a good one the unfortunate debtor is unable to pay the interest, let alone the capital, and eventually is compelled to make over his land, if he has any, in payment of his debt. This is one of the methods by which the aghas have succeeded in attaching much of their property.

The coin which is chiefly current in the villages, and in which prices for livestock and grain are normally quoted, is the Turkish lira, which before the war was worth a little less than our pound. There are very large quantities of gold in circulation. The British Government will normally only accept the rupee in payment of revenue, and this has become the currency in the towns. When I left the country, in October, 1920, about fourteen rupees were the equivalent of one lira. Indian paper money is readily accepted, the higher value notes at a premium on account of the ease with which they may be carried, while Turkish paper money is worth only 15 per cent of its face value. The weights and measures are extremely complicated and vary not only in every town, but almost in every village. Grain is measured by capacity, and each village selects its own particular vessel to be its standard. Endeavours are being made to introduce the kilogram as the standard weight throughout the country.

Some of the Arbil merchants have wide connections, possessing their own agents in Aleppo and Baghdad, and corresponding before the war with firms in Marseilles. They are expert in taking advantage of the exchanges. During 1920 Ahmad Pasha used to send large quantities of rupees to Baghdad to be exchanged for drafts expressed in English pounds. These he despatched to Aleppo and realised for Turkish gold, the lira there being worth about Rs.9. The gold was then loaded up on donkeys and brought back to Mesopotamia, a clear profit of 25 per cent being realised on each transaction.

CHAPTER VII

ALTUN KEUPRI AND FIRST VISIT TO ARBIL

DURING THE MONTH OF October, 1918, two British columns were advancing into northern Mesopotamia, one along the Tigris towards Mosul, and the other by the Kifri road towards Kirkuk. The latter town fell on October 27th: by the end of the month our troops had reached Altun Keupri on the Lesser Zab. The Mosul column was within a few miles of its objective when news arrived that the Allies had concluded an armistice with the Turks.

At this time I was at Mandali, hourly hoping to be ordered northwards. At last, on November 1st, a telegram arrived appointing me A.P.O. Altun Keupri. The same afternoon I set out in my Ford van with one servant and the minimum of kit, and reached my destination at noon on the 3rd.

Altun Keupri or Golden Bridge is so called from the famous bridge which used to connect the town with the left bank of the river. It is supposed to have been built several centuries ago at the orders of an energetic young lad called Altun. It crossed the river in one span about twenty yards wide. The arch, made of stones and gypsum on a wooden framework, was so steep that all carts and guns had to be manhandled across it. On reaching the river I found that both this bridge and the bridge on the further side of the town had been blown up by the retreating Turks. As no heavy rain had yet fallen animals and carts were able to cross the stream with some difficulty by a ford a few hundred yards below the broken bridge.

I left my van in a building and went down to the ford where, with some difficulty, I borrowed a pony and crossed. Passing through some filthy back streets I came to the main road and the Serai or Government Office. Here to my surprise I found Mr. C. C. Garbett, I.C.S., who had come from

Baghdad to take notes on the revenue systems of the districts which had just been occupied, and to give such assistance as might be necessary to the newly installed A.P.Os. He had only arrived a few minutes before me, and was already busy talking to some of the leading inhabitants and taking down notes.

The main part of Altun Keupri is huddled together on a rock in the middle of the river. There are a number of small shops on either side of the main road which passes through the centre of the town and descends beneath a tunnel-like arch to the foreshore of the right fork of the stream, which is wide but contains little water, and then climbs again up a very steep ascent to the second bridge. This road is only just wide enough in the town for a car to pass along it. A few narrow dirty lanes branch off from it, and give access to closely packed houses. On the mainland on either side of the river are a few larger and better spaced houses, but these were all deserted, having been previously occupied by Turkish troops. From May to November, while the river is low, all the way round the rock is a strip of foreshore which serves as the refuse place and latrine of the population. The houses round the edge of the rock have privies which project over it and drain on to it. In addition to the local population a considerable number of Turkish troops had encamped in and around the town for some months. Consequently the place was encircled by half a year's accumulation of filth. The flies were indescribable; a piece of food put on the table was immediately blackened with them.

Of an original population of 3,000 about 1,000 were left. The rest had either emigrated or died of starvation. They were a miserable dirty crew. The leading inhabitant was one Hassan Agha, a hateful old hypocrite and the agent of Ahmad Pasha Dizai. The Rais Baladiyah, or head of the municipality holding a post not unlike that of a Mayor in England, was Suayid Agha, an honest old fellow but very thick-headed, who used to drive me to a frenzy, as I was ill most of the time I was at Altun Keupri, and consequently did not suffer fools gladly. I remember one day I told him that I wished the river would come down in flood and carry off him, the town, and all its inhabitants.

Mr. Garbett stayed a day or two in Altun Keupri, and spent his whole time interviewing tribal and village headmen. Meanwhile I was occupied in trying to reduce chaos to order. The district allotted to me consisted of three nihayas, which had formerly been part of the Kirkuk district. They all lay to the south of the Lesser Zab, except for a few villages along the right bank. It is not an easy thing to install Government machinery when there is practically nothing to start with. I was busy, therefore, recruiting my own gendarmes and arming them, and finding suitable men to fill the various Government offices. I had many applicants for posts, but most of them were unsuitable, and I had to obtain effendis from Kirkuk to fill the more important appointments. Within a few days an Indian accountant and a supply of stationery arrived, and it then did not take long to get my office into order. I quickly recruited a force of gendarmes, composed of the most arrant scoundrels under the sun, and was compelled to arm them with some very ancient large-bore rifles collected from the townsmen, which fortunately they never had to use.

The gendarmes in Turkish times were the curse of Mesopotamia. Hardened ruffians without training and without principles, they used their authority to commit innumerable extortions. Loathed by the people and being able to earn a livelihood solely as minions of the Government, they were usually loyal while the Government's prestige remained high and could normally be relied upon to follow out instructions given to them; while some acted in critical times with the greatest bravery. On entering a new district it was necessary for the A.P.O. to raise an executive force at once, and in nontribal areas the old Turkish gendarmes were the only material at his disposal. Great efforts were made to improve them, and enlist young men, and in some districts bodies of regular police were formed; but it was always one of the A.P.O.'s greatest problems to keep their rapacity in check.

The municipal authorities of Turkish times were still in being, and great efforts were made through them to obtain labour to improve the sanitary state of the town. About two men and a dozen boys were forthcoming, but as they spent most of the day sitting down and talking to each other, the great work of cleaning the place had to be left to the rains and the floods.

On November 7th I received an order to proceed to Kirkuk and see Major E. Noel, C.I.E., who had been appointed Political Officer Kirkuk, and was generally directing policy in southern Kurdistan. I drove over on the following morning through rain and bitter cold wind. Major Noel explained to me the policy he wished adopted, the general idea being to govern through the tribal chief, and dismiss wherever possible the corrupt Turkish official and gendarme. While I was in Kirkuk a telegram arrived saying that a Political Officer was to proceed directly with a small force of cavalry and take over Arbil from the Turks under the terms of the armistice. Major Noel deputed me, and the G.O.C. Kirkuk gave me a formal note to deliver to the O.C. Turkish troops, asking him to withdraw to Mosul. After lunch I returned to Altun Keupri.

After much delay and difficulty in collecting transport I left for Arbil with one British officer and a troop of the 12th Cavalry (Indian) and two British telegraphists at 1 p.m. on the 10th. Meanwhile, to my disappointment , a wire had been received to the effect that Captain (now Major) S. G. Murray, C.I.E., had been appointed to Arbil, and that I was to return to Altun Keupri as soon as he arrived. We fixed on Gul Tappeh, a Dizai village, as our destination for the night, and I went on ahead with a few sawars to make the necessary arrangements. After meeting nobody for miles we came across a solitary Kurd driving along some bullocks and donkeys; he directed us to the village which was concealed in a hollow about a quarter of a mile away from the road. I sent on a gendarme to announce my arrival, and the whole of the male population turned out to meet me. I was greeted with a note of interrogation. The headman, Mahmud Yaba, an independent agha not closely connected with any of the big Dizai chiefs, shook hands with me and seated me on a cushion outside his guest-house. He is an ugly middle-aged man, and at first I put him down as a liar and a rogue. When I returned to Arbil I found he was unusually truthful for a Kurd, and I used often to apply to him when I required an unbiassed opinion on matters affecting the rival Dizai chiefs. One of the first things he said to me was, 'You are going to Arbil. You will find there my friend, Ahmad Effendi, the Rais Balayidah. He is a good man and will help you.' This was the first I heard of the greatest friend I have made among Eastern peoples, and one of the most faithful and high-principled men I have ever met. When I had sat down all the elders of the village gathered round me and through one of their number who could talk Persian bombarded me with volleys of questions – why had the British come? how were they going to govern? were they going to suppress the tyrannous chiefs and headmen? how much revenue would they collect? what agricultural improvements would they introduce? would they build railways? etc., etc., while I endeavoured to answer them to the best of my ability. It was rather a curious experience, sitting there that dull cold evening with dour grizzled Kurds all round me subjecting me to such a close examination. I was probably the first Englishman with whom they had ever talked. During this first visit the Dizai impressed me as rather an unfriendly and inhospitable people. Later on I grew very fond of them, and came to look upon them as the best type of Kurd in Mesopotamia, more manly than the tribes to the south of the Lesser Zab and more reasonable and intelligent than the wild men of the hills. At sunset on the muezzin's call my friends went off to pray, and shortly afterwards Mahmud Agha brought me out a welcome meal of meat and rice. The cavalry arrived about 6.30 p.m.

The following morning we set off at 7 a.m. in a drizzle. After an hour we passed a large square building, which appeared to be empty. We had ridden on some way when one of the sawars suddenly said there were some Turks on the road behind us. We went back and found the building contained a quantity of grain with a guard over it. The officer-in-charge insisted on handing over to us, and rejoining his headquarters in Arbil. We could not spare any men to relieve the guard, so I had to send for the chief of the nearest village. He proved to be a boy of about eighteen, called Ali Agha. He was clothed in a wonderful black silk costume with a twisted waistband 14 ins. broad. He undertook to look after the grain until a proper guard could be found.

For two or three hours we rode on through endless bare undulating country, until finally at the top of a rise we saw some four miles away from us in the plain a great circular

ARBIL

mound crowned with a ring of buildings. This was Arbil, the
ancient sacred city of the Assyrians, existing under the same
name as early as 1800 B.C., where kings prayed for victory
and mighty conquerors flayed their captives alive before the
altar of Ishtar. Here it was that Alexander the Great after his
victory pursued the fallen Darius, and though disappointed of
his victim overtook the royal treasure. Here, too, at one time
ruled the best-known Kurd in history, the great Saladin.

   We approached the town by the wrong road and were compelled to make our way through a narrow back street. Eventually we came to a small open place with coffee shops on one
side and the municipal offices on the other; here, despite the
weather, a large concourse of people were assembled. The
gendarmes were all drawn up, and their commandant was
the first to greet us. He was followed by the Rais Baladiyah
Ahmad Effendi, and the Turkish Mutesarrif, or Governor. I
was given tea and coffee in the Baladiyah or municipal office,
and then after seeing that the troops were properly accommodated was conducted up the great cobbled ascent to the city
on the hill. Above the entrance to the upper town is the Serai
or Government Office, whence a magnificent view is obtained
over the lower town and the surrounding plain.

   Arbil, with its battlemented heights and its great solitary
minaret, presents a unique appearance. The upper town,
built on a huge circular mound, commands the surrounding
plain like a vast fort, the outer walls being lofty and containing only small irregular windows like loopholes, except where
some of the rich aghas have constructed balconies. It is
entered by only two gates – one broad entrance on the north
passing in under the Serai, and another small door giving
access on the east. The streets within are very rough and
narrow, and cannot be used for wheeled traffic. It is said that
this town was built two or three centuries ago, and that all
the population of the countryside were compelled to labour at
the task of making even the sides and top of the mound.
Within are probably relics more valuable than all those found
at Nimrud and Asshur, but it is impossible to excavate
without destroying the town. People who have tried to dig
wells on the top have come upon such strange sights that
they have hastily ceased their work. The lower town clusters
round the south and east sides of the mound. Here is the

bazaar, which is very extensive, and contains two fine arcades in good repair, and two others in ruins, but likely soon to be rebuilt. The other shops are mostly stalls, the merchants bringing out their goods in the morning and storing them in a 'Khan' or caravanserai at night. The bazaar is well stocked and Kurds flock in from all sides, even from distant Nehri, to make their purchases.

Arbil was never the scene of a conflict during the Great War. The Russians reached Rawanduz and the British Altun Keupri and the outskirts of Mosul, but she remained untouched. Her people were able to secrete stores of grain, and consequently comparatively few perished during the year of famine.

In the fields on the western edge of the town stands a great brick minaret about 110 ft. high and 12 ft. in diameter at the base. The top has fallen off, leaving an uneven stump. Traces remain of brightly coloured tiles, and there is a certain amount of rough ornament. It is eaten away at the base and will eventually fall if efforts are not made to preserve it. No other visible trace exists of the mosque of which it must have once formed part, but the uneven surface of the surrounding fields betrays the presence of a former town. Local tradition says that this minaret was constructed in the time of the Caliphs, and that it was the centre of a former Arbil ruled by an independent Sultan.

I lunched with Ahmad Effendi. This remarkable man, who is almost forty years of age, belongs to the most respected family in Arbil, and is the cousin of Mulla Effendi, one of the leading divines of Southern Kurdistan. His father and his grandfather before him were also divines, as is his only surviving brother. In his youth he followed a legal career, holding the office of Public Prosecutor under the Turks in Arbil. Shortly before our occupation he was elected Rais Baladiyah, or Mayor. He is about 5 ft. 9 ins. in height with a pronounced stoop. His whole figure is lean and slight; his features are sharp and his nose long and hooked. His eyes are unusually bright, and he will probably sooner or later fall a victim to consumption, a disease which has carried off nearly all the members of his family. He does not wear a beard, and is usually dressed in European clothing. He is remarkable in that he is a true democrat, and really has the interests of the people, and especially the poorer people, at heart. He always takes their side against the aghas, by whom he is consequently loathed. In times of difficulty he supports the Government through thick and thin, knowing that disturbances will bring misery chiefly to the poor. Twice he saved the town in Turkish times; on one occasion when the Governor was threatened by a conspiracy of all the notables, and he persuaded Ibrahim Agha to come in and save him, and again when the tribes were preparing to sack the town just before my arrival he kept them away by innumerable artifices, and put guards on the granaries that they might not be looted. And again in September, 1920, when the trouble came, it was he above all who helped me to guide the town safely through the storm. I confided in him on all occasions, and was never deceived; his devotion to me became almost doglike, and if occasion had arisen I have little doubt that he would have laid down his life for me.

Having lunched well, about 3 p.m. I went over to the Turkish camp, which lay a mile to the west of the town, to pay my compliments to the Turkish commandant. He was a funny little man, a Caucasian, talking in spasms of unintelligible Turkish, and did not seem in the least pleased to see me. However, rapid orders were shouted to his orderly and coffee and cigarettes appeared. I handed him the note I had been given. Knowing French he could read a word here and there, and pretended that he understood all that was said. He agreed to depart the next day, but proposed that his sick should remain in Arbil. I insisted that he should leave a doctor, which he refused to do. He finally promised to take his sick with him, but after he had left they were found scattered about in houses all over the town. Accompanied by a Turkish officer I now proceeded to take over the granaries and magazines. This occupied a long time, as there were large quantities of wheat and barley in the former. A tomb in one of the cemeteries contained over 500 assorted bombs. I dined and slept in Ahmad Effendi's guest-house. It poured with rain all night, and as owing to the disturbed conditions it had been impossible to have the flat roof remudded the water came through in torrents.

The following day the whole place was under water, and still it continued to rain. I thought it polite to ride out and say good-bye to the Turkish Commandant, but apparently he believed I had come out to laugh at him departing ignominiously, under such conditions. The town was full of Turkish officials, many of whom had fled here from Kirkuk and other places, gendarmes, and discharged soldiers. In the Serai the old Turkish machinery was in working order, and I thought it better to leave things as they were till Captain Murray arrived. I only dealt with urgent matters and with the numerous wires that I received. In the afternoon all the notables called on me. I talked to them at length, but they had not much to say for themselves. On the 13th, Captain Murray arrived, and I handed over to him, setting out for Altun Keupri again the following morning, accompanied only by two gendarmes and my servant on a mule with my bedding.

I had to return via Dibakah in Kandinawah, as I had promised to visit a small military post which had been despatched there. A mile or two away from Gul Tappeh I was caught in a heavy thunderstorm and soaked to the skin, and rather against my will I had to resort to Mahmud Yaba again. He made me very welcome, and taking me into his guesthouse placed a large pile of thorns and brushwood on the fire, which burst into an enormous blaze. I changed my clothes, and as it was late decided to spend the night there. I discussed many weighty matters with the Kurds, and in particular asked questions about the quantities of Government grain which the Dizai had looted from some of the local granaries. I remember asking Mahmud Agha a question to which, after uttering a long prayer in Arabic, he replied with an enormous lie. After a simple dinner of burghul and vegetables an old saiyid called Shaikh Riza (or more popularly Shaikh i Shait or the Mad Shaikh) rode up to the door, dismounted and came in. He was a jovial old gentleman possessing an enormous sense of humour which is probably why the Kurds thought him mad; he talked with me at length, and ever afterwards considered me his close personal friend, even going so far as to consult me on his matrimonial difficulties. He would say his prayers in a loud voice, and continually interrupt them to join in the talk. He and Mahmud Agha nearly drove me mad by keeping up a loud conversation long after I had turned in, and when that had finished the old shaikh continued to cough, hoick, and spit all night.

I set out at sunrise the following morning and passed on
the way Qurshaqlu, the village of Ahmad Pasha, who had
gone away to attend some funeral ceremonies in the Khushnao country. I had to inquire the way there, and was much
surprised because nobody offered me even a drink of water —
a most unusual thing in a Kurdish village. While crossing the
Arbil Plain I heard rifle shots being fired in all directions; it
must have been Kurds amusing themselves, as they love
nothing more than expending ammunition when they have
plenty to spare. On reaching Dibakah I found that Captain
Marriott and his detachment had settled down as comfort-
ably as could be expected. I had my meals with Rasul Agha,
the least important of the four leading Dizai chiefs, who
treated me with the greatest hospitality. He is an enormous
stout man with a blatant, tactless manner but comparatively
well educated. The next day I returned to my headquarters.

During the month that followed I was busy with the normal routine at Altun Keupri and the touring of the district.
On the 18th, in a village just outside the town, I met Mahmud Agha, a chief of the Shaikh Bizaini tribe resident in the
Koi district, which was still under a Turkish governor. As he
expressed a wish to come under British rule, I wrote to Baghdad asking if I might visit this village, and received a reply
granting me permission, and asking if I would be willing in
due course to go out and take over Koi Sanjaq. I readily replied in the affirmative. On the 25th I toured up the right
bank of the Lesser Zab to Sartik, the village of the above-
mentioned Mahmud Agha. He is an active old man of seventy
with a white beard and well-tanned face, very short in stature, but possessed of considerable will-power and astuteness.
Though none too scrupulous he is a paragon of virtue compared to the other aghas of his tribe, about the most unprincipled set of scoundrels I have ever met. He became a great
friend of mine.

The next morning we crossed the river in Mahmud Agha's
private ferry, a Heath Robinsonian contraption made out of a
large number of small planks fastened together with
enormous nails and propelled by oars of unpolished wood
with a natural fork near the haft which worked against a
peg. The creaking was terrific. By dint of much baling we
reached the other bank in safety. From here a steep ascent

brought us to the top of the Shuan hills, whence a magnificent view was obtained. All around was a raging sea of rough bare hills topped to the east by the frontier snows. Below us the Zab pursued its blue serpentine course through a bed of white stones nearly a mile wide, and decked here and there with groves of green poplar. After several hours' journey through delightful upland country, whose bareness was relieved by plantations of fig, aspen and plane decked in vivid autumn raiment, we came to Redar, the headquarters of the Shuan sub-district. Here I experienced an arduous time endeavouring to apply President Wilson's principle of self-determination to two untutored Kurdish tribes. Each had at least four candidates for the chieftainship, none of whom were at all enthusiastically supported by their people. The only thing that the Kurd understands from self-determination is a state of affairs where each individual can do exactly as he likes, otherwise anarchy. In one village I even went so far as to hold an election, which was highly successful.

On November 28th I returned to Altun Keupri and began to busy myself with the issue of agricultural loans. The Turks having requisitioned nearly all the grain and most of the plough animals in the country, it became necessary to assist the cultivator to make a fresh start. I was allowed to advance considerable sums on easy terms, and I sent notices all round the district bidding the people come and fetch the money. It then proceeded to pour with rain, the river came down in flood and the flying ferry which the military had constructed had to be dismantled. I tried to cross in my own clumsy old craft, but it was carried miles down the river, and it took nearly four hours to haul it up again. I was compelled to sit with my money in Altun Keupri and watch hundreds of hungry cultivators on the other bank vainly waiting for an opportunity to get across.

Meanwhile urgent wires for the despatch of a British Political Officer kept pouring in from Koi Sanjaq. The Turkish Governor was ill, and in any case possessed no authority. Anarchy and chaos were daily increasing. I received orders from Baghdad to proceed there as soon as I could, but I delayed, as I wished to complete the issue of agricultural loans before starting. Finally, on December 12th, a telegram arrived from Koi saying that the Piran tribe had at-

tacked and were looting the town, and I wired to Baghdad
suggesting I should go out at once. At 1 a.m. that night I received a clear line message granting me permission, and in-
vesting me with summary powers to deal with the
disturbances. I hurriedly collected transport and was away
by 10 a.m. on the 13th.

CHAPTER VIII

KOI AND RANIA

OUR FIRST DAY'S RIDE brought us to Sartik, the village of
Mahmud Agha, who promised to provide me with an escort
for my journey to Koi. The next morning a band of some fifteen heavily armed cutthroats duly appeared, led by a black-
bearded cheery villain called Abbas Agha. Mahmud Agha also
insisted on accompanying us himself. Beside the tribesmen I
had with me some eight gendarmes, clad in bright blue jack-
ets and trousers, and my trusty retainer Jaafar Khan, a top-
hatted Lur from the Pusht i Kuh country. He was a stout
fellow, 6 ft. tall with a mass of curly hair, a companion and a
stand-by in a land that was strange to both of us.

We set out from Sartik in gloomy weather, and after following up the Lesser Zab for a few miles plunged into the
maze of low red sandstone hills which is characteristic of the
Koi district. For five hours we pursued our way across this
country along a track that was almost invisible, having been
washed away by the heavy rains. It was up and down, up and
down, over continual red ridges, adorned only with occasional
tufts of long dead grass, and intersected by precipitous watercourses in which stood oleanders and tall clumps of pale
reeds. The few villages in this desolate area are hidden away
in folds of the hills, and only betray their presence to the
passing wayfarer by some solitary outstanding mulberry
tree. At noon my companions halted for midday prayer by a
small stream at the bottom of a ravine. About 3 p.m. we
emerged from the hills into a small undulating plain and
soon reached the village of Ilanjaq, where we had decided to
spend the night. As it was inhabited only by peasants and
contained no guest-house worthy the name, I had to billet
myself on one of the people and provide my own food. On the
road I had received a letter from Hama Agha of Koi, and I

now wrote a reply, addressing him as Governor of the town
and announcing my arrival on the morrow.

Before we reach Koi it is necessary to explain briefly the
state of affairs that existed there. For centuries the town had
been rent in twain by the animosities of the rival factions of
the Ghafuri and Hawaizi, two Kurdish families who between
them owned most of the villages in the surrounding district.
At the time of which I am speaking the Ghafuri were led by
the above-mentioned Hama Agha, who, I was told, was 130
years old, but still in full possession of his intellect. As his
party was numerically the stronger, and his age and character earned for him considerable respect from both parties,
Major Noel had suggested that I should select him as governor.

The head of the Hawaizi, who, though weaker than their
rivals, can boast of many more able men, was one Abdulla
Agha; he was favoured by the Turks, and for some years had
possessed a predominating influence in the town. With the
decline, however, of the Turkish authority that followed on
the Armistice, the Ghafuri determined to assert themselves,
and some of the party, not including Hama Agha, seized the
opportunity to encourage Sawar Agha, chief of the Piran
tribe, to commit a series of depredations on Abdulla Agha's
property and finally to attack Koi itself, when a horde of the
Bilbasi tribesmen had succeeded in surrounding Abdulla
Agha's house and seriously wounding one of his sons. Old
Hama Agha, roused from a bed of sickness, sallied forth in
the middle of the night and stilled the tumult. This incident
occurred only two days before my departure from Altun
Keupri.

On the 15th, another cold windy day, we had to traverse
some 14 miles of bare undulating country intersected by deep
red ravines before we reached our destination. About an
hour's distance from the town I perceived about fifty mounted
men waiting for me at the top of a rise; this was the istiqbal,
or party who had come out to welcome me, including the
green-faced Abdulla Agha, wearing European clothes, and old
Hama Agha with his bland countenance and snowy white
beard, his broad hairy chest bare even to this inclement
weather. There were many others besides, none of them very
prepossessing, and it seemed to me that all their features

had turned green from the acrimony of the feuds which are
their sole interest in life. Abdullah Agha was the first to
greet me, but I immediately asked for Hama Agha, and rode
beside him, much to the chagrin of the former, who kept trying to occupy the place on my other side. It was too cold for
conversation, and we made our way in silence through grave-
yards and ruins into the town. On the outskirts I was greeted
by the Christian community with their black-robed priest at
the head, full of joy at the idea that I had come to relieve
them after centuries of oppression. My arrival in bad weather
was a fortunate omen; he who brings rain, brings prosperity.

I was conducted first of all to the Serai or Government Offices where a room had been made ready for my reception.
Here assembled all the notables and leading mullas of the
town, and after coffee and tea had been served the Mufti (a
religious dignitary), Mulla Muhammad Effendi, delivered a
long speech of welcome in unctuous Persian, to which I replied as well as I could.

It may be well to describe here the leading personalities
who took part in this welcome. First of all comes Hama Agha,
who sat still, silent except for an occasional grunt, looking
very patriarchal and smoking a pipe over 2 ft. long, with a
fluted stem and a bowl carved out of black stone. He was of
middle height, but extraordinarily broad across the
shoulders; considering his age, his physical strength was
marvellous. It is reported that during his long life even in the
severest weather he never used warm water for his bath or
daily ablutions. His real age was somewhere between 95 and
100; he had been head of his family for over sixty years, and
had had a stormy career. He could remember the struggles in
his earliest years between the Pashas of Rawanduz and Sulaimaniyah, under whose sway Koi alternately fell. In his
youth he fought the Turks, and after much bloodshed was
captured and imprisoned for fifteen years. In the struggle his
ear was practically severed from his head; the wound healed
up, but he always had an issue from his ear, which he used to
mop continually. He engaged in many conflicts with the surrounding tribes; the Hamawand attacking some of his villages he called in the Shaikh Bizaini to assist him in
expelling them. This having been successfully accomplished,
he had in turn to attack the Shaikh Bizaini and drive them

'FOR HE WAS GOT TO A SLEEPY MOOD'

back to their homes. He possessed some fifty villages in the district around Koi, and to prevent the tribes encroaching upon them was the keynote of his policy. It was always a great sorrow to him that all his sons had died in infancy and that he had no successor; eventually when he was already ninety years old one day an old mulla came and announced to him that God would grant him another son, and that he should call his name Muhammad Ziad. The child was to be separated from his mother as soon as he was born, and was not to live in Koi. This miraculous event duly came to pass, and when I arrived little Muhammad Ziad, now about eight years old, was living in a village several hours' distance from the town. Hama Agha was a fine old man, with most of the failings of his age, ever fond, when he was roused, of telling stories of the good old times, but otherwise often going to sleep in the middle of a conversation. He possessed a benign smile and was the soul of hospitality, having the reputation of being the only rich old man in Kurdistan who was not a miser. By nature kindly disposed, he was also endowed with a strong and extremely obstinate character. He was a tyrant to his relations and never forgave his enemies, continually raking up petty grievances that were years old. He was strongly influenced by personal likes and dislikes.

It is depressing to have to pass from dear old Hama Agha to the leader of the Hawaizi, Abdulla Agha. A lank stooping man of about sixty-five, with a sallow, wrinkled, and spec- tacled face, and great shaggy eyebrows dyed blue-black, he always had a revolting appearance, especially when dressed in European clothes. He was well versed in intrigue and the corrupt practices that had been rife under the Turkish Government. When I arrived he was still Rais Baladiyah or Mayor of the town, but was loathed by the majority of the populace. Even his relations were not fond of him, but they admired his intellectual abilities, which were much superior to those of Hama Agha.

The most prominent of his relations was his cousin, Jamil Agha, a really remarkable man. His father when dying had entrusted him as a son to Hama Agha, whose daughter he had subsequently married. He was therefore closely allied to both the rival houses and always stood out for reconciliation. For a Kurd he is one of the most honest and truthful I have ever met; a model of piety, he is by no means a fanatic, and is always recognised as a protector of the Jews, in whose quarter he lives, and of the Christians, some of whom cultivate his land. When quite a young man he was for four years the Mayor of the town, and is the only man who has held that office for the benefit of his fellow citizens and not of himself. Tall and upright with a high forehead his face nevertheless is somewhat weak, and he is liable in times of trouble to sacrifice his convictions for the sake of peace and quiet. He possesses two brothers, Jalal and Jalil, both scoundrels.

Koi literally swarms with white-turbaned mullas, the chief of them being Mulla Muhammad Effendi, whom we nicknamed 'The Bishop'. A tall middle-aged man he possesses great learning and a tremendous gift of the gab. Wherever he is he monopolises the conversation; fortunately he is also endowed with a very wide sense of humour, so that he can be most entertaining. He always boasts that he is the most learned man in Kurdistan, a failing common to his class. He became the Hakim i Shara or Muhammadan judge in Koi under our administration, and though his learning could never be disputed the equity of his decisions was often called into question, for he was a worldly prelate, too fond of society and the world's goods.

When the formalities in the Serai had been concluded I proceeded to a house which Hama Agha had prepared for me. The old man came in with me and endeavoured to converse with me in a curious mixture of Persian and Turkish. His voice was thick and his words difficult to catch; when I was able to reply he could rarely understand what I said owing to his deafness. After a sumptuous lunch had been produced, Hama Agha withdrew, and I spent the afternoon in interviewing various important personages. I had many problems before me, the chief of which was to make peace between the Ghafuri and Hawaizi and arrange for the government of the town in a way that would suit both parties, and to exact compensation from Sawar Agha of the Piran for the injuries he had inflicted on Abdulla Agha. I had already determined that Hama Agha should be governor, and it would be necessary to distribute the minor offices in a way that should reconcile the rival faction to his appointment.

The following day I was able to explore the town. It is very compact and lies in a hollow at an altitude of some 1,800 ft. above the sea. Hills of over 3,000 ft. in height shut it in on the east and north, and the small plain in which it stands is enclosed in the other directions by the ravined sandstone country which I have already described. War and famine had reduced its population from 10,000 to 4,000, half the houses were in ruins and the inhabitants were in a state of great destitution. Prices, which were abnormally high, fell 50 per cent within a few days of my arrival, and to relieve distress a poorhouse was instituted which accommodated nearly 300 inmates, mostly fatherless orphans. The streets of the town are narrow, consisting of two raised pavements with a deep passage in between just wide enough to take a pack animal. On the west side of the town on a large mound are the old Turkish barracks, from the roof of which I surveyed the view. The country was saturated and the little town with its mosques lay before me a uniformly dull grey, against a background of grey hills whose summits were wrapped in the folds of heavy rain clouds. I reflected on the strange concatenation of circumstances which had brought me to this remote spot and caused me to be caught in the vortex of its century-old family quarrels.

That evening while I was in the Serai a messenger suddenly arrived to say that an officer and detachment of men were about to enter the town to prepare a place for Shaikh Osman, appointed by Shaikh Mahmud as Qaimaqam, or Governor, of Koi. A few weeks previous to this Major Noel had visited Sulaimaniyah and Shaikh Mahmud had been created hukmdar or ruler of Kurdistan. Koi had been included in his dominions, but I had understood from Major Noel that I was to nominate a local man myself as governor, and I was therefore somewhat nonplussed by this announcement, especially as I had already given the appointment to Hama Agha. I was further handicapped by the fact that though the telegraph line was working the operators were natives of the country, and any message I sent was sure to become public property within a few hours.

That night Shaikh Osman arrived with his cousin Shaikh Abdulla, and an ex-Turkish officer called Rashid Effendi. I found they had been sent with an army of 400 men, of whom

A VIEW OF KOI

I only saw a portion, to assist me in restoring order at Koi, and especially in bringing to book Sawar Agha and the Piran. Shaikh Osman was an absolute gentleman, of a mild and pious disposition, small and slight in build, and with a most wonderful carriage of the body. Despite his stature I have seldom seen anybody look more regal than Shaikh Osman when he came to the Serai in his flowing robes accompanied by a long train of attendants. He could not read or write, and spoke nothing but Kurdish. He was perfectly honest in all his dealings with me, and had no ambition to become governor of Koi, though others wished to make him so. It was Shaikh Abdulla, a stronger and better educated man, who set on foot all the intrigues to oust Hama Agha and install one of the shaikhly family, assisted by that scoundrel Rashid Effendi, who spent most of his time imprisoning and extorting money from innocent Jews and Christians. I had then no idea what powers Major Noel had given to Shaikh Mahmud and his emissaries, and I was in a very awkward situation. I had a long talk with Hama Agha, and arranged that for the present his authority should be in abeyance. I then asked Shaikh Osman to govern the town temporarily with the title of 'Special Agent of Sheikh Mahmud' and gave out that he had only come to settle the feud between the Ghafuri and the Hawaizi, and would depart when this was done. No one in Koi was very glad to see the Shaikhs, and a long-standing feud existed between Hama Agha and the Sulaimaniyah family.

In the afternoon I paid a call upon the Turkish ex-Qaimaqam, who was lying in bed seriously ill. He was a tiny little man, a native of Crete, and I much pitied him left in his feeble state among such a lawless people. He was unfeignedly glad to see me, and gave me some excellent Stambul coffee, and a beastly concoction that looked like tea, but was made out of cinnamon, which he assured me was a most excellent remedy for the chill from which he was suffering. He began by saying he had a large number of 'confessions' to make to me, and would I be pleased to hear them. They proved to relate to business matters and the disposal of Turkish public moneys. He made many requests for back-pay and journey-money to take him to his distant home, and I did my best to satisfy him. Eventually the conversation came to the subject of the Piran. 'Ah,' exclaimed the Qaimaqam in a thin high-pitched voice, 'when the Government is strong they are as meek as sheep, but when the Government is weak' – and he suddenly jumped up in bed and shouted – 'they roar-r-r like a lion.'

I spent the next few days in trying to bring the rival factions to an agreement, Shaikh Abdulla doing his best the whole time to thwart my plans. My idea was to appoint Hama Agha as governor, and Abdulla Agha as his deputy. Hama Agha, however, refused to accept his hated rival, and suggested Jamil Agha. I agreed, and was about to issue an order making the appointments when news arrived that Karim Agha, a nephew of Abdulla Agha, had just burnt one of Hama Agha's villages containing a valuable store of tobacco.

It now became clear that the two factions would never make peace unless heavy pressure were brought to bear on them. I therefore conceived the idea of arresting and deporting to Sulaimaniyah the worst firebrand on each side. On the morning of the 20th I communicated my plan to the Shaikhs, who were delighted; the intrigue by its nature appealed to them, and the presence of two such hostages in Sulaimaniyah would greatly increase Shaikh Mahmud's influence in Koi. They undertook to effect the arrest, and all they asked me to do was to come to their house that night two or three hours after sunset. After dinner a note from Shaikh Osman arrived, and I proceeded to his lodging, where in excited whispers Shaikh Abdulla informed me of their plans. I was a sort of decoy, as orders were being sent to our two victims to come and see me in the Shaikh's house; on their arrival they were to be seized and despatched to Sulaimaniyah with the greatest secrecy. I sat cross-legged by the side of the Shaikh Osman for two hours, during which a great deal of excited whispering and going to and fro took place. Shaikh Osman was very pleasant, and presented me with a Kodak camera which he had taken from a German officer whom his men had killed. Soon after 9 p.m. Shaikh Abdulla came in and announced that he had successfully disposed of Muhammad Amin Agha of the Ghafuri, the grand-nephew of Hama Agha, and a young and ill-educated lout. Shortly afterwards in came our other victim, Karim Agha, and sat down. He was the nephew of Abdulla Agha, whom he rivalled in sal-

lowness. I got to know him well later on, and found him a
very capable and well-educated man. After I had asked him a
few questions relating to his uncle's health, Shaikh Abdulla
beckoned him to the door, where he was informed he must
make a journey to Sulaimaniyah, and hastily departed. I regret to say the Shaikhs' men who accompanied him deprived
him of his watch and all his money on the road. I did not
enjoy the part I played in this evening's work and it is impossible to convey in black and white the tense atmosphere of
excitement and intrigue which has caused those hours spent
in Shaikh Osman's house to impress themselves so vividly on
my memory.

Nobody knew that the two aghas had been spirited away
till the following morning, when it was supposed they had
been sent to Kirkuk. Old Hama Agha came to my office in a
rage, saying, 'What have you done with my son, the apple of
my eye? He alone was left to me, to look after my remoter villages in my old age. What have you done with him?' I replied
that he was proceeding to Sulaimaniyah for a short visit for
the good of his health. 'Well,' said the old man, 'you think to
improve matters by this action, and you have made them
worse. You have lighted the thorns beneath the pot and the
water will boil over.' 'I suppose you know,' I replied, 'that
Karim Agha has also gone to Sulaimaniyah?' This took Hama
Agha by surprise. He grunted a bit, and eventually a bland
smile spread over his childlike features.

The kidnapping of the two aghas completely changed the
situation, and both factions were now ready for a settlement.
Any odium that attached to the act fell on the two shaikhs,
who were universally unpopular. Accordingly in the afternoon all the leading men assembled in my office, where I
made a speech to them: subsequently we adjourned to Hama
Agha's house, and all agreed to accept the old man's rule,
with Jamil Agha as deputy. I instructed them to prepare and
sign a declaration to this effect ready for Major Noel, who arrived the following day and confirmed the appointments.

Having disposed of the question of the governorship, my
chief anxiety now centred round Sawar Agha, chief of the
Piran. I had been in Koi for a week, and though Hama Agha
had ordered him in on the day that I arrived, he had not appeared. His village lay the other side of the Haib us Sultan

Dagh, on Bituin, some four hours' journey from Koi. One day he had come within two miles of the town, but had suddenly taken fright and withdrawn. I believe Shaikh Abdulla sent out and warned him not to come in, for on the evening of the 22nd he came to see me, and said that it was Hama Agha who was keeping Sawar Agha away, but that if he wrote to him he would no longer hesitate. I told him to write, and as soon as he had gone informed one of Hama Agha's relations of what had happened, warning him that it was essential that Sawar Agha should appear to come in on Hama Agha's word, and not on that of the Shaikhs.

On the afternoon of the 23rd Hama Agha's nephew, Mulla Ahmad Agha, arrived at my office and said, 'Sawar Agha has come in and is in Hama Agha's house.' Hardly were the words out of his mouth when Rashid Effendi rushed up saying, 'Sawar Agha has come in and is in Shaikh Osman's house.' I replied at once, 'I am going to the house of Hama Agha to see Sawar Agha', and set out in the direction indicated. When I arrived Sawar Agha was not there; he was only in the mosque, they said, saying his prayers and would shortly be with us. After two or three minutes he was brought in. The two shaikhs never gave me any further trouble.

Sawar Agha possessed a remarkable personality. A young man of twenty-five or twenty-six, he had a few years previously, on the death of his father, become chief of the wild Piran tribe. Finely built and full of spirits he was simply worshipped by his men, whom he had led on many marauding expeditions. His smile was one of the most fascinating I have ever seen. He is about 5 ft. 9 ins. in height with regular handsome features, a ruddy burnt complexion and a short light beard. His eyes are small, closely set and very bright, always with something cruel about them. Owing to the very thick padded clothes, twisted waistband, and balloon-like trousers characteristic of the Bilbas chiefs, he appears to be stout, and walks in a very slow pedantic fashion, swinging his body round to the right as he brings his left foot forward and vice versa. Normally cheerful and gay in disposition he becomes sullen when rebuked, and behaves like a spoilt child. Though at the present time he was under the influence of bad advisers, he readily agreed to make peace with Abdulla Agha and restore all the property he had stolen. Unfortunately, just as the deeds of settlement between the parties were ready for signature the son of Abdulla Agha who had been wounded in the Piran raid died, and further negotiations were prevented by his obsequies. Major Noel insisted on leaving for Rania on the 24th, and I wished to accompany him, so it was arranged that Sawar Agha should escort us, and subsequently return with me to Koi to complete the necessary formalities.

When I took over Koi, Major Noel had agreed that such parts of the old Turkish qazas, or districts of Rania and Qala Diza as lay north of the Lesser Zab, should be within my sphere. Shaikh Mahmud had appointed one of his relations, by name Shaikh Amin, to the former place, while at the latter Babekr Agha, chief of the Pizhder, had installed himself immediately after the armistice, and been subsequently recognised by the British authorities and the Hukmdar of Sulaimaniyah. It was necessary for me to visit both these places in order to pay off the Turkish officials who were no longer required, and arrange for such appointments as might be necessary. Accordingly, at 2 p.m. on Christmas Eve, I left Koi with Major Noel and an escort of some twenty Piran horsemen, including their chief, Sawar Agha.

Our way lay over the Haib us Sultan range, which takes its name from a small ruined shrine situated beside the road at the beginning of the ascent. A long climb up a narrow and precipitous path brought us to the top, where a beautiful view awaited us. The southern face of the range on which we were standing is very steep and regular, and presents the appearance of a blank grey wall, the northern slopes, on the other hand, are broken up into a series of spurs and depressions thickly clad with dwarf-oak and tufts of dead grass. Beyond is another low range and then the great green plain of Bituin, bounded on the north by a series of rugged peaks and to the east by a long black ridge, broken at the southern extreme by a defile known as the Darband i Ramakan, through which flow the waters of the Lesser Zab. The whole landscape was topped by the shining snows of Galala, Kandil, and other imposing heights. We had now left behind us the bare foothill country, and entered the real Kurdistan, where Nature moulds her material in the grand style. An easy descent by a road lined thick on either side with bushes – a sight I had not seen for years — brought us to a small depression containing a clump of fine tall oaks, marking as usual the site of a cemetery; from here we climbed over a low ridge and found ourselves on the edge of the plain. After an hour's journey, during which we forded a considerable stream, we reached Sarkhuma, the village of Sawar Agha. As it was now dark we could see little of our surroundings. Instead of being conducted to the ordinary diwankhana we entered a small room in our host's private house, where we found awaiting us Mamand Agha, chief of the Ako, and certain of Sawar Agha's relations, including his five-year-old son, a delightful rosy-cheeked boy called Qadir. An excellent meal was produced, consisting of the usual pilau, some savoury forcemeat, and a bowl containing a mixture of thick gravy, lumps of meat, rice, and fresh grapes. We spent the evening in conversation, asking innumerable questions about the surrounding villages, their inhabitants, and their methods of agriculture.

The following morning I was up at sunrise. The fresh morning air, the wide green plain around threaded with silver streams, the lofty precipitous hills that encircled it with their coronets of gleaming snow, and the cloudless blue sky over all combined to make a scene that is unforgettable. I found that the building in which we had passed the night was situated halfway up a large mound, on top of which was the main guest-house. The village, which lay at the western foot of this eminence, consisted of some forty mud huts of the usual type with about thirty conical erections made out of reeds. In the neighbourhood were several springs, the site of which was marked by clumps of bramble and other shrubs; while a hundred yards to the east was a wide stream uniting just beyond with the river we had crossed the previous night. The course of both was marked by a variety of shrubs and reeds, the haunt of the wild boar which abounds in these parts. I visited one of these springs for a wash, expecting to find it very cold, for there was a slight frost on the ground, and pleasantly surprised when I dipped my hands into tepid water.

We left for Rania at 9 a.m., accompanied by Sawar Agha and thirty Piran horsemen; some 8 miles in front of us lay a rocky ridge with perpendicular strata which tailed out across the plain in a series of sweeping curves. Our escort were most

picturesque with their gaily coloured tasselled caps, thick
padded coats, felt waistcoats, and enormous pantaloons, each
individual laden with at least four bandoliers of ammunition,
a rifle, a pistol, and a dagger. They were finely mounted on
restless snorting steeds, and every now and then the gayer
spirits would show off two or three at a time, galloping across
our front almost touching our ponies' nostrils as they passed,
then suddenly turning and galloping back again, at the same
time swinging their rifles round their heads and firing off
wild shots into the air. Occasionally, to show his skill, a man
as he is galloping will take aim with one hand at the rider in
front of him, often going so far as to press the muzzle into the
centre of his back, a performance which has been known to
cause serious accidents. As we drew near the rocky ridge previously mentioned, a stream of horsemen could be seen descending its slopes. Our escort now formed themselves into a
long line on either side of us, one or two still galloping up and
down in front, while the opposing party, consisting of some
fifty horsemen who had come out from Rania to meet us, did
likewise, advancing slowly towards us to the tune of the zurnai and the accompaniment of the frequent discharge of rifle
shots. These two parties of Kurdish horsemen in their gay
fantastic attire meeting thus this bright Christmas morning
on the green sunlit plain with the great snow heights all
round presented a spectacle which cannot easily be forgotten.
When we met, the usual introductions followed, for the welcoming party included many important chiefs: first came
Shaikh Amin, the governor of Rania, a stooping, shifty-look-
ing individual, his crafty eyes half hidden by the tassels
which hung down from his silken head-dress; next was the
great Babekr Agha, chief of the Pizhder and governor of Qala
Diza, the most powerful man in Southern Kurdistan, a
gentleman of the first water, of medium height but sturdily
built, possessing a great hooked nose and the kindest of
smiles. He was wearing riding boots and bright blue pantaloons, with a handkerchief concealing his right eye (which
the public never saw), and an embroidered scarf tied under
his chin. Next followed Agha i Baiz, the titular chief of the
Bilbas confederation, a dear white-haired old fellow who entertained the Turco-Persian Frontier Commission just before
the war, and still talks of the fat brown cigarettes they gave

him; and finally, Ka Hussain, son of Baiz Pasha of the Mangur, in black garments of the finest material, with a white
twisted waistband and an enormous black head-dress surrounding a tasselled cap wrought in white and gold, a
delightful boy of seventeen, on whose ruddy countenance the
soft down just showed. These were accompanied by their dependants and relations, hardy warriors and young boys all
arrayed in their best. We proceeded *en masse* to Rania to the
tune of the zurnai, Ka Hussain and others performing feats
of horsemanship in front of us.

Rania proved to be a small village unhealthily situated by
a large spring and surrounded by rice fields. It is intensely
hot and malarious in the summer and autumn, and in the
winter and spring literally swarms with fleas, which make
sleep out of the question. Here we were greeted with low
bows and courteous gestures by the Turkish Qaimaqam,
Shaikh Muhammad Khalis, son of the Kurdish poet Shaikh
Riza. Later in the day we called upon him. He was a well-
educated and artistic man, calling himself a darwish or religious mendicant, and living very humbly. He read to us long
passages of his father's poetry, and protested bitterly at being
evicted from the governorship of Rania, as he was a Kurd and
no Turk. I had much business to transact in this place, and
occupied myself in dismissing and engaging officials and gendarmes, and assessing and paying pensions, while Major
Noel talked with the assembled chiefs.

We spent the night in Shaikh Amin's miserable flea-
infested quarters, and the following morning about 11 a.m.
Major Noel left for Rawanduz and I for Qala Diza, accompanied by Babekr Agha, Ka Hussain and a large escort. Just
outside the village we put up two jackals, which Ka Hussain
pursued firing his rifle at them wildly. Our way lay along the
foot of an almost perpendicular ridge of black rock with a serrated top, known as the Kewa Resh or Black Comb, until we
reached Darband, the defile of the Lesser Zab, where is situated a deserted village with a ruined fort which some eighty
or more years ago was occupied by Hama Agha, then only a
boy, and acting as agent of the Pasha of Rawanduz. He collected tribute from the surrounding tribes, and baj or toll
from passing caravans. This Darband is a most important
place, commanding as it does the only road, except for some

exceedingly rough mountain tracks, which connects Persia and the Pizhder Plain with Bituin and Koi. The river passes deep and clear through a narrow gorge, where the road for a quarter of a mile is rocky and difficult; after the rains an abundant spring wells up from the very centre of the track. From here we followed up the right bank of the Lesser Zab, which is bordered by a broad belt of marshy land, thick with reeds and bushes and affording grazing to large numbers of ponies, cattle, and buffaloes. A strong wind blowing from the snows raised clouds of dust all along the river's course. On our left lay a strip of undulating arable land bounded by mountain masses rising to a height of over 10,000 ft. Passing several villages mostly consisting of from ten to twenty conical reed huts, about 2.30 p.m. we reached Qala Diza. Here we were literally surrounded by great snow-capped mountains towering straight above us and separated by no intervening ranges. Babekr Agha was my host, and produced an excellent dinner finishing up with some delicious pears with walnuts and bastuq, a jelly-like substance made out of grape syrup and flour. I quickly found him a man of the soundest opinions; he talked always with a drawling voice, speaking slowly and deliberately and never wasting his words. I failed to discover what ailed his right eye, and he never referred to it. He is about fifty years old, one of the most delightful and kindest of men it has ever been my fortune to meet.

The next day I set out on my return journey, and in due course reached Koi, where I found all well. Hama Agha, despite his age, had visited the office every day, and was busy raking up every old grievance he could remember, despite the fact that on my arrival a notice had been issued proclaiming a general amnesty in respect of all crimes committed before December 1st. I spent many hours in trying to persuade him to let bygones be bygones. He would reply by retailing endless reminiscences. 'Of course when I was a young man, such and such a thing happened' – and it took a long time to make any progress.

On the 30th a settlement was made between Sawar Agha and Abdulla Agha, in which the Piran chief agreed to pay blood-money for the latter's son and to return all stolen property or its equivalent value. It was easy to make him promise; to exact payment was an entirely different matter.

CHAPTER IX

VISIT TO THE KUSHNAO, AND OTHER TOURS

THE FIRST THREE WEEKS of January passed quietly. I began to shape the administrative work of the district into a regular routine, and always found plenty of official business to occupy my attention. In the spirit of the policy that was being adopted I endeavoured to act in everything through the local aghas, but as with one or two exceptions they were all both inefficient and corrupt, it was difficult to go ahead very fast. My chief stand-by was Jamil Agha, with whose assistance I managed to keep old Hama Agha on the lines and prevent any acts of gross injustice. I spent most of the day in my office, retiring before sunset to my house, where, after the evening meal, the notables used to visit me and talk. I frequently dined at their houses, and was on very good terms with all of them except Abdulla Agha, who used to come to my office from time to time and ask what job and salary I intended to give him. It became my object to lessen his influence as much as I could, and correspondingly increase that of Jamil Agha, in the hope, which proved vain, that the latter would come to be recognised as the head of the Hawaizi.

Excellent order prevailed in the town and surrounding districts. Prices in the bazaar fell rapidly; new shops opened and everything began to look up. The poorhouse to which I devoted much care saved large numbers of the population from starvation; dismissed Turkish officials and dependants of soldiers taken prisoner or killed in the war were allotted pensions, while it became both politic and necessary to grant subsistence allowances to the numerous mullas whose endowed property had fallen into ruin during the war, and to devote funds to the keep of the takias or religious hostels. Many said, and I believe truly, that if the British Government had delayed sending a representative for another

month the town would have been deserted and left a heap of
ruins, while thousands would have died of starvation. Plen-
teous rain gave promise of a good harvest, and all were filled
with new life and hope.

On the 23rd I set out for the Khushnao country, accompanied by a fatuous old clerk I used to take about with me,
called Mulla Rasul, and a few gendarmes. Our road lay over
similar broken sandstone country to that I have already described. We reached Banaqalat, our destination for the first
night, at 5 p.m. and were entertained by two old Kurdish
farmers Chokha Hawaiz and Chokha Saleh. They were
simple cheery individuals, especially the former, who indulged in broad jokes. Somewhat to my embarrassment a
deaf and dumb imbecile appeared and began to take a great
interest in me, grunting, grinning, and nodding his head
towards me.

The next morning, after enjoying a breakfast of bread and
furu, or beestings, the first milk from a ewe after the birth of
a lamb, we set out at 8 a.m. for the Girdi village of Hajji Usu,
where a fussy little old man called Hassan Agha provided us
with lunch. Hence we proceeded over the same sandstone
country to Ashkafsaqa, the village of Aarib Agha, chief of the
Koi section of the Girdi. The country was beginning to show
signs of spring, the weather being abnormally mild, everywhere plants were forcing their way through the soil, and I
saw some white and mauve anemones in flower and a yellow
blossom on a shrub like laburnum. Aarib Agha, an old weak-
looking man, met us on the road with his cousin, Shaikh
Muhammad Agha, a burly, heavy-browed scoundrel whom we
always called 'The Villain'. They accompanied us to Ashkafsaqa, where I was very hospitably entertained. Though the
Girdi are a small community, their chiefs consider themselves superior to any of the aghas of the surrounding tribes.

On the 25th we proceeded northwards and soon reached
the defile or darband through the big limestone range which
bounds the sandstone country on the north-east. Beyond this
we were in Khushnao territory, and an entirely fresh landscape greeted our eyes. On our right front rose the great
mass of the Safin Dagh, its summit wreathed in cloud, while
beneath it a long valley ran southwards in the direction of
Koi. To the left lay a confused tangle of hills between which

and the Safin Dagh there stretched out before us a broad valley interrupted here and there by spurs and covered with a
large variety of trees and shrubs. Many vineyards could be
seen on the surrounding hillsides. The dull red of the sandstone is no longer the predominating colour, its place being
taken by the limestone's more cheerful whites and yellows
and blues. The Khushnao country is the pleasantest that I
know in Kurdistan, and it is no wonder that its inhabitants
so love it that they cannot bear to be detained on the Arbil
plain for more than two or three days at a time. Shortly after
passing the defile we perceived coming towards us, accompanied by a considerable following, a stout middle-aged
gentleman with bulging eyes, who proved to be Miran i Qadir
Beg, a personage whom we shall often meet. 'Miran' is a title
always adopted by the leading Khushnao chiefs.

It is necessary here to make a short digression into
Khushnao politics. The last chief of the Mirmahmali, the
senior tribe of the confederation, was one Miran i Baiz Beg, a
man so stout that on one occasion it took him four days to
ride to Koi, a distance of 33 miles, and he killed three ponies
in doing so. He had died of influenza at the beginning of the
previous November; his sons were not yet of age, and the succession lay between his two brothers, Qadir Beg and Rashid
Beg. Of these the elder, Qadir Beg, was the son of a different
mother to the previous chief, and as at the time of Baiz Beg's
death he, too, was suffering from influenza and thought he
was on his deathbed, he made no objection when he heard
that the relations of Baiz Beg's mother, who was also Rashid
Beg's mother, had installed the latter as Mir. Meanwhile the
country came under British rule, and a policy of governing
through salaried tribal chiefs was instituted. Qadir Beg recovered, and realising the position it was possible to acquire
under the new order of things, repented of his act of resignation. I was now visiting Shaqlawah to decide whether he or
Rashid Beg should be appointed Governor of Shaqlawah and
chief of the tribe.

Like most of his family Qadir Beg is of an enormous bulk,
being both tall and stout. His face is large and round, and he
wears a beard. We always called him Henry VIII, owing to
the striking resemblance he bears to the portraits of that
monarch. He is completely uneducated, talking nothing but

Kurdish, and as a result is liable to come under the influence of odious clerks and scheming relations. In times of trouble he finds it difficult to make up his mind, and is borne in this direction and that by floating breaths of rumour, but, on the whole, he is honest and well intentioned. He is certainly a leader of men, and assisted by a good adviser would make a model ruler.

He was now residing at his village of Qalasinj, while Rashid Beg was in Shaqlawah looking after his late brother's family and property. We repaired to the former place and awaited lunch, which Qadir Beg delayed, hoping I would be compelled to spend the night with him. I grew impatient and insisted that I should leave for Shaqlawah without any lunch, if it was not produced at once; on this a series of trays were brought in and placed before us down the centre of the room, and after the servant had uttered the grace, 'Bismillah', 'In the Name of God', we all fell to work. Two other chiefs whom we shall afterwards meet were present at this meal. One of them, the arch-traitor Miran i Saleh Beg, was head of the Miryusufi, though several disputed his title. A bluff, burly, 'hail-fellow-well-met' type of man, for some months he was a personal friend of mine. He feigned the greatest affection for me, and continually used to boast how he was not a Kurd, and how free he was from the treacherous and bloodthirsty practices of his race; I always knew he was a bit of a humbug, but it was a long time before I saw him in his true light.

The other chief was Mustafa Agha, of the Kora, who, though he is reported to have put away several brothers and other relations, is the mildest and kindliest of men. The hours I spent under the big mulberry tree outside his village are among the pleasantest of my recollections of Kurdistan, and to him and his men I owe my life on at least one occasion. He was the most unselfish and faithful Kurd I ever met, and curiously enough he was the close friend of Ahmad Effendi of Arbil.

The road to Shaqlawah lay through magnificent scenery, for the clouds now withdrew their folds and revealed the snowy beauties of the Safin Dagh. We passed by narrow lanes through vineyards and orchards, then out into an open valley where oak trees and hawthorn lined our course. Arriving at a

small village situated on the precipitous bank of a mountain
stream we were greeted by an old man in a fez wearing a
Russian officer's greatcoat. He proved to be one Khurshid
Beg, a Hakkari chief of some prominence, who had been
driven by Russian depredations in Northern Kurdistan to
take refuge with the Khushnao. He had been a colonel in the
Kurdish cavalry raised by Abdul Hamid, and possessed an
unenviable reputation. He became the plague of my life, always boasting to me of his high descent and great position in
his country, and complaining of the meanness of the al-
lowance granted him by Government. He was a foolish old
man, and a terror to the few refugees who had survived with
him, permitting none of them to be seated or to smoke in his
presence. I afterwards endeavoured to settle him and his men
in a deserted village, but they would not work for their livelihood; they eventually left for their own country in the spring
of 1920.

We now rounded the north-western extremity of the Safin
Dagh, and began to climb upwards towards Shaqlawah,
which we did not reach till dark. We were greeted just outside by Miran i Rashid Beg and two sons of the late Baiz Beg,
Umr and Sulaiman. Rashid Beg is a tall man with black
beard, not so stout, but more flabby than Qadir Beg. His eyes
have a shifty look. He is a well-educated man and can speak
Turkish, Persian, and a little Arabic besides his native Kurdish. He is much cleverer and more versed in intrigue than
his somewhat simple-minded brother. I never liked him; as
Major Noel said, he was too much of a lawyer.

I spent the whole evening in discussions concerning the
chieftainship. Rashid Beg admitted his rival's right as elder
brother, but begged that whatever happened he would not
take up his residence in Shaqlawah. He stated that he himself must stay there to look after Baiz Beg's property and womenfolk, and one place would not hold them both. He
eventually fell down on his knees and besought me with tears
in his eyes not to do anything that would cause dissension between him and his brother. I had by this time made up my
mind to appoint Qadir Beg as Governor, in which capacity it
was essential for him to reside at the headquarters of his district, but it was not till the following morning that I was able
to persuade Rashid Beg to give way. It was then arranged

A KOI MULLA

THE KUSHNAO CHIEFS

Rashid Beg   Qadir Beg   Saleh Beg

that he and Qadir Beg should repair to their aged uncle, Aziz
Beg, at Balisan and swear before him an oath of mutual fidelity. This was never done, and the friction caused by the
jealousy of the two brothers was a source of constant anxiety
to the successive A.P.O.s. at Koi.

Before I left I formally appointed Qadir Beg as Governor
of Shaqlawah, with authority over all three branches of the
Khushnao and the Kora tribe; while Rashid Beg became official chief of the Mirmahmali section, and Saleh Beg of the
Miryusufi. On the whole, Qadir Beg proved a most successful
ruler.

I was assisted in the negotiations by Hajji Nauras Effendi, a native of Rawanduz, and ex-mudir of Shaqlawah. A
little undersized man of Persian descent with a head like a
turkey's, he mingled more than a usual share of Oriental cunning with an intense nervousness. Most of the time he was
with me on this occasion he trembled from head to foot, and
stuttered when he spoke, for fear, I imagine, that I might inquire into his past misdeeds. The day I left Shaqlawah he returned to Rawanduz, where we shall shortly find him.

On the morning of the 26th I had time to explore my surroundings. Shaqlawah, which contains some 3,000 inhabitants, about half of them Christian, is situated on the
northern slope of the Safin Dagh, which provides for the town
a lofty background of precipitous rock now covered with snow.
It is divided into two halves by a spur, on which is situated
the church. The houses are built one on top of the other, so
that a man steps from his front door on to his neighbour's
roof. By the main path through the town there are some tall,
picturesque white buildings, the residence of the Mirs, and a
small mosque surmounted by a brass hand. Numerous
springs bubble up in and around the town, and rush down to
water the extensive woods and gardens which stretch along
the valley below for several miles. Here are big plantations of
poplar and orchards of apple, pear, peach, apricot, fig, pomegranate, and other fruits interspersed with lofty walnuts and
chinars or plane trees. These gardens are delightful in the
summer, but somewhat dreary and dark in the winter. Hajji
Nauras conducted me to the summer palace of the late Baiz
Beg; it is not a particularly striking building, but outside it
stand two enormous chinars, which, from existing poetry, are

known to have been growing in the same spot 500 years ago, and a fine water tank which has only recently been discovered and re-excavated.

We now went on to the church, despite Hajji Nauras' nervous protests that it was not worth seeing. I wondered what he had done with it, and when I arrived I found it in a very dilapidated condition and full of raisins and grain, part of the Government share of the crops which he had stored there. From the church we proceeded to the Christian quarter at the southern end of the town. Here in an open space I found assembled four or five priests with a crucifix, a surpliced choir of very dirty little boys, and a large concourse of people. As soon as I appeared they all struck up a hymn, and much to my embarrassment the whole procession followed me round singing 'Alleluia' with raucous voices. Crowds of women – mostly old and ugly – clung round me, kissing my hands and my clothes. Poor people – I am afraid they must have been bitterly disappointed of the high hopes for the future which they entertained on this occasion.

I was unable to leave Shaqlawah until late in the afternoon, when I set out on my return journey to Koi, following the main route along the eastern slope of the Safin Dagh. Our way lay continually among trees and along lanes with lofty hedges; the mud was thick, and in many places the track had become a stream of water. We passed a large number of oaks bearing a curious gall-nut, shiny black and the size of a golf ball. Two or three hours after dark, having once or twice followed a stream in mistake for the road, and only found out our mistake when we came to precipitous waterfalls, we arrived at our destination, the village of Iran. I spent the night with one Ali Beg, who had frequently been in revolt against the Turks. He treated me very hospitably, which was unusual, for his village being situated halfway on the road between Koi and Shaqlawah he was often overwhelmed by guests, and did not encourage them by lavish entertainment. Here I found Miran i Ahmad Beg, chief of the Pizhgali, a broken-down old man with no will of his own. His tribe had once been powerful, but a few years previously had offended the Turks, who called in the Piran and laid all its villages waste.

The following morning I left early for Koi, and after half an hour's journey reached the village of Nazanin. The villagers made me sit down and produced a tray of figs, raisins, and pomegranates. Here, too, were extensive fruit gardens with plantations of poplar and chinar. The pomegranates of Nazanin are supposed to be the best in Kurdistan. We now descended to the sulphurous stream of Jali, which has its source in a long and intricate cave in the hills above. By the side of it was a warm spring full of fishes; its water left a blue-grey deposit and had a strong chemical smell. The Kurds bathe here to cure skin complaints.

On my return to Koi I found that Sawar Agha had not arrived, though before my departure I had instructed Shaikh Amin to bring him in. I therefore mobilised a small army, and sent word to Babekr Agha at Qala Diza, who collected some of his tribesmen and moved down to Rania. The threat proved sufficient, and Shaikh Amin came into Koi at once, bringing with him Sawar Agha and two other of the Piran headmen who were wanted, viz. Agha i Mam Zindin and Maraz. They all lodged in Hama Agha's house, where I sent and arrested Sawar Agha and one of the headmen, but the other, Maraz, could not be found. Some wag told my retainer, Jaafar Khan, that he was lodging with Mulla Muhammad Effendi 'the Bishop'. Jaafar Khan, therefore, went round and demanded him, much to the fury of that divine, who replied that his house was not a den of thieves. About this time somebody descried a solitary horseman crossing the Haib us Sultan range, and we never saw Maraz again. Agha i Mam Zindin had a delightful little boy about ten years old, who kept on coming to see me and begging for his father's and Sawar Agha's release. I eventually acceded to his request, proper security having been provided that they would make no attempt to leave Koi without my permission. Within a few days all outstanding matters were satisfactorily settled and they were allowed to return to their villages.

At the end of January I was compelled by family affairs to apply for leave to England, which was duly granted. Prior to my departure I set out on a tour with Captain R. E. Barker, who had recently arrived as my assistant, to introduce him to the outlying districts of Rania and Qala Diza. We commenced our journey on foot, crossing the Haib us Sultan by a differ-

ent and shorter route to that which I had previously
traversed; on the further side we passed the demesne of Chinarok, where 'the Bishop' possesses a delightful summer retreat, a recess in the rock whence spouts a spring of ice-cold
water, surrounded by chinar and wild-rose. The Kurd has an
appreciation of the beautiful rare amongst Eastern peoples.
All down the hillside were extensive vineyards, and the
whole country was gay with a carpet of green spangled with
white, mauve, and crimson anemones. At the foot of the descent we came to the village of Qasrok, where we were entertained hospitably by Mam Qaranai, an old cousin of Sawar
Agha's. He had some delightful children, who presented me
with a tasselled Bilbas cap, in return for which I promised to
bring them some toys from England.

There were thunderstorms all night, and the next morning we set out in a driving rain; the first river we forded
successfully, but the second was too much for us, and we were
compelled to stop at Sarkhuma, where little Qadir made
many inquiries after his father, who was still detained. After
a meal we started off again in the hope of crossing the river
higher up, but the rain came down in torrents, with great
peals of thunder and the most vivid lightning, and we were
forced to take refuge in a little hovel at the village of Kani
Maran, where we dried ourselves in front of an enormous
fire. The weather cleared slightly, and we tried to get on
again, but were held up by a deep, though narrow, stream.
With some difficulty we managed to ford it on our ponies,
while despite the cold – for it was snowing in the hills a
couple of hundred feet above us – two Kurds stripped stark
naked and carried over our kit for us. About 4 p.m. we arrived opposite the village of Puka, where some of the inhabitants came out and showed us a ford, so that we were able to
cross the main river without mishap. As soon as we had
reached the further bank the stream came down in spate,
and separated us from our baggage animals, which spent the
night in another village.

Our host was a homely old gentleman called Ibrahim
Agha; he was obviously a poor man, and commanded but a
small following, though he protested that before the war he
could turn out forty horsemen. We were lodged in a very
small room full of household furniture, and separated only by

a screen of matting from several buffaloes. A pair of remarkably fine greyhounds occupied a place near the door. We partook of a good, though simple, meal, and being very tired were able to sleep despite the buffaloes and the fleas.

The next morning we set out in beautiful weather along the northern edge of Bituin; the hills were covered in a fresh coating of snow nearly down to the plain, and dispersing clouds were clinging round the mountain tops. Passing through a defile in the range of hills which juts out across Bituin we came to Sarkapkan, the village of Mamand Agha, chief of the Ako.

A little hunched-up silent man, I had rather disliked him when I met him at Sulaimaniyah; he had an evil reputation for oppression and cruelty, and had lost his hold on the greater part of his tribe. On better acquaintance he proved to be unusually polite and intelligent for a Kurd of these remote parts. His guest-house was clean and large, and everything was done in the best style. We were now in a narrow valley north of Rania, just under the rocky slope of Kewa Resh. Our next destination was some 14 miles by road, but could not be more than six over the hill. We therefore determined to walk, and send our baggage round.

We hoped to see some ibex on the way, and persuaded Mamand Agha to provide us each with a stout Kurd and a good rifle. After lunch we duly set out with our two guides, short stocky savages with striped coats and trousers and long woollen stockings. We ascended by a winding rocky path, and about halfway up came to the first snow. Just near the top we saw three ibex; Captain Barker was in front, and his guide, who was carrying his rifle and did not understand the game, tried to shoot at the animal himself. Captain Barker in fury wrested the rifle from him, by which time the ibex were miles away. We climbed in all some 2,500 ft.; on top the air was bitterly cold, and the bushes were gleaming white, their branches being coated with frozen snow. The further side of the hill was thickly wooded and literally alive with chikor or hill-partridge. About sunset we reached our destination, the village of Dugoman, so-called for two pools which are its sole water supply. Here lived Baulul Agha, chief of one of the sections of the Ako, who was much surprised to see us arrive thus on foot, for a Kurd of the better class never thinks of walking. He is a fat, jovial old man, a sort of Falstaff, except that he does not drink. We were shown into the guest-room, his women-folk peeping at us round the corner, and were waited upon by three of his sons, while he fondled the fourth, a child of five. During the course of the evening I was handed a letter which, I found, came from some religious students quartered in the village, who expected from me some contribution towards their maintenance.

Leaving Dugoman early the next morning we followed along the northern edge of the Pizhder Plain and soon entered Mangur country. Such villages as we saw were small and poverty-stricken. At 11.30 a.m. we reached Sharwait, the residence of young Ka Hussain, whom, much to his embarrassment, we caught bathing. When he had dressed he showed us into a fine new guest-house, only built a year or two before by the late Baiz Pasha. The view of the surrounding hills was magnificent. Galala towered above us – a vast black precipice crowned with snow, while beyond it could be seen the Zernikiau ridge and the crest of Kandil, the latter the king of these snowy peaks, and said to include even distant Tabriz in its wide survey. At Sharwait is a large hot spring. We reached Qala Diza just before sunset, and I spent till midnight discussing important matters with Babekr Agha. The following morning I said good-bye to him, and I have never seen him since. He remains in my memory as the wisest and greatest of the many tribal chiefs I met during my two years in Kurdistan.

On returning to our headquarters I handed over my duties to Captain Barker, for my successor, Captain Beale, had not arrived, and after elaborate farewell ceremonies took my departure for Baghdad.

It was with the greatest regret that I turned my back on Koi. I had grown to love the funny little out-of-the-way town and its strange inhabitants. For a time their customs had almost become my customs, their likes my likes, their feuds my feuds; and it was with a sense of emptiness and depression that I found myself in the outside world again. I think my two months in Koi were the pleasantest I spent in Kurdistan.

CHAPTER X

ARBIL AGAIN

MY LEAVE COMPLETED I returned to Mesopotamia via Aleppo, reaching Mosul on June 30th. Here I received orders to proceed to Arbil and relieve Major Murray, as A.P.O. I arrived on July 3rd, but Major Murray did not leave till the 13th. Between these two dates several alarming events occurred, and when I took over, Arbil was not altogether a bed of roses.

The Arbil district, though except for its headquarters predominantly Kurdish, had not been included in Shaikh Mahmud's domains and, as a consequence the Dizai chiefs had not, like their neighbours of the Khushnao, received any lucrative official appointments. They had no love for the hukmdar of Sulaimaniyah, and in fact affected to despise him, but to see men whom they considered of less importance than themselves drawing large salaries and covered with honour was a bit more than they could endure in silence. The revolt of Shaikh Mahmud, in May 1919, was the beginning of the reaction, in Northern Mesopotamia, and though it ended in failure it showed that it was possible to defy the new Government, and sent out waves of unrest over the country. The Dizai chiefs remained firm, hoping perhaps that their loyalty would be rewarded by an improvement in their status; but they were again disappointed. Next came the barley estimations; the officials responsible grossly underestimated the crops, and Enver Effendi Mudir of Makhmur reported the fact to Major Murray, who carried out a re-estimation in certain areas. This gave the Dizai aghas an excuse, and Ahmad Pasha persuaded his three confrères to sign with him a manifesto which they despatched to the A.P.O.; in it they stated that all the Government officials were corrupt and inefficient, that from motives of private enmity they had caused the crops to be over-estimated, and that the district would be far better managed if they themselves were appointed as officials. On receiving this missive, Major Murray ordered its authors into Arbil. On some insufficient pretext they refused to come. A stronger note was then sent them; but partly in a spirit of defiance, and partly in fear of dire punishment if they did come in, they still remained obdurate. This was the situation when I arrived. Many efforts were made to make the Dizai chiefs see sense; but these were counteracted by evilly disposed people in the town, who sent out messengers to them urging them to revolt, and assuring them that they would all be executed or transported if they came to Arbil. The aspect of affairs grew daily more alarming, and most of the Government officials in the Dizai country left their posts.

In the town the situation was also disquieting. The arbitrary and tyrannical actions of the gendarmes and town police were a cause of general discontent among the populace. A branch of a secret society with wide ramifications was ceaselessly active with anti-British propaganda, and certain of the leading notables were its most ardent supporters. The chief of these was Hajji Rashid Agha, a man who in Turkish times had often given trouble to the Government, and openly looked forward to the arrival of the British, and who when the British did come was the first to demand the return of the Turk. He is a tall, fine-looking old man who clings stoutly to his old Oriental traditions, but he has little education and less brains. His sole pastime is land-grabbing, and he blusters too much to become a really dangerous enemy. His eldest son, Ataullah Agha, a weak-kneed degenerate who wears European clothes, and may be seen any day slouching round the bazaar with his beads, was also active in the anti-British movement. Of a far different calibre was Ali Pasha. A stout man, still quite young, with delightful manners and superior education, he had made his money and received his title during the war. He had been an active member of the Committee of Union and Progress, and on the coming of the British had been honest enough to say frankly that he preferred the Turk. Subsequently he never indulged openly in anti-British propaganda, and at times I was deceived into thinking that he had really become reconciled to the new Government. But he was an absolute master of intrigue, and

with his fat, pleasing smile and facile conversation he
cloaked innumerable designs for my ruin. He rarely committed himself, and it was only an accident that finally gave
him away. It is interesting to note that both Hajji Rashid
Agha and Ali Pasha supported bands of highway robbers,
who in Turkish times had been their paid bullies. With them
they had kept the neighbourhood of Arbil in a state of terror;
the Turkish qaimaqam was quite unable to suppress them,
and usually ended by himself becoming a tool in the hands of
these powerful aghas.

The anti-British movement was also supported by a number of corrupt ex-Turkish officials, who had lost their appointments, and certain of the lesser notables who found it
difficult to earn a livelihood by honest means. Among these
latter was Hajji Suayid Agha, a noted drunkard, and his
family.

On July 9th an event occurred which, though alarming at
the time and unfortunate in the loss of life that resulted,
really served to clear the air and prevent any further serious
trouble in the town for more than a year. That morning I had
received a complaint from the above-mentioned Hajji Suayid
Agha that his son Yunis had the previous evening been pub-
licly insulted by a policeman in the Arab theatre. I accordingly gave instructions that all the people should appear
before me the next day, in order that I might inquire into the
matter.

But Hajji Suayid Agha thought otherwise. Bent on creat-
ing a disturbance, on the evening of the 9th he invited to sup-
per Abdulla Effendi, an ex-Turkish official, Bubu the Jew,
who kept a drinking tavern, and Amin the Barber. His son
Yunis, and Ahmad Beg, the son of the Khushnao chief Saleh
Beg, were also present. The older men imbibed freely, and
when the meal was over the whole party adjourned to the
theatre. Hajji Suayid Agha and his cronies went to the very
back of the house, and placing one bench on top of another,
sat in an exalted position playing cards and sipping 'araq.
About halfway through the performance Hajji Suayid Agha,
who is a big man, suddenly leapt to the floor overturning
both the benches, and started to abuse the performers in foul
language, ordering them to cease playing. He then addressed
the audience, cursing them for not assisting his son against

the police on the previous evening. The people seeing that there was going to be trouble began to leave the house, while Sergeant Methuen, closely followed by Sergeant Kennard, went up to remonstrate with Hajji Suayid Agha. The last named refused to sit down and be quiet, on which Sergeant Methuen tried to pull him out of the theatre; a general uproar ensued, several shots were fired in quick succession, Sergeant Methuen fell dead, Hajji Suayid Agha himself was seriously wounded, while Sergeant Kennard and one of Hajji Suayid Agha's men received slighter injuries. Two native gendarmes who happened to be in the theatre were seen crouching under their seats, but Iz ud Din, the bashchaoush of the police, did splendid work, arresting all Hajji Suayid Agha's party, except Yunis and Ahmad Beg, who had been sitting in another part of the theatre and had managed to effect their escape. Fortunately the people showed no inclination to join in the disturbance.

Yunis Agha was found the next day hiding in a cellar, and was shot at and seriously wounded, just as he was in the act of surrendering, by the same Abdul Wahab who was supposed to have insulted him. Neither he nor his father became fit for trial for several weeks. Under the belief that Yunis was responsible for the murder, I released Abdulla Effendi, Bubu, and Barber Amin on bail. Ahmad Beg had fled to the hills, and it was a long time before I could persuade his father to bring him down to Arbil. When he came he dropped a hint which caused me to send a party to search the house of Abdulla Effendi; in an obscure corner they found a heavy iron box, on the discovery of which its owner heaved a sudden sigh. Within was found a pistol of the same description as that with which Sergeant Methuen had been killed – for the bullet was extracted from his heart. Other evidence was forthcoming, and after the trial, which took place in September, Abdulla Effendi was hanged, while Hajji Suayid Agha and Yunis were sent to prison, the former for five years and the latter for life.

We buried Sergeant Methuen, whose loss we felt keenly, just outside the Christian village of Ainkawa, on a mound beside the tomb of one of the local saints. A cross now marks his grave, which the inhabitants of the village tend carefully.

We must now return to the question of the Dizai. There began to be talk of military action, a thing which at all cost we wished to prevent, as the Dizai chiefs had so far done nothing unforgivable, the country was well populated and prosperous, and punitive measures were calculated to bring misery on thousands of innocent people. On the afternoon of the 10th, therefore, with Major Murray's consent, I paid a personal visit to the Dizai chiefs and endeavoured to bring them to their senses. I set out in a car with a Government official called Enver Effendi. Reaching the village of Mirguzar I was stopped on the road by a little middle-aged man, who proved to be Hajji Pir Daud Agha, one of the four big chiefs. He informed me that the other three were in his guest-house. I therefore stopped the car and went in with him, seeing no sign anywhere of hostile preparations.

This was the first time I had met the three most important of these chiefs, and I must introduce the reader to them, as they will dog our footsteps throughout the remaining chapters.

First of all comes Ibrahim Agha, a man of seventy, but appearing younger owing to the black dye in his hair and beard. He was of medium height with high forehead, black sparkling eyes and a prominent nose. The lines on his face betokened the numerous troubles and sorrows he had encountered during his eventful career; after a life of fighting and strife he had arrived at old age with a character refined as if by fire to the purest gold. Possessing a commanding personality he was practically worshipped by his relations and his subjects; their homage he returned by a warmth of affection and a solicitude for their comfort that is rare in a Kurd. He was a clever old man, and a born diplomat, excellent in the art of conversation and possessing a considerable fund of humour. Locally he was a maker of history, for thirty-eight years previously, in the days of his father, he had led a party of Kurds across the Qara Choq Dagh and founded Makhmur, where after several years of fighting first against the Shammar Arabs, and then against the Turks, he had succeeded in establishing himself. Several others followed him, and it was thus due to his initiative that the Qara Choq desert became inhabited and cultivated. Subsequently he had been involved in many fights with the rival Dizai chiefs and, as previously narrated, had lost his eldest son. His then only surviving son, Mushir Agha, was a light-headed spendthrift of twenty, who had not yet begun to take life seriously; it is reported that Ibrahim Agha in his early years similarly sowed his wild oats; so there is a hope that he may develop.

Ibrahim Agha was really paramount chief of the whole tribe, and all except the immediate relations of his rivals acknowledged his authority. With his brothers he owned some thirty villages, while many others looked up to him as their chief. He and his relations were known as the Baiz section of the Dizai, from the name of his father, and it is remarkable what a fine set of men they were; I could name seven or eight who both in physical appearance and character were infinitely superior to any men who could be found in the rival sections of the tribe, with the possible exception of Ahmad Pasha's eldest son Khidhr.

We now pass to Ahmad Pasha, a talkative, stout little man of over sixty, ill-educated and ill-behaved, and more of a successful merchant and profiteer than a tribal chief. Often nicknamed 'Kah-farush', or 'straw-merchant', his sole motive in life is the accumulation of wealth, in which he possesses no scruples: his inability to hold his tongue and his complete lack of tact make him neither desirable as a friend nor dangerous as an enemy. His career is illustrative of the man. In his early years, being penniless, he eked out a living by keeping gaming tables in the Arbil coffee shops. Growing tired of this occupation he one day stole a pair of mules and, escaping to Kandinawah, which was then just beginning to be populated, proceeded to found a village. He attracted cultivators to himself, but the first year's harvest proved to be a complete failure. He applied to the Turkish Government for a loan to enable himself and his fellows to buy seed for the next spring. Receiving a considerable sum to distribute amongst the cultivators, he kept it all to himself and proceeded to issue it in loans at enormous rates of interest. After this everything prospered with him; with his relations he is now owner of some eighteen villages and is said to possess £200,000 in gold in his house, besides having large sums out at interest. With his wealth he had always been able to buy the support of the Turkish Government in his land-grabbing designs or his quarrels with Ibrahim Agha, who, extorting little from his tenants and lavishing his money in hospitality and the support of his relations, was a comparatively poor man. Consequently Ahmad Pasha, when he found that the British Government cannot be bought, quickly showed an anti-Government bias, and was probably the prime mover in the present troubles.

Hajji Pir Daud, a little rather good-looking man of fifty-five years of age, with keen dark eyes and long silky moustaches, was of a very different type. He had a beautiful soft voice – I have never heard anyone read Persian poetry so exquisitely – and the heart of a devil. He and all his family – who are mostly red haired and undersized, and many of them diseased – are known in Arbil as 'mal'un', which literally means 'accursed' but is better translated as 'a bad lot'. Well educated and a cunning schemer he allied himself with Ahmad Pasha in the anti-Government movement, and provided the brains as did his partner the money. Lecherous unprincipled scoundrel that he was, he always made a great show of piety, and had performed the 'hajj' or pilgrimage to Mecca, but only, it is said, because his own country got too hot for him. With his relations he possesses some eighteen villages.

The fourth chief, Rasul Agha, we have already met; compared with the others he is a nonentity.

These were the people whom I found in the guest-house at Mirguzar. They were all by now in a state of panic, and clung closely together, each afraid that one of the others might try to get into Arbil first alone and obtain some advantage over his companions. I was unable to offer them any definite terms, for I had not yet taken over from Major Murray, and they therefore imagined that all sorts of horrible punishments awaited them. I suggested to Ibrahim Agha that he should come with me in my car, but the others would not let him go. Finally, after much conversation, they all agreed to come the following day to the house of Mulla Effendi at Badawa, just outside Arbil, and there discuss terms with Major Murray.

The Dizai aghas did not keep their promise to come in on the following day, and it was not till after Major Murray had left that they plucked up courage and assembled at Badawa. They stayed there several days, but were so suspicious of my intentions that they withdrew every night to one of their own villages. Using Mulla Effendi and Ahmad Effendi the Rais Baladiyah as mediators I let them know my terms, which were the payment of a fine of 200 rifles and the surrender of a deposit of £T.1,500 for six months, with the proviso that they should remain in Arbil on security till the terms had been fulfilled. Despite the visit of armoured cars to Qurshaqlu and of an aeroplane to Badawa they still hesitated and haggled. I endeavoured to detach Ibrahim Agha, promising him special consideration if he were the first to come in; but Ahmad Effendi, who acted for me, was never able to speak to him alone. After three or four days of fruitless negotiations and goings to and fro, on the morning of the 20th the Dizai chiefs left Badawa and took the road back to their villages.

I was in despair; there was now nothing for it but to ask for military action. But that evening, shortly after sunset, as I was sitting alone on the roof, I was surprised to see a stately but rather dejected figure riding towards the house; before he had reached the door Ahmad Effendi rushed up in an excited state to say that it was Ibrahim Agha. It was a very nervous old man that climbed up the steps to my roof; but I was so overcome with joy that the crisis was past that I received him more like a prince than a man in disgrace. He partook of tea and coffee, and we quickly became friends; before he left to spend the night in his house in the town, he promised to send word to the other chiefs, bidding them come in the following day.

Ahmad Effendi, though unable to speak to Ibrahim Agha alone while he was at Badawa, had managed to confide in one of his servants; during their ride back that day the old chief had been compelled to turn aside from the road to obey a call of nature, when the servant succeeded in delivering to him our message. He seized the first opportunity to give his companions the slip and return to Arbil.

The next day about lunch-time Rasul Agha came in, the sweat streaming down his face, and was followed a few hours later by Ahmad Pasha and Hajji Pir Daud.

In due course the rifles were brought in and the deposit surrendered all except £50, over which a violent quarrel arose, Ibrahim Agha and Rasul Agha insisting that Ahmad

Pasha should pay it, and Ahmad Pasha and Hajji Pir Daud saying that it was part of the contribution due from Rasul Agha. Ahmad Pasha eventually paid, but for the rest of my time at Arbil the two above groups were at continual enmity with one another.

The Dizai aghas having paid their fines, it was determined to meet their grievances as far as possible by offering Ibrahim Agha, Rasul Agha and Hajji Pir Daud appointments as official magistrates in the three Dizai sub-districts. The first two chiefs accepted, but Hajji Pir Daud insolently declined, and, as it was known that Ahmad Pasha did not wish to serve, I nominated in his stead Ibrahim Agha's second brother Rahman Agha. Ibrahim Agha was recognised as official chief of the whole tribe. All the appointments were thus in the hands of Ibrahim Agha's party, which from this time onward I unhesitatingly supported; and I had my reward, for it was they who saved me and Arbil when the crisis came.

The chief of the Arbil Girdi, Jamil Agha, showed no sympathy with the Dizai in their opposition to the Government authorities. I therefore took an early opportunity of visiting him and thanking him for his loyalty. He lives in the village of Buhirka, which lies in a hollow near the Bastura Chai, the north-eastern boundary of the district. Jamil Agha belongs to the worst type of Kurdish chief, vain and avaricious, boastful and fond of show, thinking of nothing but his own advancement. With grey hair, but a young and unwrinkled face, he possesses a fine physique. But a low forehead, dark and shifty eyes, and a sullen mouth betray the man. At first he rather deceived me by his fine speeches and grandiloquent promises; later, I learnt that he was one of a large class who would only serve me well so long as they were convinced it was to their own advantage to do so. He possessed a fine guest-house into which he had introduced a number of plush-covered chairs made by the most fashionable carpenter in Arbil. He provided me with an unusually elaborate meal, after which a dear old white-bearded fellow of seventy endeavoured to yodel us some well-known folk-songs. In the course of the evening we discussed the behaviour of certain turbulent spirits in the Rawanduz district. 'Ah,' said Jamil Agha, 'they are nonentities. If you leave it to me I will march tomorrow with two hundred men and quickly dispose of them.' As a matter of fact, his tribe could not produce more than fifty rifles, and if I had taken him at his word he would have been ready with a hundred excuses.

The Dizai trouble being settled, my attention was urgently called to revenue matters, for the state of affairs that had existed had seriously interfered with the wheat estimations. Full returns had been received, but it was obvious that the estimators had recorded not their own calculations, but what the aghas had told them or paid them to write. In the last days of July I therefore set out on horseback with Khoja Sibi of Ainkawa and a revenue official to check the work that had been done, and visited some thirty villages in the Qush Tappeh nahiya. The heat was intense, and we used to work from 5 a.m. to 11 a.m., and 3 p.m.to 7p.m. It is difficult for anybody living in northern climes to picture what it is like riding over these arid plains at this the hottest time of the year. The sun's pitiless rays strike fiercely from above and are thrown back by the earth's bare surface with almost equal intensity. Everything is swallowed up in a dancing haze, through which passing travellers may be seen wrapped up as though in a snowstorm. For the hotter the day becomes the more clothes does the native of the country put on, well knowing how dangerous it is to expose his body to the scorching air. The work of estimation is by no means easy. The corn is found in an unthreshed heap; it is necessary after walking round each heap to judge of its size, to examine carefully whether it be closely or loosely packed, to pull out a handful of corn in order to determine the proportion of straw, and finally to rub out a few grains in the hand, to discover their weight and quality. This having been done an estimate must be formed of the total weight of grain the heap will produce when threshed. Experts like Khoja Sibi can usually arrive within 10 per cent of the total; amateurs, though after a little experience they may work out nine heaps with fair accuracy, will err grievously at the tenth. At a large village there may be a hundred heaps to deal with, and there are few things more tiring than walking round them and estimating them in the intense heat.

Life at Arbil passed quickly and pleasantly, work being plentiful and really more than I could cope with single-handed. Every morning I received an average of thirty petitions, dealing with every imaginable subject; many of them I was able to pass on to local officials, but there were always several matters into which I had to inquire myself. I made a practice of leaving my office at least once every morning, and visiting the verandah outside where the complainants used to wait; here I interviewed them personally, and in this way everyone who wished was sure of seeing me. Otherwise many petitioners would have been sidetracked by corrupt officials. Land suits and criminal cases were my special province and took up much of my time, while there were nearly always two or three chiefs from outside staying in Arbil who would visit me every morning for long interviews. In addition there was the ordinary correspondence to be dealt with, and routine matters connected with revenue, the municipality, the hospital, education, etc. I always tried to devote to touring as many days as I spent in my office. At the end of August the Political Officer Mosul sent me Lieut. A. F. S. Curtin to assist me in my work, and he was relieved in October by Captain J. R. L. Bradshaw, just returned from leave, who had previously been assistant to Major Murray. He remained with me for more than a year, and I owe a great deal to his equability and painstaking perseverance.

I was assisted in the maintenance of law and order by a body of about thirty-five town police, under Mr. H. C. Robbins, a regular sleuth-hound in the detection of crime, and some 150 gendarmes, trained by Sergeant Kennard, who quickly recovered from his wound, and commanded by a native officer. From October onwards this last post was held by a Syrian Arab called Saiyid Ali Effendi. A lively young man of twenty-six with an uncertain temper and apt to sulk, he was a most energetic worker and as brave as a lion; I was very fond of him, and he became, I believe, most devoted to me. On one occasion I should probably have perished but for his resource and courage, and he several times distinguished himself by acts of heroism. Sergeant Kennard did splendid work in training the gendarmes, despite constant attacks of fever, and both he and Mr. Robbins were still at Arbil when I left in the autumn of 1920.

Friday and Sunday afternoons were holidays, and on the former it was the custom for the notables of the town to visit me and discuss matters of interest over some tea and coffee. I

used to call this my Parliament, as it gave me an opportunity
for consulting public opinion on Government matters. The
regular attendants were Mulla Effendi, Saiyid Abdulla
Pasha, the Mufti, Ali Pasha, and Hajji Rashid Agha, with a
few others of less note.

Of these Mulla Effendi is by far the most important; I
often used to visit him at his house at Badawa, the scene of
the negotiations with the Dizai chiefs. It is a lovely place
shut in by orchards and vineyards with, on the east side, a
small water-tank surrounded by flower-beds thick with
whatever blooms happen to be in season. Close by roses and
jasmine perfume the air. The building is of two storeys, in
each of which there is a large open room facing north; that
below contains a fountain while the upper one is separated
from the open air by a finely carved screen of walnut wood.
There are various inner rooms, beautifully carpeted, some of
them containing fine inlaid furniture. The whole style of the
building is highly ornate, the ceilings being painted in a
mosaic of the brightest colours with occasional patches of
mica. Mulla Effendi spends his days in the Great Mosque of
Arbil, and betakes himself to this retreat in the evening. His
real name is Abubekr, but he is always known as Mulla
Effendi or Mulla i Gichka, the Little Mulla. Short in stature
he possesses refined and aquiline features, and the tranquil
look of a really pious man; I have never seen such a pair of
delicate hands as his. He wears normally a long grey gown
stretching to his feet, and a fez wound round with pale blue
muslin. He is respected throughout Kurdistan for his piety
and learning; his ancestors for several generations before
him have earned a similar reputation, and it is said that
none of the family, which owns large properties, have ever
yet laid a complaint against any man. Mulla Effendi is
trustee for the endowments of the Great Mosque; he normally
leads the services there and preaches the Friday sermon. Unlike most of his class he is decidedly progressive, reading
modern periodicals from Egypt and Turkey, and talking with
intelligence on political and scientific subjects. I asked him
one day his attitude with regard to the situation in Mesopotamia, and he replied, 'Everyone wishes to see his mother
country independent. At present, however, we are split by
mutual jealousies, and there is nobody fit to govern. We want

you to look after us until security is restored, and we are
capable of governing ourselves.' He remained true to this
policy throughout, and though, as became one of his cloth, he
refused any official position, he always supported the
Government with his influence to the utmost of his power,
and it was he more than anybody else who led public opinion
in Arbil. Ahmad Effendi, his cousin and my faithful adherent,
acted very largely on his advice. Mulla Effendi's whole family
are consumptive; he had lost his wife and three daughters
through this complaint and has only one little son of five left.

Of the other notables we have already met Ali Pasha and
Hajji Rashid Agha. Saiyid Abdulla Pasha is the Naqib or
leading saiyid of the town, a homely old gentleman who may
usually be seen abroad on a remarkably fine roan mule with
an expression exactly like its master's. He is rich but avaricious, and having no convictions will adopt the policy which
he thinks most calculated to preserve his money-bags intact.
He is well educated and has visited Egypt, Syria, and Constantinople. The Mufti is brother to the Rais Baladiyah, a
talkative old man; he used to come and read Persian with me
every day. His companions regard him as an amiable bore.

In the first week of September the Qurban 'Id was celebrated. This is the greatest of the Muhammadan festivals,
and was observed by us with a four days' holiday. The town
presented a brilliant scene, everybody wearing their best
clothes, the children especially appearing clad in silks of
many hues and laden with gold ornaments. It was like a
country fair in England: beside the road, just below the fort,
were set up swing-boats and joy-wheels where rides might be
had for one anna; while opposite them were stalls containing
sweets and knick-knacks; the scene was one of universal
gaiety. At 8.30 a.m. on the first day of the festival I paid a
formal visit to the Serai; my arrival was announced by the
discharge of a gun, and I found Saiyid Ali at the door of my
office with a guard of honour from the gendarmes. When I
had taken my seat the callers arrived; the first instalment included the greater and the lesser notables and the leading
merchants, probably about thirty in all. I shook hands with
them, and they each partook of a sweet, a cigarette, a cup of
tea, and a cup of coffee, while I wished them the compliments
of the season and endeavoured to converse on light subjects.

Next filed in the Government officials, and the same thing
happened over again, the only impression that was left on me
being a succession of paws, some hard and horny, and some
limp and clammy. In the third and last instalment came the
Christians and Jews.

The next day it was necessary for me to return the calls of
the notables; there were ten or eleven houses to visit and a
quarter of an hour was spent in each. On arrival I was first
served with a cup of coffee, usually sweetened, next came a
plate of sweetmeats, then either a glass of sherbet or a cup of
tea, and finally a cup of bitter coffee. It takes some time to
recover after being subjected to this treatment ten times in
the course of a few hours.

At the beginning of October I was granted three days'
leave, and visited the Khushnao country in order to breathe
again the fresh mountain air. I travelled by car as far as the
Bastura Chai, where my pony awaited me. As soon as I
crossed the stream I was in the territory of Mustafa Agha of
Kora, and was greeted by his brother Rasul Agha, who took
me to the village of Siwaka and gave me tea and coffee. Setting out again we passed a ruined fort with a village and a
delightful fig garden just below it, and began to ascend a
high ridge. The top proved to be a plateau covered with oak
trees, beneath one of which we found a large earthenware
vessel full of water, provided by the piety of Mustafa Agha for
the benefit of passing travellers. From here there was a fine
view out over the hill country, while the village of Kora could
be seen nestling in a little valley below. We descended and I
found that Mustafa Agha had spread cushions for me under
the shade of a great mulberry beside a babbling flower-
decked stream. The samovar was before me. Kora is situated
on a mound at the higher end of a long, narrow valley; at the
foot of the mound is a considerable brook along both banks of
which stretch gardens of fig, pomegranates, and other fruits
interspersed with tall chinars and graceful poplars. I have
encountered few more beautiful villages during my sojourn in
Kurdistan, and it is a regular Paradise to a traveller who
comes to it direct from the bare Arbil plain. Mustafa Agha attended to my wants most carefully, and it was with great difficulty I could persuade him to allow me to continue my
journey to Shaqlawah.

Half an hour's ride brought me to the village of Khurshid Beg, the refugee chief described in the last chapter, who brewed me some very strong tea; from here onward the road was already familiar to me. It was nearly dark when I reached Shaqlawah. I found that Miran i Qadir Beg had built for himself an enormous chardaq or bower in an open space in the gardens, and had furnished it with numerous mattresses, cushions, and carpets, and some finely carved wooden tables. Here he kept court surrounded by numerous attendants. He was intensely jealous of his brother Rashid Beg, and if he could prevent it would allow no traveller to lodge in his guest-house. He was now very much in the hands of an unscrupulous clerk called Ahmad Midhat Effendi, who traded on his master's inability to read and write. I received a warm welcome and partook of the usual hospitable fare.

The following day, after my bread and mast, I went for a walk through the gardens descending to the stream at the bottom of the valley. It was very beautiful, and the leaves overhead were beginning to take on their autumn hues. Most of the inhabitants of Shaqlawah were at the top of the walnut trees shaking down the nuts. The fig, plum, pear, and pomegranate trees were still laden with fruit.

In the afternoon I determined to cross the Safin Dagh, which reaches a height of 6,500 ft. above the sea, and visit Saleh Beg's village Khoran. Three of Qadir Beg's men accompanied me, and we took a difficult path in the hope of encountering some ibex. After several hours' exhausting climb, during which we came on a small rocky glen with a spring surrounded by pear trees laden with the most luscious fruit, we did at last see a herd of eight or nine silhouetted against the sky on the rocks above us, but they were too distant for a shot, and I was too exhausted to pursue. On the top to my surprise I found a broad plateau covered with dry grass and the withered remains of tulips and other flowers which had blossomed in the spring. The view was superb. Over the plains the lower course of the Greater Zab and a portion of the Tigris were visible, and it was said that on a clear day we could have seen Kirkuk and Mosul; while eastwards there lay spread out the whole of the Harir plain, with its numerous villages and a portion of Bituin, surrounded by tier on tier of rough gigantic hills. We followed along the crest for some miles, passing the pits, now empty, which supply Arbil with snow in the summer, and then began to descend steeply till we came to the vineyards laden with fruit, and an icy cold spring, which was most welcome, as I had had nothing to drink for some hours. Saleh Beg's son Ahmad Beg met me on the road, and we reached Khoran just as it was getting dark. My host conducted me to a sort of verandah supported by rough tree trunks, where he treated me with a very homely hospitality. I spent two nights at Khoran, after which Saleh Beg accompanied me down to Kora. It was the tenth day of Muharram, and I found that both Saleh Beg and Mustafa Agha were fasting, having been told by some wandering darwish that it was the best day on which to make up for a lapse in Ramazan. At lunch, however, they decided they would choose some other occasion and partake of the meal with me. While I was at Khoran, Saleh Beg told me long stories of how he used to humbug the Turkish officials and avoid paying revenue, and I noticed how prosperous his village appeared; we found eventually that he was playing the same game with us. His cheery familiarity and warm protestations of friendship were all part of his stock-in-trade, and when he found that we would not overlook his peccadilloes he became a most treacherous foe.

On my return to Arbil I was busy estimating the rice crops until the end of the month, when matters of some importance compelled me to make a journey to Baghdad.

CHAPTER XI

FORMATION OF THE ARBIL DIVISION

UP TO NOVEMBER, 1919, the Arbil District formed a part of the Mosul Division; of this Lieut.-Colonel G. E. Leachman, C.I.E., D.S.O., was Political Officer until early in October, when he was relieved by Mr. H. Bill, I.C.S. For some time proposals had been on foot to form a separate Arbil Division which should include the Koi District, at present under Sulaimaniyah, and the Rawanduz District, the A.P.O. of which was independent and corresponded direct with Baghdad. This arrangement had many advantages, as the only good road to Rawanduz lay through Arbil, while Koi could communicate much more easily with that town than with Sulaimaniyah, from which it was separated by the Lesser Zab. Accordingly, on October 29th, I left for Baghdad in order to discuss the above proposals with Colonel Wilson, in the hope that some decision would be reached. Colonel Wilson, however, was unwilling to embark on the new scheme until Mr. Bill had had time to visit Arbil and make his recommendations. Meanwhile events happened which entirely altered the situation.

I took with me on this journey the Rais Baladiyah Ahmad Effendi, who was much interested in the train by which we travelled from Sherqat, as he had never seen one before. We spent four or five days in Baghdad.

On the evening of the 3rd, an hour or two before I was due to leave, Colonel Wilson called me aside and informed me that G.H.Q. had just received news to the effect that Mr. Bill, P.O. Mosul, and Captain K. Scott, M.C., A.P.O. Aqra, had been murdered at Bira Kapra in the Zibar country. This news was as stunning as it was unexpected, and it was not till some days later that any details became available.

Aqra is the headquarters of a district which is enclosed on its southern and eastern sides by the Greater Zab, and separated only by that river from the Rawanduz District. The

town is situated on the slopes of a ridge which is a continuation of the Kewa Resh range which bounds Bituin, and the
Harir Dagh, the lofty rampart which overlooks the Dasht i
Harir. Westwards of this ridge and along the northern bank
of the river dwell the Surchi, fellow-tribesmen of the Dasht i
Harir Surchi, while the hilly country to the east and the valley of the Greater Zab above its bend to the north-west is occupied by the Zibaris. East of the river at Barzan, formerly in
the Rawanduz District, dwells Shaikh Ahmad, a young man
of twenty who is well known to be half mad. Of holy origin
his family have for some time exercised only temporal sway,
their supposed sanctity giving them great influence over the
surrounding country. They were often a thorn in the sides of
the Turks, who on one occasion mobilised the Kurds of the
Arbil and Rawanduz districts and attacked them. The then
ruling shaikh, a brother of Shaikh Ahmad, fled to the north,
where the Shikak imprisoned him and handed him over to
the Government: he was brought to Mosul and executed. The
Zibaris and Barzanis with their neighbours, the Shirwan
tribe, are known throughout Southern Kurdistan as the
Diwana or Mad People. They are reputed to be the most savage of all the Kurds, respecting neither God nor man.

On November 1st Captain Scott, who had been newly appointed A.P.O. Aqra, in the company of his Political Officer
Mr. Bill, paid a visit to Bira Kapra, the centre of the Zibar
country, for the purpose of discussing certain matters with
the local chiefs Faris Agha and Babekr Agha. These latter
took offence at something that was said in the course of the
conversations, and that night plotted to murder their guests,
sending across the river to Shaikh Ahmad to come and assist
them. The following morning they and their men together
with a brother of Shaikh Ahmad rode out with the two officers as if in the usual manner they proposed to escort them
a mile or two along the road. As soon as they were well clear
of the village one of them fired a shot which instantly killed
Mr. Bill; Captain Scott drew his revolver, which was shot out
of his hand. He then took refuge behind a rock, and with a
rifle which he had seized from his escort succeeded in ac-
counting for one or two of his assailants; but deserted by all
his gendarmes except one, he was soon overpowered and
killed. The tribes then, roused by the sight of blood,

proceeded to swarm over the mountains and descend on Aqra; quickly expelling the gendarmes they looted the town and devoted themselves to a mad destruction of Government property. Some of the Surchi, especially one Shaikh Raqib, came in to assist them, but the most important chief, Shaikh Obaidullah, remained at his village of Bajil. After remaining in Aqra two or three days, and glutting themselves with the plunder, the tribesmen returned victoriously to their homes.

When I arrived in Arbil on the 4th nothing was known of these events, and they did not become public property for several days, such a formidable barrier is the Greater Zab. On the 5th I received a wire appointing me to officiate as Political Officer of the new Arbil Division which was formed, with effect from November 1st. The Districts of Koi and Rawanduz were in the charge respectively of Captain C. A. G. Rundle, M.C., and Captain F. C. de L. Kirk, who now resided at Batas in the Dasht i Harir. I determined to visit both districts on the first possible opportunity, but meanwhile events at Aqra made it imperative for me to stop at Arbil.

The news of the murders and the sack of Aqra, even when it became known, had little effect in Arbil, but the case was certain to be different in the Rawanduz district, which was already somewhat disturbed. Captain Kirk, hearing that Shaikh Obaidullah of Bajil had so far remained loyal to the Government, determined to visit him in order to strengthen his resolution – for his defection would undoubtedly have a very serious effect on the Surchi south of the river – and find out what he could about the situation. He accordingly crossed the Greater Zab at Kandil with a small escort, and boldly made his way to the disturbed district. Much alarmed for his safety I despatched Captain C. E. Littledale with a party of gendarmes to assist him. Captain Littledale had arrived at Arbil a few days previously to take charge of the gendarmes of the Division; he had formerly been at Mosul. Owing to his intimate knowledge of the Aqra district he was a few days later recalled to act as A.P.O. to the column which set out to avenge the murders. He returned to me again early in January. Captain Kirk reached Bajil in safety, and having assured himself of the Shaikh's fidelity proceeded through most dangerous country to Aqra itself, which the tribesmen had now abandoned. Having remained there a few hours he withdrew in the direction of Mosul and soon reached safety. Captain Littledale followed along the same route, and in one place only escaped falling into an ambush through the careful vigilance of Saiyid Ali Effendi who accompanied him. Meanwhile I had a most anxious time at Arbil – for it is far more wearing to know that others for whom one is responsible are in danger than to be in danger oneself – and was much relieved when I heard that all concerned were safe. Saiyid Ali Effendi was promoted to the rank of Yuzbashi, or Captain, for the part he played on this occasion. While Captain Kirk was away I received numerous messages for Captain D. C. E. Tozer, M.C., the military commander at Batas, where there was a small detachment, that the surrounding tribes were about to attack his post; but fortunately nothing alarming occurred, and I do not think the threat was ever a serious one.

A military expedition shortly afterwards visited Aqra, Bira Kapra, and Barzan. Some villages were destroyed, but the murderers escaped, for it is impossible for a slow-moving column to catch the wily Kurd in his mountain home.

On the 18th I at last set out to visit Koi, taking the shortest route from Arbil through the village of Hajji Usu. Two hours from my destination I was met by a large istiqbal or welcoming party which included all the notables except Hama Agha, who rarely went out now, and Abdulla Agha, who was in Baghdad. Captain Rundle met me just outside the town, and my first action on arriving was to visit Hama Agha, whom I found much the same, except that he was a bit older and sleepier. I remained in Koi two or three days, during which I had long talks with most of my old friends.

Koi had changed very little since I left it in February. I had been succeeded as A.P.O. by Captain T. C. Beale, who had held the appointment till May, when he took over Rawanduz. He was followed by the present A.P.O., Captain Rundle. In April, Rania and Qala Diza had been formed into a separate district with headquarters at the former place, and Captain Barker had been appointed A.P.O. My successors had dismissed some incompetent aghas whom I had been compelled to employ under the former regime, otherwise the local personnel were practically unchanged, Hama Agha, Jamil Agha, and 'the Bishop' still retaining their offices. 'The

Bishop' greeted me with great hilarity. 'Last time,' he said, 'when you came you brought rain; this time if you do not bring it we shall have to duck you.' Fortunately a few drops fell during my stay, so I escaped this indignity!

The revolt of Shaikh Mahmud was naturally followed by a period of considerable anxiety; the A.P.O. was cut off from his headquarters, could get no news, and had to act on his own responsibility. Old Hama Agha adopted an uncompromising attitude; hearing that some of the notables were about to hold a meeting to consider the situation, he threatened forcibly to break up such a meeting if it took place, saying that no consideration was necessary, it being essential for all to support the Government. His influence kept things straight. Abdulla Agha played a double game endeavouring to keep in with both sides; the A.P.O. detected his chicanery and he was deported to Baghdad for a year. Miran i Qadir, Beg of Shaqlawah, received letters from Shaikh Mahmud and spent many hours in anxious thought, but remained loyal.

Koi was now in a much more prosperous state. The bazaar was full and trade had revived. The majority of the population, who had formerly appeared half-starved and dejected, now went about their business cheerfully. It had been found possible to apprentice many of the orphans in the poorhouse to local tradesmen, and only a few inmates now remained. The appearance of the town, too, had greatly improved, much of the rubbish and debris having been cleared away, and great efforts having been made to repair the water channels. Unfortunately Koi proved to be very unhealthy during the hot weather, all the officers stationed there suffering from fever, while the continual reshabahs, or black winds, which blow with gale intensity almost every day and night throughout the summer months made life most unpleasant.

Though I was now in no way connected with the government of Rania and Qala Diza, events there naturally interested me. The revolt of Shaikh Mahmud had caused a crisis in this area, and the situation had only been saved by the untiring efforts of Captain Barker and the unswerving loyalty of Babekr Agha. The opposition party in the Pizhder was still causing a lot of trouble; in the early autumn a column of troops had proceeded to Darband to support Babekr Agha, and their presence compelled the disaffected chiefs to remain in the hills until the roads were closed by snow and greatly eased the situation. With the assistance of the same troops Sawar Agha was successfully arrested and deported to Baghdad; he had been most active in the anti-Government movement at the time of Shaikh Mahmud's revolt, and one of his relations had fired at Captain Barker one day as he was crossing the river just by Sarkhuma. I saw much of Sawar Agha subsequently, as after spending some months in Baghdad he was entrusted to my care at Arbil.

From Koi I made my way to Shaqlawah along the western slopes of the Safin Dagh, spending a night with Saleh Beg at Khoran on the way. We encountered a heavy hailstorm just outside this village and it was bitterly cold all night. I had lunch with Qadir Beg at Shaqlawah, and found him much disturbed because he thought I showed undue favour to Saleh Beg. Apparently the latter had gone about boasting that it was entirely owing to his influence with me that Qadir Beg had ever been appointed Governor. I hastened to reassure him that in my eyes Saleh Beg counted for nothing compared with himself.

From Shaqlawah we descended by a rough but beautiful road through the gardens to the stream below, by the side of which we passed through a gap in the ridge that fronts Shaqlawah. Crossing yet another ridge by an easy track we descended on to the upper or southern end of the Dasht i Harir. This remarkable expanse occurs like Bituin in the middle of the hill country, where, so geological experts say, its position is abnormal. It is roughly cone-shaped, the Greater Zab forming its base; on the west it is bounded by a series of well-wooded ridges, while to the east the traveller is confronted by the unbroken and almost sheer rocky face of the Harir Dagh, which rises nearly 3,000 ft. above the plain. A short but rough pass connects the Dasht i Harir with the valley of Balisan which runs down into Bituin. The length of the plain is about 20 miles; its surface undulates considerably, especially round the edges, and is intersected by many small streams. At its upper end are many picturesque little villages, each with its fruit gardens and plantations of poplar, which belong to the Khushnao. Along the eastern edge is a line of villages mostly the property of the notables of Rawanduz, while the northern end near the river is occupied by the

Surchi. The Khushnao villages are under the administration
of the A.P.O. Koi, while the rest of the plain forms part of the
Rawanduz District.

The migratory tribes were now beginning to descend from
the hills, and we passed several encampments of the
Khailani, who were well armed and looked very fierce. They
are noted thieves, but have no reputation for bravery. Before
sunset we reached Bashur, the last Khushnao village, whence
a canter over three miles of level country brought us to
Batas. This village, which contains some sixty houses, is built
on the extremity of a low outcrop at the foot of the Harir
Dagh. Behind it an abundant stream waters extensive gardens of fig and pomegranate, and then curving round the end
of the outcrop flows through a small plantation of poplar, and
below the houses out into the plain. On the further side of
this stream, just above the bend, is situated the house of Abdulla Pasha.

When I arrived I found the military had occupied a large
artificial mound, excellent for defensive purposes, about half
a mile away, while Captain Kirk and his office were miserably housed in the village itself. He had been compelled to
leave Rawanduz in August under circumstances which will be
related in the next chapter, and the settlement at Batas was
only intended to be temporary. While I was here a telegram
was received directing that at the end of the month Captain
Kirk should proceed to Aqra, where order had been re-estab-
lished, and take over as A.P.O. After his departure the office,
until it was closed in January, was in the charge of Mr. Scott
of the Telegraphs, assisted by the head clerk, Mr. Turner.

The day after my arrival we called on Abdulla Pasha,
using the path to his house where his son, Suayid Beg, had
been murdered a year previously. Abdulla Pasha is another
remarkable nonagenarian, being very nearly, if not quite, as
old as Hama Agha. Unlike the latter, who was physically big
and strong, but mentally in his dotage, he possesses a small
frail body with trembling hands and shaking head, while his
mind is still very active. He is always talking and frequently
repeats himself. He has a thin, short beard, a little pale,
wrinkled, and rather blotchy face, with dark eyes and dyed
eyebrows. He is about 5 ft. 3 ins. in height, and is always
shabbily dressed in a long gown with an old overcoat and a

very ancient gold embroidered head-dress, and stumps about with a long stick. He is extremely miserly, and is reported to sleep every night on his money chests. His long official career under the Turkish Government, for which he was rewarded with a Pashaship, has made him a remarkably wise and astute old man. After holding various offices in the remoter parts of the Rawanduz district, he was for eleven years Qaimaqam at Arbil, and for a time acted as Mutesarrif (the head of a liwa or division) at Sulaimaniyah. Owing to his intimate knowledge of the Kurds and their ways the Turkish Government frequently resorted to him when they were in difficulties; on one occasion he was sent to Sulaimaniyah to make peace between the local shaikhs and the Turkish governor, and on another he received a decoration from the Shah of Persia for settling a serious quarrel among the frontier tribes. For an ex-Turkish official he was an unusually straightforward and honest man; he remained a firm friend of the British Government, and his advice could always be relied on where neither his private enemies nor his money-bags were concerned. His only son had been killed a year before, and his grandson Ismail Beg was now in Rawanduz.

The situation at Batas was now satisfactory. The Surchi, even if they had contemplated hostile action a few weeks previously, were sufficiently cowed by the presence of the punitive column in the Aqra district. Our chief anxiety was centred round the Harki, who were already moving down the Rawanduz gorge, and whom it would be difficult to control if they once got out of hand, for they could muster 600 men, well armed, and the best fighters in this part of Kurdistan.

On November 24th I returned to Arbil via Mawaran and Kora. The former of these is a picturesque village situated in its own narrow little valley, and separated from the Dasht i Harir by a single high ridge. For several centuries it has been the headquarters of a distinguished family of mullas, known as the Haidaris. It once contained two or three hundred houses, and was surrounded by miles of gardens, but the water that used to irrigate them is used up in the Shaqlawah gardens, and now only a small stream trickles down the valley, broadening out into a limpid as it passes the village. One of the Haidaris is in Constantinople, and recently held the office of Shaikh ul Islam, and several other members of the family are in Arbil; its representative at this time in Mawaran was one Aziz Agha, a rough unlettered Kurd, who subsequently murdered three gendarmes in his guest-room in cold blood. It is curious that on the very day that I am writing these words I have received a letter to say that the village has been totally destroyed in revenge for this deed.

From here a climb over another ridge brought us to the main Arbil–Shaqlawah road, and we were soon lunching with Mustafa Agha at Kora.

I returned to Arbil that evening, and a day or two later was down with a severe attack of fever, only recovering just in time to welcome Colonel Wilson, who arrived at Arbil by aeroplane on November 29th. On the same day Captain Kirk came in from Batas, being on his way to Aqra, and from now onwards I administered the Rawanduz district directly. Colonel Wilson, who had come to see Captain Kirk and to discuss with me certain matters relating to the future of Kurdistan, returned on the 30th to Baghdad, when I set out in my car on a visit to Major Soane, at Sulaimaniyah. It was now several months since Shaikh Mahmud had been removed, and under Major Soane's vigorous rule the whole spirit and appearance of the place had changed. Returning to Arbil three days later I set out again for Batas, being in high spirits and full of hope that circumstances would allow me to proceed to Rawanduz, the place about which I had heard so much, and which for months I had been longing to see.

CHAPTER XII

RAWANDUZ AND THE GORGE

BEFORE PROCEEDING WITH THE narrative it will be as
well to outline briefly the previous history of this remarkable
place, Rawanduz, which for the next ten months was to be
the centre of my thoughts and ambitions.

Though traditions exist dating back to the seventeenth
century, few details are forthcoming until the accession to
power in 1826 of Muhammad Pasha, usually known from a
defect in one of his eyes as the Blind Pasha. The head of the
local ruling family he quickly consolidated his power in the
Rawanduz district and within a few years overran and occupied Rania, Koi, Arbil, Aqra, Amadia, and Zakho, even
penetrating as far as Jezira and Mardin. In 1838 the Turkish
authorities, becoming alarmed at his increasing power,
despatched a large force, which easily defeated him. He was
captured and put to death. The district is covered with the
remains of the forts which he erected to ensure the obedience
of the tribes and protect them from the aggression of the
Babans of Sulaimaniyah.

His relations succeeded in maintaining a state of semi-
independence for ten years, after which the Turkish Government administered the district directly, usually maintaining
there a garrison of not less than 800 men. They had little
control over the remoter tribes, and their revenue collectors
were always accompanied by a body of troops. Before the war
the town could boast of more than 10,000 inhabitants, with
mosques, baths, and extensive bazaars.

Early in 1916 Rawanduz was occupied by the Russians
and a rabble of Christians from Persia and Armenia, who
with the Russian soldiery laid waste the countryside, com-
mitting every conceivable outrage. The whole town was laid
waste and became a heap of ruins, except for the upper or
residential quarter, where the Russian officers were billeted.

Such terror and loathing did the Russians inspire by the ravages that all the Kurds from Arbil, Koi, and Rania combined to resist their advance, and several thousand of them joined the Turkish forces, which were entrenched on the Kurrek Dagh overlooking the town. Nearly every Kurdish chief of my acquaintance was there, including even old Hama Agha, who is reported to have slept soundly through the most critical moments. I have heard universal complaints about the behaviour of Turkish officers on this occasion, and after a few days the Kurds withdrew in disgust; it is probable the Turkish commander found it impossible to feed them, and that such a large undisciplined host was more of a hindrance than a help. The Russians were unable to capture the strong position on the Kurrek Dagh, and after two or three months were compelled to withdraw. The Turkish army then re-occupied the town, and before long destroyed the little that was left, hewing down for firewood the valuable fruit trees which the Russians had spared. By the time of the armistice in 1918, it is probable that only 20 per cent of the original population of the district survived; these were in an advanced state of destitution, and the majority would certainly have perished but for timely British intervention.

A few days after the occupation of Arbil by the British, as he was crossing the stream on the way to his father Abdullah Pasha's house at Batas, there perished Suayid Beg, the only strong man of Rawanduz, shot by unknown assassins concealed in the neighbouring gardens. He was universally recognised as the leading man in the district; he had once or twice been governor under the Turks, and his influence among the tribes was enormous. If he had survived it is likely that the British Government would have been saved much trouble and expense, for with him perished the only local chief capable of controlling the district. He left one son, by name Ismail Beg.

The first British A.P.O. was appointed to Rawanduz late in December, 1918; Major Noel, however, arrived a few days later and undertook the organisation of the local government. The chief posts were distributed amongst the notables of the town, it being found impossible to make any one of them supreme, while tribal chiefs were given salaries and appointed magistrates of the sub-districts in which they resided. Agricultural loans were liberally distributed, enabling the starving population to support themselves through the winter and sow small quantities of grain for the next harvest.

Three A.P.O.s in succession administered the district until early in July, when Captain F. C. de L. Kirk was appointed. He found himself faced with a very dangerous situation. The rising of Shaikh Mahmud had been a serious blow to British prestige throughout Kurdistan, and at Rawanduz the Government had little but prestige to support it. The nearest garrison was at Arbil some 68 miles away, and though a considerable force of gendarmes existed, they were rather retainers of the aghas who commanded them, than servants of the Government, and in this way became a positive danger. The local chiefs, who had been saved from starvation by liberal salaries and agricultural loans, began to grow restless when the loans ceased, and the salaries were reduced, and soon saw that the Government possessed few means of coercing them if they misbehaved. Finally Nuri, the son of Bawil Agha, a young gendarme officer of commanding personality, who had acquired a great influence over his men at the time of the Sulaimaniyah rising, refused to obey the orders of the A.P.O. Under these circumstances, in face of the recent murders at Amadia, and taking into consideration the enormous expense incurred in running the district and the little return it gave, it was decided to evacuate Rawanduz and remove the A.P.O.'s office to Batas. A column of troops was despatched to enable Captain Kirk to leave the town in safety. Nuri was arrested, but within a few minutes of his capture tore himself away from his guard, and hurtled down the mountainside. All efforts to recapture him proved unavailing. On August 10th the column withdrew through the gorge without molestation and established the A.P.O. at Batas, a small detachment remaining with him to support his authority.

The inhabitants of Rawanduz were much dismayed at the withdrawal of the Government, against which they felt little or no hostility. Within a few days all the leading notables visited Captain Kirk at Batas. At their request Hajji Nauras Effendi, whom we have previously met at Shaqlawah, was nominated Government representative in the town. A few necessary officials were appointed to assist him, but all the

tribal chiefs were deprived of their salaries with the exception of Shaikh Muhammad Agha, chief of the Balik, who was responsible for keeping open the Persian road, and had always loyally supported the Government. The Dasht i Harir was administered directly from Batas, while the nahiya of Dera, consisting of the hilly country between the Arbil district and the Dasht i Harir, remained under the Mudir, Yahya Beg.

The people of Rawanduz and the surrounding district, like naughty children who had been punished, continued for a few months on their best behaviour hoping thereby to persuade their fairy godmother the Government to return. Nuri lived in exile in a village a few miles outside the town. He was once bombed by an aeroplane, which a few minutes afterwards crashed in the Dasht i Dian opposite Rawanduz, the pilot and Captain Kirk, who was acting as observer, making their way back safely to Batas.

The murders at Bira Kapra at the beginning of November entirely changed the situation, and highway robbery became the order of the day, the chief culprits being Yusuf Beg, Muhammad Amin Beg of Dargala, which lies on the Persian road, and certain opponents of Shaikh Muhammad Agha in the Balik tribe. With the despatch of a military expedition to Aqra matters improved slightly, and Mir Muhammad Amin Beg came in and deposited a security for future good behaviour. The Balik malcontents, however, showed no sign of repentance, while Yusuf Beg's tyranny increased, and he began to nurture designs for making himself overlord of Rawanduz. His father-in-law, Hajji Nauras, was quite unable to restrain him or cope with the situation generally, and sent in frequent requests that he might be allowed to resign. These disorders had already caused much uneasiness to neighbouring A.P.O.s, and if allowed to continue unchecked would infect the surrounding districts.

When, therefore, I left Arbil for Batas, on December 6th, I proposed, if possible, to proceed thence to Rawanduz, in order that I might find some means of preventing further disturbances and, if the situation allowed, bring to book the offenders. I also hoped to set up some more stable form of Government.

I set out by the main road, being able to travel the first 18 miles as far as Dera in a car. Dera, so called from a Christian monastery which some centuries ago existed in this neighbourhood, was once a considerable village, but being situated on the main road, completely vanished during the war, leaving only a substantial fort on a mound, one of the relics of the Blind Pasha. Majid Agha, brother of Jamil Agha, chief of the Girdi, had, however, acquired a large part of the village land partly by purchase and partly by seizure, and was now living in a temporary hut he had erected just below the fort. An elderly disappointed man, with a weather-beaten beardless face, he was wearing at this time of the year a sort of close-fitting blue frock-coat done up tightly with brass buttons bearing the Persian Lion and Sun. Being older than Jamil Agha he should have been chief of the tribe, but was rejected on account of his sour and miserly disposition, which ill compared with his brother's more free and open personality. The two were at perpetual enmity with one another, Jamil Agha especially descending to the most petty tricks to annoy his rival. Personally after some months' experience of both I preferred Majid, finding him by far the more honest and truthful of the two. One of his ambitions was to become Mudir of Dera, and he therefore gave great trouble to the actual occupier of that post, Yahya Beg, and whenever I visited the place there was always a squabble as to which of the two was to entertain me.

Yahya Beg is the great-grandson of Rasul Pasha, the last independent ruler of Rawanduz, and through his mother the grandson of old Abdulla Pasha, and cousin of Ismail Beg. Born and educated in Kirkuk and unlike a Kurd both in appearance and manners, with a white pasty face and nervous jerky speech, I was at first not at all favourably impressed with him; afterwards I found him to be a most capable and devoted servant of the Government, and one of the few men I could really trust. His contempt of the Kurds and frequent bad temper in dealing with them made him unpopular in the district. After providing me with a simple meal in the Fort, he set out with me for Batas.

For the first few miles we passed over a succession of low ridges of sandstone and limestone, until Duwin was reached. This was once the seat of a powerful ruling family, but now

nothing is left except a ruined fort where the road passes
over a range of hills. The surrounding country is occupied by
the Zarari tribe, a mean and ignorant people, whose villages
are not visible from the road. The further slope of the Duwin
ridge is covered with shrubs and grass, and is a beautiful
spot for flowers in the spring; here we found a large encampment of the Harki on their way down from the hills. The
wicker-work screens that form the walls of their black tents
were rolled back, and men, women, and children could be
seen basking in the sunshine, all very picturesque, but
ragged and dirty; great fierce, hairy dogs barked at us as we
passed, and large numbers of ponies and cattle were grazing
up and down the slope. Crossing a considerable stream, the
same which has its source at Shaqlawah and passes
Mawaran, we ascended through country well covered with
small oak trees, and traversing a small green plain containing a sulphurous spring came to Babachichek, a small village
with a gendarme post and a coffee-shop where caravans on
the road usually spend the night. Passing here through a gap
in a precipitous range of hills we descended steeply to the
Dasht i Harir, where after an hour's ride over undulating
country we left the main road and completed the remaining 5
miles to Batas.

I spent altogether four nights there, two of them in the
camp and two of them in Abdulla Pasha's house. The first
night I repaired to the camp, where I was hospitably entertained by Major Middleton of the 87th Punjabis, who was
now in command. The next morning I called on the old Pasha
and found that a letter had arrived for me from Muhammad
Suayid Beg of the Baradost, saying that with the help of the
neighbouring tribes he had cut off all the roads of escape
which were open to the murderers of Mr. Bill and Captain
Scott, and could catch them if the Government would assist
him. The Pasha also informed me that Ahmad Agha of the
Shirwan had visited his grandson in Rawanduz and made
similar promises. I therefore wired to Baghdad asking permission to proceed to Rawanduz in order to interview these
chiefs and, if possible, make arrangements to apprehend the
murderers. The permission was duly granted, and Major
Middleton was instructed by the military authorities to move
up as far as Kani Wutman at the mouth of the gorge in my

support. I telephoned down to Arbil for Saiyid Ali Effendi to
come up with as many mounted gendarmes as he could collect. He duly arrived on the 9th, and with the men he
brought and those already at Batas I had an escort about
fifty strong. Before I left, considering it advisable to have one
tribal chief, whom I knew, to assist me, I sent word to Jamil
Agha of the Girdi to join me as quickly as he could with fifteen men.

Early in the morning of the 10th I at length set out with
my cavalcade. For 4 miles our road lay through a valley
formed by the Harir Dagh and a long outcrop of rock; we
passed three or four small villages, and the going was rough
and stony. Reaching the main road we ascended the Spilik
pass and found ourselves in a different and much grander
country. On our left was a thickly wooded mountain mass
which is known as the district of Serchia; to our front lay the
saddle-shaped Kurrek Dagh, some 7,500 ft. in height and
now snow-capped, while on our right were the eastern slopes
of the Harir Dagh well covered with scrub-oak. Half-right between these two ranges we could see up the whole length of a
narrow valley shut in at the top by a lofty bluff like a gigantic pillar, and with a silver stream winding down its centre.
Our road ran along the base of the Serchia heights, and
about 2 or 3 miles from the Spilik pass we saw on our left a
solitary coffee-shop. Above it hidden away was the village of
Kalikin, where dwelt the famous brigand Hamada Shin.
Another 2 or 3 miles and we climbed a rough path to the village of Kani Wutman, which exists chiefly for the benefit of
passing caravans, and contains three khans for their accommodation, curious circular buildings with no windows to
admit the light, and very low roofs supported on numerous
rough tree trunks. In this village were stationed gendarmes
and a Customs post for checking caravans coming in from
Persia. From here a wonderful view could be obtained of the
valley previously mentioned, while a few miles ahead all progress seemed to be blocked by an enormous wall of rock, the
offshoot of the Kurrek Dagh. Only one V-shaped crack could
be perceived in it, and it is by this that the road enters the
Gorge.

Descending steeply from Kani Wutman we soon came to
the small plain of Khalifan and the bank of the stream which

had so long been visible flowing down its valley. A canter over a mile or two of grassy level country, and with the stream we entered the gloomy portals that give access to the Gorge.

I had heard so much of this famous place that it was with strange feelings of mingled awe and exhilaration that I entered it. The ominous line kept running in my mind, 'All hope abandon ye who enter here.' Outside all had been warm and sunny; it was now dark and bitterly cold, small pools in the road being covered with ice. The passage of the Gorge takes from two and a half to three hours, the distance being about 10 miles. For the first three of these the road descends with the stream, having first crossed it by means of a very rickety bridge. It is hemmed in on the right by black tree trunks and confused grey boulders, above which rises a sheer cliff, growing higher and higher until it must reach some 2,000 ft. This is faced on the opposite side by a similar cliff, the distance between them being in places not more than a hundred yards. The road winds in and out amongst enormous boulders, turning the most unexpected corners, now led along the edge of the stream by a causeway tucked in close against a rock 30 ft. high, now emerging in a small open space where caravans can rest and small patches of mash, a sort of pulse, are cultivated. After 3 miles the road leaves the stream and begins to rise; here a detached piece of cliff stands in the middle of the gorge like an enormous pillar, and just beyond may be seen another gorge branching off from the opposite side at right angles. The path here begins to zigzag steeply up the cliff, and on looking down the traveller is surprised to see that he is now going up-stream, for he has reached the Rawanduz Chai, which with the stream he has previously followed flows down the above-mentioned side gorge to the Greater Zab. For 4 or 5 miles he continues to climb until he sees the Rawanduz Chai, a thin silver thread 1,500 ft. below, while above him to the height of more than a thousand feet towers a sheer cliff. On the opposite side he is faced by another great cliff some 3,000 ft. in height. Trees and grass grow in abundance wherever they can gain a hold of the sides of this wonderful rift, for the lower slopes are not quite sheer and the road winds in and out along spurs and re-entrants. The first time I rode through the Gorge I was so overawed by its majesty that I felt almost depressed, and the whole time

THE GORGE OF RAWANDUZ

lines from Browning's 'Childe Roland' kept running in my head, while I pictured Rawanduz as the Dark Tower. Never have I seen Nature so terrible as she is here. With what fearful stroke can she have cloven these mountain masses, or with what years of labour delved these mighty chasms! At the highest point of the road there is a sort of cleared platform, the site of the most advanced Russian outpost. From here it may be observed that the main gorge turns to the right, while straight ahead a smaller gorge runs into it from the opposite side. If the traveller looks carefully he will see at the upper end of this the ruins of a considerable bridge which once spanned the stream that runs down it and the village of Balikian. Beyond this may be obtained a delightful glimpse of a stretch of green plain bounded by vast snow-capped mountains. We now begin to descend and soon turn to the right, in which direction the Gorge now runs straight for a mile, finally making another sharp bend to the left. In this mile the cliffs on either side, though not so high, are more sheer, and the stream is often seen several hundred feet perpendicularly below the road. The opposite cliff is bare and lined with horizontal strata; a small path runs along the bottom leading to little caves in the rock, outside which may be seen pieces of burnt wood and the dung of animals. Where the main gorge turns to the left, a short side gorge branches off to the right and up this our path turns. Here a great volume of water descends foaming by a narrow course lined with willows, planes, walnut trees, wild roses, and brambles. The road crosses it three times, the last crossing being just below the fount of Baikal.

This spring defies description, and with the Taj Mahal at Agra ranks as one of the two most splendid sights it has, up to the present, been the fortune of the writer to see. Within the narrow gorge enclosed by gaunt black cliffs and just below the V-shaped cleft by which the traveller again emerges into the outside air, there springs suddenly from a point in the rock some 50 ft. above a fountain of water foaming white, which spreads out fanwise and swells every moment with an increasing roar as it rushes down the steep slope, finally contracting at the bottom into a narrow voluminous stream which leaps noisily from boulder to boulder down its short gay course to the Rawanduz Chai.

Even in the middle of summer its waters will freeze the throat, while the fine spray which hangs about the spring like a mist renders the air delightfully cool. A small open space with a few walnut trees provides a resting place for the weary wayfarer.

It was with a feeling of relief that I climbed up through the cleft into the open. We now found ourselves entirely in a basin surrounded by hills, where presumably but for the exit through which we had just passed a lake would have been formed. Turning to the left past the ruined village of Baikal we began to ascend a ridge on the top of which we espied a party of armed men. They proved to be some of Hajji Nauras' gendarmes who had come to meet us. From here I had thought Rawanduz was certain to be visible, but it was not so. For two miles the road wound in and out along a hillside until we rounded a spur, and there it lay just in front of us. I was too interested in the sight to study a man who was tending a water channel at the side of the road, and hastily moved away as we came along. It was Nuri. Just outside the town I was met by Ismail Beg, with whom I had arranged to lodge, and was conducted to his house through a narrow street past rows of wild staring faces. Another chapter had started in the history of Rawanduz – how was it to end?

CHAPTER XIII

YUSUF BEG

SURROUNDED BY A CROWD of armed men I entered Ismail Beg's house, and climbing up some very narrow stairs was shown the two rooms he had set apart for me. One of them, which contained only a table and a chair and a few rugs on the floor, was to be my office; it was a bright and airy room with two windows looking out into the street, and a door leading on to a small verandah. The other, intended for my private use, was a small dingy room with an enormous stove in the centre and two very diminutive windows. The walls were hung all round with beautiful silk Persian rugs, and mattresses and cushions were spread out on the floor. Several articles of furniture were displayed for my edification, including a modern coffee-making apparatus, a chiming clock, and several massive silver mugs, curiosities collected by the late Suayid Beg. A third room was allotted to Saiyid Ali Effendi and visiting tribal chiefs. Saiyid Ali kept a constant watch on me while I was in Rawanduz, and two or three gendarmes usually dogged my footsteps.

Ismail Beg was a young man of nineteen or twenty, clothed in European costume with a red fez. He possessed good-looking, though as yet rather weak, features, and his build was slight and delicate. Gifted with an easy and refined manner, he was absolutely without conceit, and made a charming and attentive host. Conscientious and always striving to do the right thing, he was nevertheless too soft for the part he was called upon to play; and unsophisticated well-bred gentleman though he was, there lurked in his character a wild strain, probably due to fear, which impelled him to the most bloodthirsty acts. He was haunted by his father's murder, and imagining himself to be in perpetual danger of a similar assassination, strove to remove his enemies by every means in his power. His father had treated him in a most extraordinary fashion; whether afraid of the power he might eventually acquire, or ashamed of him as a weakling, he had kept him away from the outside world, not allowing him to appear in the guest-house or even teaching him to ride. He had not, however, stinted him in education, for he knew Turkish and Persian well, had read a good deal of history, and had even started to learn French. As a result of his father's folly he grew up a hot-house plant, too much under the influence of his mother, who fed his fears and suspicions, visiting his room frequently during the night to see that he had not fallen a victim to the assassin. Finally, he was as lavish as his father had been miserly, bestowing gifts freely on all his guests, and providing the most sumptuous meals I ever met in Kurdistan.

I arrived about noon and sat down in the office while lunch was being prepared. Suddenly I heard a commotion going on on the verandah outside and an old voice saying repeatedly to the gendarmes, 'Go and tell the hakim [i.e. Political Officer] ki az am – that it is I.' I guessed who it was, and was delighted to hear the 'az' or 'I', which is characteristic of the north instead of the 'min' of the south. After I had had my lunch I allowed him to come in, a little old man with a fierce grey beard sticking out in all directions, keen eyes and aquiline nose, wearing a shabby grey overcoat over the usual long gown, and a loosely tied cheap cotton head-dress. It was the father of Nuri, Bawil Agha, who for half an hour treated me to a tale of woe, complaining bitterly of the misfortunes which had befallen him and his son, and of the poverty to which he had been reduced. He boasted proudly that he was the oldest and most honourable of the notables of Rawanduz. What he really wanted was pardon for his beloved son, and I promised him that if Nuri made his 'dakhalat', i.e. surrendered himself to me, I would grant him easy terms. Bawil Agha is a tragic old man, and a Nemesis dogs him and his. It is curious how heavy is the hand of Fate in this wild mountain spot. The whole atmosphere is unreal and sinister, and it seems as though some malignant fiend were at work determined to preserve the ancient savagery of Rawanduz and to thwart all plans for her advancement and prosperity.

In the afternoon I received in turn all the leading notables and chiefs who happened to be in Rawanduz. First of all

came Shaikh Muhammad Agha, chief of the Balik, the two
words Shaikh Muhammad being a common name in Kurdistan, which implies no sanctity in its bearer. In many ways,
both in appearance and character, he much resembles,
though he does not equal, Babekr Agha of the Pizhder. He is
fifty years of age, of medium height, heavily built, with a
round face and slightly hooked nose. He stoops somewhat,
and has a deep, thick voice with a very deliberate manner of
speaking. He dresses in the ordinary costume of a hill Kurd,
usually in sober colours. A wise and extremely cautious man
he had become chief over the heads of two elder brothers,
who much resented and often resisted his authority. He was
my chief adviser during the six stormy days I now spent in
Rawanduz, and I acquired a great respect for his honesty and
simple kindly ways. He was the one chief who had supported
previous A.P.O.s in Rawanduz through all their difficulties.
On receipt of the news of the Sulaimaniyah rising, and before
it became public, Captain Beale and Captain Kirk had visited
him at his village, Walash, and tested him by speaking well
of Shaikh Mahmud and encouraging him to join in his praise.
He had not, however, fallen into the trap, and had given them
convincing proofs of his loyalty. He told me how his father,
who had lived to be 110, one day summoned his numerous
sons and gave them the following advice: 'There is', he said,
'always a Government, though sometimes it is weak and
sometimes it is strong. When it is strong, obedience counts
for nothing. When it is weak, that is the time to show your
loyalty.' On his advice Shaikh Muhammad acted. I talked
with him at great length, and asked his views on the local situation: he confirmed what I had heard several times, first
more than two months previously from Saleh Beg of Khoran,
that Yusuf Beg was at the root of all the trouble. If he could
be removed most of the difficulties would disappear.

After Shaikh Muhammad Agha had left there came in together Hajji Nauras Effendi and Karim Beg. Hajji Nauras I
have previously described. His grandfather, a Persian, had
been armourer to the Blind Pasha, as one or two old guns
about the town testified; he was therefore regarded by the
other notables as rather an outsider. He had maintained his
position for the last four months chiefly through the influence of Yusuf Beg, to whom he had a few years previously

ISMAIL BEG

MUHAMMAD ALI AGHA

unwillingly married his daughter. Yusuf Beg supported him as long as it served his ends, and kept him in a state of terror with his foul tongue. The disorders of November tried his nerves sorely, and he did not know which to fear most, Yusuf Beg or the Government. He talked much in his usual rapid and spasmodic style, explaining his absolute inability to cope with the situation and begging me to accept his resignation. I adopted a 'wait and see' attitude. Karim Beg, a dumpy figure in European clothing, need not detain us.

Next came Muhammad Ali Agha with his brother the Khalifa Rashid. The former is a well-built, middle-aged man, with a low forehead and a long vacant face. He wears the ordinary dress of a hill Kurd and is in character a simple old farmer, without much character or brains. He owns several villages and keeps about twenty armed retainers. His brother wears the long gown and white head-dress of a divine – Khalifa being a title given to a man who repents after a wild youth and takes to a religious life. He was a most inoffensive old man.

These were followed by the Qazi and the local divines, including Mulla Suayid Effendi, a simple, pious man with no worldly ambitions, who remaincd loyal to the Government, even in its darkest days.

Last of all was announced Yusuf Beg. The eldest of six brothers who owned a group of villages on the further side of the Rawanduz Chai, he had been appointed by Major Noel chief of the surrounding district, and had subsequently obtained very great influence in Rawanduz and the neighbourhood. He possessed a strong personality and a violent and persuasive tongue, with which he kept all men in a state of terror. The appointment of his father-in-law and tool, Hajji Nauras, as governor of the town had increased his power. His tyranny knew no bounds, and to strengthen his own position he devoted his energy to sowing dissension amongst the other chiefs and aghas. His morals were notorious, and he would often enter the houses of the poorer classes and tear a wife from her husband's arms. Though regarded with universal detestation none were bold enough to oppose him. With the Bira Kapra murders and the consequent fall in the Government's prestige, he had developed the idea of setting himself up as an independent ruler; he sent men to the assistance of the Barzanis and encouraged his brothers and the malcontents of the Balik to commit outrages which terrorised the district. A few days before my arrival he had formed a league with Karim Beg and Mir Muhammad Amin Beg of Dargala with the intention of deposing his father-in-law and setting himself up in his place. He proposed to collect land revenue from the surrounding country and Customs from all caravans, and had already made preparations to enlist a force whereby to maintain his authority. When he came to see me I knew little of the above, though I was aware of his power and his bad influence. He was a tall, finely built man with a long, hatchet-shaped face terminating in a very resolute chin. His features ugly in repose were made handsome by his winning smile. Long tassels from his head-dress dangled over his eyes, and he talked with a fascinating lisp about the Hukumat i Blitania or Blitish Government. Had I previously known nothing of him I should have been captivated by his personality. Our conversation was of a formal non-committal nature.

The following day I had an opportunity of exploring the town, or rather what is left of it. Rawanduz is situated on a narrow spit of land, which descends in three stages. Behind it is hilly country terminating in the ridge over which I had passed the previous day. It is enclosed on both sides by two vast ravines, each many hundred feet deep. That on the eastern side comes down from the Vale of Akoyan. By the upper town it is a wide chasm with sheer sides of smooth grey rock, but further down it dwindles away until, where the Persian road crosses it just above its junction with the Rawanduz Chai, it is possible for an agile man to leap across it. The other side of the spit is bounded by the gorge of the Rawanduz Chai, which here plunges into the heart of the mountains.

The surrounding scenery is magnificent in the extreme. To the north is the Vale of Akoyan, terminated by a group of snowy peaks, and bounded to the right by the Kurrek Dagh, which crops out on this side into a series of peaks like the teeth of an enormous saw, and on the left the great smooth mass of the Hindawain Dagh, which rises over 8,000 ft. and for many months is covered with snow. This mountain occupies most of the view to the east until the valley of the

Rawanduz Chai meets our gaze, presenting a long vista of
rugged peaks ending with the giant Argot nearly 11,000 ft. in
height. Beyond the Rawanduz Chai, but close at hand overlooking the town, is the peak of Zuzik, which reaches 8,000 ft.
The river here is little more than 1,500 ft. above sea level, so
that it may be realised how imposing these heights appear.
Northwards across the Chai is a line of low hills, the most
prominent of them being crowned with one of the Blind
Pasha's forts; behind them comes a little circular plain, the
Dasht i Dian, then line on line of rugged mountains fading
away into the distance. Westwards over the rising ground
may be seen the chasm-split Balikian Dagh and the saddle-
shaped summit of the Karch Dagh. Whether clad in winter's
white raiment or bathed in the sunshine of summer I know of
few more picturesque sites than Rawanduz.

Ismail Beg's house was in the only surviving part of the
town — the upper or residential quarter. Here along either
side of the cobbled street were grouped a number of houses
large and small, all badly in need of repair, with a few shops
and occasional intervening gardens. Other houses are built
away from the street on the hill slopes among the fruit trees.
Descending we passed the telegraph office and a few coffee-
shops, one of them kept by a swarthy man in a blue coat,
with a pronounced cast in his eye and the most villainous
face I have ever seen, known as Mustafa Rewi or Mustafa the
Fox, and came to an open green space bounded on its further
side by a 500 ft. drop into a ravine. Here was the proposed
site of a bazaar, planned by a previous A.P.O., the trenches
for the foundations being already dug, while on our left lay a
large new house built by Hajji Nauras out of his perquisites
as Mudir of Customs. Descending again steeply for nearly
half a mile by a cobbled road down a rocky slope we came to
the lower town, packed closely together at the very end of the
spit of land, with the remains of houses perched up 200 ft.
sheer over the river. All was now a heap of ruins, a few walls
here and there more solid than the rest attesting the former
presence of splendid mosques and bazaars. Away to the right,
just near the river bank and across the small bridge over the
ravine by which the Persian road enters the town, was the
residence of Muhammad Ali Agha, spared because found useful by the Russians as a kitchen, with a few habitations

round it recently erected for his retainers. But for these there was not a single house standing. Such was the handiwork of the Russians and the Christians who followed them. At the extremity of the spit is a narrow gateway giving access to a wooden bridge some 20 ft. long, 100 ft. below which, between sheer cliffs, flow the narrowed waters of the Rawanduz Chai. Beyond a cobbled ascent leads to the road which passes across the Dasht i Dian to the home of the Diwana or Mad tribes.

I spent much of this day in interviewing the local gentry and receiving petitions which were mostly applications for Government appointments from seedy ex-Turkish officials, or demands for redress from merchants whose property had been looted on the Persian road or elsewhere. My only new visitor was Mir Muhammad Amin Beg of Dargala, a most picturesque brigand. Short in stature, with swarthy, deeply lined features and a short black beard, the most noticeable thing about him was his large head-dress bound round with a beautiful gold and black silk handkerchief, the fringes of which hung down over his forehead. He wore the wide bell-mouthed striped trousers that are typical of the Rawanduzi, and was covered with bandoliers of ammunition. He is not a bad man and is much less fierce than he looks.

I held long conversations with Shaikh Muhammad Agha, and spent several hours in anxious thought. Hajji Nauras had resigned, and I was very much averse to re-appointing him. It was certain none of the other local aghas would accept his office if Yusuf Beg was allowed to pursue his career unchecked. It was therefore necessary to concede everything to Yusuf Beg, despite his known villainies, and offer him the post of governor or else get rid of him.

Having only fifty gendarmes with me, and knowing so little of the local situation and the attitudes the various aghas would adopt in the event of trouble, I was inclined to the former course. Fate, however, stepped in and settled the matter for me the following day in the most dramatic fashion.

In the afternoon I paid a call on Hajji Nauras, who showed me into a long, finely appointed guest-room and served me with tea in a glass with a silver stand. Yusuf Beg was present, and announced his intention of returning to his village that evening. I asked him to stay another day, hinting that it might be to his advantage to do so.

That evening I had my first interview with another stormy character, fated to bring disaster on his house, his town, and very nearly on me. Tired out with endless arguments in Kurdish in a small overheated room I strolled out with Saiyid Ali Effendi, my Arab officer, and climbed a small gravestone-covered hill above the town. Two trees stood on its summit, beneath which we halted, admiring the magnificent scenery and enjoying the fresh air. Presently I saw approaching Bawil Agha with a young man by his side and two armed retainers following close behind. I knew the young man must be Nuri, so I adopted a Napoleonic attitude and awaited him. In due course he arrived and stood before me, half shamefaced, half defiant, while Bawil Agha grunted out a string of remarks, asking me to forgive him and treat him well. This was a strange surrender. Here was Nuri fully armed with a revolver and dagger, and two men with rifles standing just behind him, while I had nothing except a small pistol in my pocket, and there were no gendarmes at hand. He was certainly a striking figure — tall and very slight, but wiry, with the most piercing black eyes, somewhat fanatical, set in a long, sallow face. His features were wonderfully regular and refined by much suffering; he bore the look of a leader of lost causes. 'What sort of a dakhalat is this?' I said to him, pointing to his arms and attendants, and told him to go away and come to me the following morning and make a proper submission, promising him easy terms if he did so. With scarcely a word he saluted and went, Bawil Agha muttering the while.

The next day, December 12th, was a memorable one. I spent the morning in my room transacting business and interviewing anyone who wished to see me. About noon I was passing through the small verandah that overlooked the street when I heard a sort of 'hooroosh' going through the town, men running in all directions, confused shouting, the bolting of doors and the shutting up of shops. It was a sound, or rather an atmosphere, that none who have not been in a wild Eastern town when some sudden disturbance breaks out can appreciate. My gendarmes swiftly collected and loaded their rifles, and everyone in the house stood still, tense, and alert.

No shots were fired, the noise ceased as suddenly as it had begun, and the people resumed their normal occupations. I immediately sent out to inquire what had been the cause of the panic. While I was at Batas Abdulla Pasha mentioned that Yusuf Beg had driven off a flock of sheep belonging to one of his tenants, Khurshid Beg, the headman of the village of Bapishtian, and that he had given the latter a note addressed to his aggressor asking him to return the animals. It transpired that Khurshid Beg had just then met Yusuf Beg outside Hajji Nauras' house, and handed to him the letter claiming the animals. Yusuf Beg had immediately accused the poor man of maligning him to the Pasha, and showering a torrent of abuse on him had called out to his retainers, who fell upon the unfortunate Khurshid Beg and his followers with the butts of their rifles. A struggle ensued, and just as the parties were turning their rifles round to open fire, Hajji Nauras had rushed out of his house in his usual state of nervous excitement and implored them both to desist. They then separated and went their ways.

I was perfectly furious at the news, and saw in it a deliberate attempt of Yusuf Beg to flout my authority and endeavour to terrify me into leaving the town. I sent messengers to both parties requesting them to come before me immediately in order that I might hear both sides of the case and settle their differences. I summoned Ismail Beg, Shaikh Muhammad Agha, and Hajji Nauras to my office to assist me in the arbitration, and told Saiyid Ali to stand in the doorway and keep a party of gendarmes in readiness outside, instructing him to disarm all who entered the room. Presently the two adversaries arrived. I heard Yusuf Beg arguing at the door, but, nevertheless, he surrendered his revolver and dagger. I made him sit on my left by the window while Khurshid Beg took up his position at the end of the opposite side of the room, near the door. Yusuf Beg tried to address me, but I turned to the other, and told him that as he was plaintiff I would hear his story first. He began to speak, but every minute Yusuf Beg interrupted with denials of his statements. I asked him several times to wait his turn; but finally, as he would not desist, I suddenly swung round to him and commanded him roundly to hold his tongue. He then asked permission to leave the room. I abruptly ordered him to stay, on which he got up and started to move towards the door. I signalled to Saiyid Ali, who was upon him like lightning. A struggle ensued, for Yusuf Beg had the strength of a lion. Saiyid Ali, however, excelled himself, and with a mighty effort pushed him down against the wall beside the window. Yusuf Beg then suddenly turned his head and looking out to the street below shouted to his men, 'Come and kill the infidel.' Saiyid Ali was on him again, pushing him away from the window, dancing round him in a fury and swearing at him like a cat, enumerating in rapid succession his various crimes: 'Was it not you who attacked the caravan at Baikali? Was it not you who — ?' until I stopped him. Meanwhile five or six gendarmes with fixed bayonets were in the room, and Yusuf Beg gave up the struggle, lying limp and sullen against the wall. I now left my chair, and looking out of the window saw twenty or thirty gendarmes with their rifles ready collected in the street, while just in front of them were figures flitting in and out behind the walls and hedges. So close were the opposing parties that one gendarme actually seized the muzzle of his adversary's rifle. Not a shot was fired. Fortunately Yusuf Beg only had about eight retainers with him. Hajji Nauras' men were afraid to join them, their master being in the room with me, so after a minute or two they ran away to carry the news to their villages and raise their tribe.

Meanwhile I paced anxiously up and down the room considering what would be the upshot of the business. One thing was clear, that any attempt to leave the town would be disastrous. Hajji Nauras, who hitherto had been in a state of muttering terror, suddenly flung himself before me and clung to my knees, begging me to release his son-in-law, who, he promised, would give no further trouble. The others present added their voice to his, more as a matter of form than from any sympathy with the tyrant. I finally ordered Saiyid Ali to bind Yusuf Beg and lock him up in another room, setting a strong guard over him. After much thought I decided that that night I would despatch him to Major Middleton, who was now with a company of infantry at Kani Wutman, with a request that he would forward him on the first opportunity to Arbil.

Meanwhile all the aghas of Rawanduz came to me with the offers of their services in the event of an attack by Yusuf

Beg's tribe. They were dangerous friends, but I kept with me
Muhammad Ali Agha and Mir Muhammad Amin Beg. We
passed the afternoon in a state of terrible suspense; but in
the event of an attack I knew I had one trump card, namely,
Yusuf Beg, and I let it be known that I would have him killed
as soon as the first shot was fired.

In the evening all the notables in Rawanduz came in turn
and implored me earnestly to release the man. This is a
curious custom. A man will come and plead for his bitterest
enemy if he is in the hands of the Government, which, as I
have before mentioned, is regarded as a sort of inhuman
monster into whose clutches no Kurd should allow his fellow
Kurd to fall. In the present instance the petitioners were par-
tially actuated by the fear that I would eventually release my
prisoner, and that he would then oppress more than before
any who had not supported him in his extremity. I remained
obdurate. Finally, after the evening meal, a deputation of all
the notables waited on me begging me to release the man,
and asking me if I did not release him what I proposed doing
with him. To avoid arousing their suspicions I talked glibly of
a fine of so many rifles, and a deposit of money, asking them
to wait till the morning, by which time I should have made
up my mind as to the amount to be demanded. They then
asked that Yusuf Beg should be allowed to speak to me. At
first I refused, but they became so importunate that I sent
for him. He was dragged in bound and guarded. Grovelling
before me with a sickly smile on his face he proceeded to lisp
forth vows of eternal devotion to the 'Blitish Government', all
his vehement spirit wilted away with terror. He was now a
ghastly sight. I replied, accepting his protestation with gratitude, and saying that I had the nature and extent of his
punishment under consideration, while the bystanders reassured him with the hope that he would be a free man the
next day. He was taken away and I did not see his face again.
When my visitors had left I sent for Saiyid Ali and arranged
for the escort to leave with the prisoner at midnight.

That night I retired early but could not sleep. Shortly
before twelve I heard from a room close at hand a series of
terrible shrieks, intermingled with prayers to the Almighty
and calls for assistance to Shaikh Muhammad Agha, Ismail
Beg, and others. The 'hawar', or tribal call for help, is used in

cases of extreme need by one Kurd to another. Normally it must be obeyed, but now no response came to Yusuf Beg's agonised yell. The noise went on for from five to ten minutes, and was succeeded by many tramplings in the courtyard below. I descended and found Saiyid Ali, who informed me that it had taken five strong men to gag and carry down the prisoner, and that he had bitten two or three of them on the hand in the process. He had refused to sit on a pony and had thrown himself off each time the attempt had been made to seat him; finally it had been necessary to bind him to his mount. Saiyid Ali pointed through the doorway, and in the darkness I could dimly descry a huddled mass on one of the ponies outside.

I passed a restless night, but at length fell asleep. At 7 a.m, I was suddenly awakened to see Saiyid Ali standing beside me with a pale and anxious face. 'What!' I cried, 'has he escaped?' 'No,' replied Saiyid Ali; 'he is dead.' Much alarmed by the news I enjoined the utmost secrecy. Yusuf Beg alive was a hostage of considerable value in my hands; whereas his death was likely to rouse his tribe to immediate revenge.

The exact nature of his end remains a mystery. Saiyid Ali related that about a mile from Rawanduz the gendarmes noticed that his body ceased to heave; and on examining him found him dead with blood flowing from his mouth. He attributed his decease to suffocation, as owing to his violence it had been necessary to gag him very tightly. He had struggled like a wild animal while being bound to the pony and during the first few minutes of the journey, and completely exhausted had been unable to inhale sufficient breath to revive himself.

His escort, which was twelve strong, was under the command of a certain Rasul Chaush, a Kurd of Sulaimaniyah possessing an unusual amount of common sense. On discovering the death of his prisoner he proceeded on his journey as if nothing had happened. While in the gorge, perceiving a party of men approaching, which proved to be Jamil Agha of the Girdi and his followers, whom I had summoned, he managed to conceal his whole cavalcade so that no awkward questions should be asked. Arriving at Kani Wutman before dawn he insisted on the sepoys waking Major Middleton and handing him a note in which I had written briefly, 'Herewith Yusuf

Beg. He is a very dangerous man, his escape would have disastrous consequences. Please have him carefully guarded and
forward him to Arbil on the first opportunity.'

Major Middleton immediately got up, and received a great
shock when he found the prisoner a corpse. He told me afterwards that he had never seen anything more hideous than
Yusuf Beg's face in death. He wished to send the body down
to Batas; but Rasul Chaush managed to convey to him that
the greatest secrecy was essential, and insisted that the body
should be burned immediately. Some sepoys were despatched
for spades, and Yusuf Beg was there and then interred while
it was still quite dark, only Major Middleton, a few sepoys,
and the escort being aware of what had taken place.

The news did not leak out till I chose to announce it more
than forty-eight hours later, though the mystery of Yusuf
Beg's whereabouts, and the fact that nobody had seen him on
the road and the inhabitants of Kani Wutman had sent word
that he was not with the military, soon caused people to suspect the truth.

I confided only in Shaikh Muhammad Agha, who was at
first alarmed, but subsequently agreed that nothing better
could have happened, saying that Yusuf Beg's death would
have an effect equivalent to the despatch of two divisions of
troops to Rawanduz. When I assured him that it was entirely
against my will that he had perished, he smiled as if to say,
'We know all about that', and replied, 'Of course.' The deputation who the previous night had begged for his release, knowing only that he had been deported, now waited on me and
thanked me 'for ridding Islam of this infidel'. My men informed me that all the townspeople were delighted, and that
the day was being celebrated as an 'Id or festival in Rawanduz.

I passed a day or two in a state of considerable suspense,
but Yusuf Beg's tribe remained in their villages. His brothers
began to collect a force, but desisted on receipt of a message
from Hajji Nauras that Yusuf Beg was in safety and would
probably be released, while any attempt on their part to interfere would only make matters worse. Those who were of
any importance were three in number, Rashid Beg, Bekr Beg,
and Begok (or the little Beg). Bekr was only Yusuf Beg's half-
brother, and had been the subject of much persecution at his

hands. He is a weak, honest man. The other two are his full brothers, the former of them being also weak and characterless; Begok, however, I never saw, for he was a hot-blooded young man and lived only to revenge his brother's death.

On the morning of the 13th, Jamil Agha arrived with some fifteen men. He immediately asked me why I had not told him to bring 200, and afterwards boasted how his arrival had saved me and the situation. He was an old friend of Bawil Agha's, and soon began petitioning me to accept Nuri's submission; under existing circumstances the fewer enemies I had the better; I therefore agreed to forgive Nuri on the receipt of a small money deposit. He came in to me on the 14th, this time unarmed, and I held a long conversation with him. He asked to be reinstated in Rawanduz as a gendarme officer; I offered him a similar post in Arbil but, after what had happened, could scarcely reappoint him in Rawanduz.

During my last three days in Rawanduz I made many efforts to recover the property of the unfortunate men whose caravans had been looted in November. The principal offenders were the men of Mirga, a hotbed of thieves which the Turks had often endeavoured to destroy. This village lies just below Shaikh Muhammad Agha's residence in the Balik country, and its inhabitants, some fifty families in number, are nearly all his relations. Being of 'chiefly' descent they consider it beneath their dignity to cultivate the soil; they have, therefore, only two means of livelihood, sponging on Shaikh Muhammad Agha, who often pays them most of his salary to keep them quiet, and looting or taking toll from the caravans that pass along the Persian road. Having no means of punishing them, at Shaikh Muhammad Agha's suggestion, I sent out to them Khalifa Rashid, who was universally recognised as a man of peace, to negotiate with them. Terrified by the news of Yusuf Beg's arrest they promised to restore all the looted property they could collect on condition of their pardon; they gave back, however, but little of the plunder, most of which they had already consumed.

On the evening of the 13th arrived the chiefs of the Shirwan and Baradost, accompanied by a following of some fifty of the wildest Kurds imaginable, grim, weather-beaten hirsute savages. The Shirwan aghas were three in number, the paramount chief being a fine white-bearded old man with a limp, called Ahmad Agha. He had a kindly smile and a thick rough voice very difficult to understand. Simple in his ways he was an honest man; his words carried conviction and his subsequent actions proved his fidelity.

Muhammad Suayid Beg, chief of the Baradost, is a little wrinkled weak old man with a whiny voice. I immediately nicknamed him 'the old woman', of which he unfortunately came to hear and vowed revenge, saying he would soon prove to me that he was a man and no woman. However, he never carried out this threat. He has very little influence with his tribe, who were nearly exterminated by the Russians, and have no reputation for martial ardour.

On the night of their arrival these chiefs all dined with me, Ismail Beg producing an enormous spread. Simple old Ahmad Agha stumped in on his stick and took a low place, from which he was with difficulty persuaded to come up higher. After the meal I discussed the situation, and discovered that they had come in with two main ideas, firstly, to be on the right side in case the Government took any further punitive action; and secondly, to obtain a renewal of their salaries, which had been cancelled on the evacuation of Rawanduz in August. Ahmad Agha promised, and I think sincerely, to do his best to apprehend the murderers, but owned that he was too weak to do anything without the assistance of Government forces. Muhammad Suayid Beg, who was frightened and distressed at the imprisonment of his relative, Yusuf Beg, cried ditto throughout with a feeble voice.

During the 14th and 15th my mind was much exercised in making arrangements for the future government of the district. Yusuf Beg was gone, and Hajji Nauras without him would be worse than useless. I talked with Shaikh Muhammad Agha at length on the subject, offering him the post of governor, which, as I expected, he refused. Being a tribesman he loathed and despised the town and its ways, and was naturally averse to living among and endeavouring to control such an intriguing and blood-thirsty crew as the aghas of Rawanduz. He discussed the whole situation with me, insisting that it was essential for a British officer with a considerable armed force to reside in Rawanduz if any attempt was to be made to control the district. He inveighed against

THE ONLY ROAD TO RAWANDUZ FROM THE NORTH

the appointment of Kurdish princelings like Shaikh Mahmud, and kept on stigmatising the race to which he himself
belonged, saying again and again, 'The Kurd is a savage, and
believes only what he sees.'

Eventually, as a temporary expedient, he suggested that I
should ask Ismail Beg to accept the post of Government representative. To my objections that he was too young and too
unseasoned to control such a turbulent district, he replied
that we could only hope that office would make him into a
'Piao' or man. Owing to his father's memory all the tribes
wished him well; and he was not yet engulfed in the intrigues
and quarrels of the Rawanduz aghas, and on the score of his
wealth and liberality was well suited to the position. Early
on the 15th I asked him if he would undertake the responsibility, and he consented.

On the afternoon of the 15th I summoned all the notables
to a conference at which the Shirwan and Baradost chiefs
were also present. Having announced the news of Yusuf Beg's
death, which was acclaimed with some fervour, I expressed
regret at Hajji Nauras' resignation of his office, and stated
that I had chosen as his successor Ismail Beg, who, I knew,
had given offence to none, and whom all loved and respected
on account of his late father's memory. Those present unani-
mously approved my choice, and Shaikh Muhammad Agha
and Ahmad Agha made speeches calling upon all to stand by
Ismail Beg and join in an endeavour to retrieve the ruined
state of Rawanduz instead of making it worse by private
jealousies and feuds. A Quran was then fetched, and all
without equivocation swore on it an oath of allegiance to
Ismail Beg, except Bawil Agha, who added a condition to his
oath, swearing, 'I will play fair by Ismail Beg, as long as he
plays fair by me.'

Early on the 16th, having left with the new governor instructions for the collection of revenue and other necessary
matters, and having appointed a clerk with previous Government experience to assist him, I took my departure for Arbil,
being accompanied to the top of the ridge by all the notables
of the town and the tribal chiefs who had assembled there.
Entrusting Ismail Beg and the peace of the district to their
care and promising to revisit them in two months' time, I
bade them farewell, and was soon retracing my steps down

the gorge, enumerating the while all the events of the past few days, and feeling a certain satisfaction in the way they had concluded. At Batas I found the old Pasha awaiting me at the door of his house quivering and smiling with pleasure. 'Of course,' he said, grinning with delight, 'Yusuf Beg is my relation, but there has never been much affection between the two branches of the family.' I reached Arbil on December 18th, glad to be once again amongst friends in a civilised place.

CHAPTER XIV

THREE QUIET MONTHS

ON MY RETURN TO Arbil I found that Captain Bradshaw had moved into our new house which had just been completed, having been designed and started by Major Murray. It was situated a little over half a mile from the town on the crest of an undulation, and was surrounded by open cultivated ground. The windows on the north-east gave a fine view of the Safin Dagh. Its chief defects were its exposed position and the fact that all the windows looked outwards, instead of inwards into a courtyard, as is the custom in Oriental houses. We were therefore compelled to keep sentries patrolling round it all night.

We spent a most cheerful Christmas Day, the notables of the town fully entering into the spirit of the festival. At 9 a.m. a deputation from the Christian village of Ainkawa was announced. A party of about a dozen priests and elders was shown in and half an hour passed in greetings and conversation. After breakfast the Rais Baladiyah called accompanied by twenty or thirty of my local staff. We entertained the British non-gazetted officials to lunch, and afterwards adjourned to the aerodrome to attend the sports which were organised by Lieut.-Colonel B. M. Carroll and the officers of the 87th Punjabis. Some of the gendarmes and police participated, while all the notables and most of the population came out to watch. On the conclusion of the sports the notables and chiefs visited our new house, and after partaking of tea and coffee were allowed to look over the building. The Mess of the 87th Punjabis very kindly entertained Captain Bradshaw and myself to dinner, when we were regaled with the usual Christmas fare. On Boxing Day a game of polo was played, after which Mushir Agha, the son of Ibrahim Agha, and some of his men were handed the sticks. They managed to knock the ball about quite successfully, and I feel sure the

Kurds would take to polo if taught how to play. During the last week of the year I asked all the notables to lunch in turn, while they returned the compliment by inviting me to their houses.

Early in January I paid my first visit to Shaikh Mustafa Effendi, who lives in the Khaniqa, a sort of combined mosque and hermitage, at the eastern extremity of the town. With a pale face, square black beard, and deep-set abstracted eyes, he is one of the gentlest and most pious of men I have ever met. His features bear traces of his asceticism and long hours spent in prayer, and he is one of the only two men I know whom I could call living saints. Though lower in rank than Mulla Effendi, owing to his complete abstraction from everything worldly, he owns an almost greater reputation for sanctity. He became a great friend of mine, and having a natural aversion to attending the ordinary meetings of notables, would often visit me privately in my house.

On January 7th Captain Littledale returned to Arbil, having the previous day ascended in an aeroplane and bombed Bajil in the Aqra district, the village of Shaikh Obaidullah of the Surchi. From this time onwards the Surchi were continually in revolt against the Government; they were a festering sore which would not heal, and eventually spread to and infected the Arbil Division. The A.P.O. Aqra had sent for Shaikh Obaidullah to appear at the district headquarters, as his attitude of late had been unsatisfactory, and it was known that the Zibari chief Faris Agha, one of the murderers of Mr. Bill and Captain Scott, had recently visited him. He refused to obey the summons, and, all efforts to bring him in proving fruitless, aeroplane action was demanded. Accordingly, on January 6th, a machine was despatched with Captain Littledale as observer, and Bajil was bombed and machine-gunned; Shaikh Obaidullah himself was wounded, while a chief of the Khailani named Aziz i Hudi, who was visiting him, was killed with two of his relations. The Surchi mobilised their men and adopted a threatening attitude, while the Zibari came over the hills to assist them. I very much feared that the trouble would spread south of the river, for there were tales of an intended attack on Batas. By January 12th the news from the Aqra district had become so alarming that I proposed collecting a tribal force from the

Dizai and Khushnao, and attacking the Surchi shaikhs; but a few days later the situation quieted down and I abandoned the idea of immediate action.

Fortunately, when the Surchi trouble was at its height the Harki and Zarari chiefs were present in Arbil, and I did not allow them to depart until the situation had assumed a less threatening aspect. The Harki were now encamped in strength in the neighbourhood of Dera. Their paramount chief, Tahir Agha, a man with a great reputation for truthfulness and honesty, promised me the assistance of the tribe whenever I needed it, while Ahmad Khan, a picturesque villain, formerly the friend of Yusuf Beg, and his instrument in the attempt to intimidate Captain Beale and Captain Kirk in the spring, swore oaths of eternal fidelity and devotion. I did not trust this man an inch, cheery scoundrel that he was, but fortunately his influence in the tribe was limited, and I never had anything to fear from him. He was followed about everywhere by an extraordinary flat-chested creature known as Sharif Zhin, Sharif the Woman. Lanky and wiry she dressed always in a man's clothes, and carried a rifle and ammunition; in physical strength she was supposed to be a match for any individual of the opposite sex. Similar Amazons are said to be found elsewhere in Kurdistan, but she was the only one I ever met. The behaviour of the Harki was exemplary throughout their stay in my area; they paid their taxes in full and made large profits by supplying transport to the military authorities.

Ahmad Beg Zarari, with his long, ugly face and shifty eyes, is certainly not prepossessing, and is as cunning as Satan. Being chief only of a small tribe within easy reach of Arbil he kept on good terms with me, and on one or two occasions undertook negotiations with the Surchi shaikhs, to whom he was related by marriage.

On January 11th, Ismail Beg and Shaikh Muhammad Agha arrived on a visit from Rawanduz. I found that all had been quiet since I left, though Hajji Nauras and Yusuf Beg's brothers were supposed to be corresponding with the Surchi.

I now had collected in Arbil nearly all the important chiefs of the Division, and my time was fully taken up with interviewing and entertaining them. I was much bent on raising a tribal force to punish the Surchi and the murderers of Mr. Bill and Captain Scott, and for some weeks kept this object in view. All the chiefs promised me their assistance, but hesitated when it came to action, and I found eventually that no reliance could be placed in tribes unless they were accompanied by a regular military force.

On January 18th I paid a visit to Mosul to consult with the Political Officer, Lieut.-Colonel L. F. Nalder, C.I.E., about the tribal situation. Plans were made for columns of gendarmes and tribesmen from Aqra and Arbil to invade the Surchi country, and a few days later a force from the former place succeeded in burning the village of Shaikh Raqib, who had murdered some gendarmes during the trouble in November. Rain and the rising of the Zab prevented action from Arbil.

About this time I submitted proposals to Baghdad for the formation in the Arbil Division of a regular striking force in addition to the gendarmes, who were meant for police duties only. It was my object to raise a body at least 200 strong for the purpose of garrisoning Rawanduz and undertaking any operations amongst the tribes that might be necessary. In due course the proposals were sanctioned, and to Captain Littledale was entrusted the task of raising the new Arbil Levies. He worked hard and recruits were readily forthcoming; the staff available for training them was, however, exceedingly small, and there were many delays in obtaining equipment.

February was a bitterly cold month. The first snow came on the 5th, there was more on the 8th, and a very heavy fall in the night of the 10th. The following morning it lay 3 ins. deep all over the face of the country. Further heavy falls occurred until the afternoon of the 13th, when a violent wind set in and it began to thaw. This weather arrived just at a time when I had been contemplating tribal operations, which, of course, it rendered impossible. All I could hope to undertake was a three or four days' raid without tents or other impedimenta, and fine dry weather was essential for such an expedition. In March, with the melting of the snows, all the rivers would rise and become impassable. I therefore had to postpone all thought of interfering with the Aqra Surchi till the late summer. Incidentally the same conditions prevented

the Surchi from interfering seriously with me until the same
season.

Early in February I visited the village of Luhaiba in
Kandinawah, and met for the first time Khurshid Agha, the
eldest brother of Ibrahim Agha. To a certain extent he resembled Ibrahim Agha in appearance; he was of the same
height and possessed an even more charming smile, but his
whole frame was much more spare and wiry, and his face
longer and thinner. He wore a grizzled beard of medium
length which he refused to dye, and he was in every sense a
much rougher man than his brother. Ibrahim Agha was the
statesman, Khurshid the warrior. He had always led the
forces of the Baiz faction in the field, and was noted for his
stubbornness and his uncompromising attitude towards his
enemies. He was a strong dour man given to violence; where
Ibrahim Agha relied on diplomacy, he would cry, 'Burn,
plunder, kill.' He was devotedly attached to his brother, and
the two taken together were admirably suited for controlling
the tribe's destinies. Khurshid Agha lacked brains and reasoning power; when he once conceived an idea he stuck to it
right or wrong; and his hatred of his family's enemies,
Ahmad Pasha and Hajji Pir Daud Agha, was undying. He
was dour and laconic, and at my first meeting I thought he
compared unfavourably with his more polished brother. He
was at the time, however, suffering from ill-health, which he
ascribed to the cigarettes he could not refrain from smoking;
and I later found that he possessed a heart of gold. Of his five
sons the eldest Ali Agha, known usually as Alu, was about
thirty years of age. A noted brigand in Turkish times he had
now sobered down somewhat, though still hot-blooded and inclined to be wild; in physique and intellect I always thought
him the finest of the younger Dizai aghas.

From Luhaiba I proceeded to Makhmur, where I spent the
night with Ibrahim Agha, to whom a son, his seventeenth,
had just been born. His only other surviving son, Mushir
Agha, was present. He stood before us a gay cavalier in rid-
ing-boots and enormous breeches, with a brilliantly coloured
coat and the tassels of his silk head-dress dangling over his
forehead. About twenty years of age he was 6 ft. tall, and
possessed a short, scraggy beard and high-pitched voice. He
was a wild young man noted for his extravagance, and was

now on one of his frequent visits to his father to beg for money; for he had recently been set in a separate establishment some distance from Makhmur.

On the night of February 23rd–24th occurred an event of rather an alarming nature. We did not retire to bed till nearly midnight. At about 12.30 a.m., just as I was dozing off to sleep, I was suddenly aroused by a shot. As is usual with me when I am in a half-asleep state and am disturbed by something, I gave vent to a succession of yells. When fully awake I thought that some sentry had probably let off his rifle by mistake, and would have settled down to sleep again had I not heard Captain Littledale's voice shouting and more shots. I seized my pistol and rushed out. The first person I encountered was the gendarme sentry. To my hurried inquiries he replied that as far as he knew nothing was the matter, only the Alai Commandant (i.e. O.C. Gendarmes) had apparently seen something and gone rushing after it into the blue. Hardly had he finished speaking when Captain Littledale rushed up in his pyjamas with a large revolver in his hand. It appeared that he had been without a light in the lavatory, which was in the same wing as my room. Hearing the shot and my yells he had looked out of the window and seen two Kurds just by my window, one with a pistol pointed into the room. He hurled himself through the lavatory window towards the men, who fled; he just succeeded in getting hold of one of them, but could not maintain a sufficient grip, so that he escaped. Shouting to the sentry he started in pursuit, but the night was too dark for him to see in which direction they had run. The sentry, who had either been asleep or was purposely looking in another direction on the opposite side of the house, ran up, fired a few shots at random into the air and continued his rounds until he met me. Having sent a message to Saiyid Ali to scour the country I returned with Littledale to my room to see what damage had been done. All the household was now roused and had collected. My windows were closed and the glass unbroken, and we were much mystified until Bradshaw pointed to a photo of one of my relatives on a table on the opposite side of the room. There was a hole through it; behind it we found a dent in the wall, and on the floor below a little leaden bullet, which must have been fired from some very old-fashioned and inferior type of pistol. Examining the window we discovered a natural fault in the wooden frame between the panes. It was blackened round the edges. Apparently my unknown assailant had aimed at my feet (being unable to see which way I was lying), but the shape of the fault in the wood had prevented him from firing straight, and the bullet had travelled horizontally across the room, passing through the photograph and striking the wall on the opposite side.

In the morning I acquainted Ahmad Effendi with the above events, and he became much agitated, sending for an expert tracker and sparing no efforts to discover the identity of the assailants. Owing to rain which fell in the morning the tracker met with little success, proving only that the attacking party numbered three, one mounted on a pony, one on a mule, and one on foot, and that they came from the northeastern corner of the district. My suspicion rested on various people in turn, but from the primitive nature of the weapon used and the crude methods adopted I am inclined to think that a certain Hamada Shin, whom I had released from prison the previous day, was responsible. He had been brought before me some six weeks previously at Batas charged with stabbing an old woman. A tall, spare, wild-looking man with blue-grey hair and beard, he had been a noted brigand in Turkish times. When told of the complaints against him, he ranted and raved, seizing his head-dress from his head and throwing it on the ground, and generally adopted such a truculent attitude, that I was compelled to send him to Arbil and imprison him. A few days after the attempt on my life he openly defied the authority of the Mudir at Dera and on an attempt being made to arrest him again fled across the Zab and joined the Surchi.

On February 26th I set out on my second visit to Rawanduz, accompanied by Captain Littledale, Captain F. G. C. Dickinson, who had recently arrived to assist me at Arbil, and another officer. We experienced a certain amount of difficulty with snowdrifts in the Gorge, otherwise our journey was without incident. In Rawanduz the snow was only an inch or two deep, and had thawed in places, but the surrounding mountains were thickly covered and presented a magnificent scene. Ismail Beg met us on the ridge and entertained us with his usual hospitality. I found the place very quiet and there was little business to detain me.

In the afternoon of the 29th we rode out with Ismail Beg, Muhammad Ali Agha, and their followers across the Dasht i Dian or Christians' Plain to the village of Balikian. The plain, which measures some 6 miles by 4, is surrounded by an amphitheatre of vast mountains: it contains the site of the aerodrome, where we found a portion of an aeroplane engine, all that was left of the machine which crashed here the previous September. Balikian, which is inhabited by sixty or seventy families of a semi-nomadic tribe of the same name, is situated at the foot of a precipitous range of hills on the bank of a considerable stream, in which stand the piers of a bridge built by Muhammad Pasha and fallen to ruins some years since. A few miles below the stream enters the mountains and joins the Rawanduz Chai within the Gorge. The two headmen of the village, both possessing the name of Sulaiman Agha, had been the first to come into Rawanduz and offer their assistance after the death of Yusuf Beg; they were simple folk and their men belonged to the wildest and most savage type of Kurd, short, sturdy fellows with bell-mouthed trousers, thick, well-worn coats, and tasselled caps. After partaking of tea, bread, and mast, we returned by a slightly different route, passing Bapishtian, where dwelt the Khurshid Beg, who had been Yusuf Beg's adversary on the occasion of my previous visit. Just outside the village is a grove of oak trees with curious stunted branches; the offshoots of these are cut every year and stored as fodder for the sheep and goats when the country is snow-bound. From a hill close by we obtained a magnificent view of Rawanduz and the ravines which enclose it.

That evening Ismail Beg entertained all the notables to dinner, and I made the usual speech to them. After the meal Fatima Khanum arrived and asked for an interview. Her husband had died just before the British occupation and left her the owner of considerable property situated in the villages of Akoyan and Faqian, at a distance of some two or three hours from Rawanduz. Major Noel had made her chieftainess of the valley to which the villages belonged; some of her male subjects, however, considered it an indignity to be placed under feminine authority, and so much trouble ensued that a subsequent A.P.O. found it necessary to depose her. Latterly difficulties had arisen over the question of her daughter. Fatima Khanum held somewhat advanced ideas of women's rights; she herself had started her career by making a runaway match, and in the previous autumn she had betrothed her daughter to Shaikh Mazo of the Surchi, much against the will of her brother Taqi ud Din Beg, who considered that he as a man had the sole right of disposing of the girl's hand. He started to use violence and it became necessary to imprison him for a period. Shaikh Mazo was just preparing to carry off the bride thus secured to him by Government intervention, when his uncle Shaikh Obaidullah was bombed and the whole family came out in revolt against the authorities. It was now necessary to tell the lady's mother that the match must be postponed till a more suitable opportunity, and to warn her that I had heard that she had sent a present of ammunition to her beloved Mazo. She came to see me in the usual blue dress worn by Kurdish women, with a capacious hood covering her head and drawn across her features, allowing me only an occasional glimpse of a very large and ugly mouth. She appeared very much embarrassed and talked to me mostly through Ismail Beg. On the 2nd we set out on our return journey to Arbil.

March passed uneventfully in the Arbil Division, the only cloud on the horizon being the Surchi trouble in the Aqra district. The time of the Government authorities was fully occupied with routine matters, the details of which would probably prove wearisome to the reader. This narrative is largely a record of extraordinary events, which befell the writer in person, and though the intervening periods are passed over in silence, it does not follow that matters of grave importance affecting Mesopotamia as a whole were not occurring elsewhere.

CHAPTER XV

VISITS TO RAWANDUZ AND
THE PERSIAN FRONTIER

TOWARDS THE END OF March the military post at Batas
was moved up to Kani Wutman at the lower end of the Gorge.
On the last day of the month the commandant announced to
me over the telephone that he had received word from Abdulla Pasha that 400 men had crossed the Zab and were preparing to attack his post. I did not believe this report for one
minute, though I knew that trouble was brewing again in the
Aqra district. It subsequently transpired that Hamada Shin
had set out from the Surchi country north of the Zab with
some forty men and had started to cross the river, intending
to settle up old scores with certain villages near Kani Wutman; Shaikh Obaidullah hearing of his plans, and having
business for him elsewhere, had recalled him.

Three days later news arrived that the Surchi had attacked and cut up a military convoy in the neighbourhood of
Aqra. A punitive column was despatched from Mosul, but
meanwhile in conjunction with the Zibaris the insurgents descended again on Aqra itself. The gendarmes were successful
in holding their own, and the tribes were only able to occupy
a part of the town, from which they withdrew on the arrival
of the troops.

These disturbances were calculated to have a most unset-
tling effect in the Rawanduz district. Accordingly, on April
8th I set out with Captain Littledale and some seventy levies,
which it was proposed to station over the crossings of the
Greater Zab at Kandil and Bardin, lest the Surchi should use
this route to invade my area, whether for purposes of aggression or in an endeavour to escape from the column that was
about to visit their territory. Captain Hamilton of the 94th
Russell's Infantry also accompanied me for the purpose of ac-
quiring a knowledge of the country. At Dera I interviewed the

Harki chiefs, who undertook to prevent a hostile force crossing the river in that neighbourhood, and thence proceeded by
the main road to Babachichek, where we found the levies
who had been sent on ahead. The country was now at its
best. Everything was green, the shrubs were all showing
fresh leaves, and the descent from Duwin was magnificent,
being carpeted with anemones and other flowers, amongst
which I noticed a blossom very similar to the bee-orchis. We
spent the night at Babachichek, where I was joined by
Mustafa Agha and a small tribal escort. I tried to sleep outside, but rain, wind, and dust compelled me to move indoors
and surrender myself to the fleas.

The next morning we started out across the lower end of
the Dasht i Harir, passing over rolling grassy downs gay with
flowers, and intersected by high-banked streams. Only those
who have lived for ten months of the year in a brown parched
world can fully appreciate the beauty of the lush green grass
which covers this country in the spring. We found the Surchi
chief, Ali Beg of Khurra, encamped in his black tents on an
open grassy place near his village. He provided us with an
excellent meal, after which we proceeded to Kandil on the
river bank; opposite us lay the country of the hostile Surchi,
a confused tangle of low hills overlooked to the east by the
gaunt mass of the Aqra Dagh. One or two villages which had
not joined the insurgents had hoisted white flags as a signal
to aeroplanes that they were friendly. We found Kandil quite
empty, all the inhabitants being in tents at this time of year;
the river could only be crossed here by small rafts supported
by inflated skins, each carrying about six men. We decided
that Bardin would be the best position for the levies to occupy. This village belonged to Shaukat Effendi, a native of
Mosul, who had long ago settled in the Rawanduz district. He
is a most unpleasant man, middle-aged, hump-backed, and of
a sour disposition. It is related that in his early years he was
a chaush, or sergeant, of gendarmes, and made himself so unpopular with the people of Rawanduz that they seized and
beat him, causing injuries that gave rise to his present de-
formities. He amassed considerable wealth and afterwards
became Rais Baladiyah of Rawanduz. When Captain Kirk
evacuated the town he retired to his village, where he has
since resided. He always feigned the greatest attachment to

RAWANDUZ GENDARMES

GORGE OF THE GREATER ZAB AT BARDIN

the Government and provided me with much useful information about the Surchi; but he probably gave even more valuable intelligence to the enemy, and true to the policy which he had followed all his life kept himself in with both sides.

Bardin is situated just below the gorge by which the Greater Zab breaks through the range of mountains known to the south as the Harir Dagh, and to the north as the Aqra Dagh. The cleft, which must be some 5 miles long and in the centre nearly 3,000 ft. deep, was visible from my house at Arbil; its sides are composed of black precipitous rock. A very difficult footpath runs through the gorge on the south side, but I believe the north side is quite impassable. On the opposite bank to Bardin and nearly a mile higher up is the village of Bekhim, situated almost within the entrance of the gorge; a little above it is a small beach from which rafts can be launched. This was the place it was most necessary to watch, as it was here that Hamada Shin had started to cross a few days previously.

Shaukat Effendi gave us lunch, Hajji Shaikh Muhammad, the mukhtar of Kandil, also being present. He is an old man with a white beard, famous far and wide for his miserliness. In the various disturbances that took place he refused to identify himself with any party, and consequently was left to enjoy his riches in peace. After the meal I said good-bye to Captain Littledale and set out for Kani Wutman, accompanied by Captain Hamilton and Saiyid Ali. Mustafa Agha and his men I sent on to Batas, as I did not think I should require them for the journey to Rawanduz. Crossing a low ridge we passed the village of Amokha, situated in a secluded valley of its own, whence we ascended the main range of hills and entered a confused and thickly wooded country. After an hour or two, just as we were becoming anxious about our whereabouts, we came suddenly to a little village of mean hovels built of mud and stone, situated by a sulphurous spring which welled up from a stone tank and watered an exiguous fruit garden. Around were a few vineyards, now green, and some patches of black soil reclaimed from the oak forests for the cultivation of sparse wheat and barley crops and tobacco. The village was shaded and concealed by tall chinars and willows. Here we were greeted by the old woman who had been brought to me in Batas in a state of collapse and was supposed to have been wounded in seven places by Hamada Shin. She told us the name of the village – Kani Gulek or Flower Spring – and pointed out the road to Kani Wutman. After climbing a thickly wooded hill, where in some open marshy depressions we found acres of narcissus that filled the evening air with their scent, we arrived before sunset at our destination. I was hospitably entertained by Lieut. Hunter, M.C., of the 94th Russell's Infantry, who detailed to me all the latest scares.

The next morning I set out with Lieut. Hunter to explore the country north of Kani Wutman, and especially to inquire where it would be possible for a hostile force to cross either the Greater Zab or the Rawanduz Chai in the neighbourhood of their junction. The district through which we passed was wild in the extreme, and, as it has probably never before been visited by a European, merits a somewhat lengthy description. Following the same road as that by which I had come the previous day as far as the village of Kani Gulek, we continued along the valley of the Rawanduz Chai, keeping several thousand feet above the stream. Our path ran along sloping country with a sheer rock face of the Sairawa Dagh, which attains a height of 6,000 ft., overlooking us on the left, while below us an outcrop of the main range presented a series of jagged peaks like some vast saw. The whole slope between the cliff above and these peaks was well wooded, chiefly with small oak trees. Across the Rawanduz Chai there faced us the rough black slopes of the Biau Dagh, with its long crest silhouetted against the sky. Patches of snow still remained on its summit. A few minute villages could be distinguished here and there on the mountainside, and the district is called the Mahal i Biau, being occupied by a section of the Surchi tribe under the leadership of one Haris Agha. The area through which we were passing, known as Serchia, was also inhabited by the Surchi under the nominal chieftainship of Hamada Shin, with whom, however, most of his subjects were at variance.

After an hour's ride from Kani Gulek we reached Gauras, pleasantly situated amongst vineyards and pear trees, the latter in full bloom. Just below the village a few pleasant green fields had been reclaimed from the forest which otherwise shut it in. The village is inhabited by only three poverty-stricken families of the wildest type of Kurd, rough, savage creatures more like bears than human beings.

The road now plunged into a thick forest of really big oaks, the trunks of which attained a diameter of over 2 ft. They were interspersed with wild pear in full bloom and hawthorn, with an undergrowth of various thorn shrubs and tufts of grass. The day was hot and sultry and it was delightful to breathe again the smell of woods in summer. Beside the road were small springs and marshy places surrounded by patches of vivid green, decked out with many kinds of flowers, including narcissus, squills, fritillaries, and orchids. Descending steeply through this forest we passed below the line of peaks, and came to the village of Sawer situated quite near the junction of the rivers. In the fork on the further side of the Rawanduz Chai was quite a large patch of green meadow land uncultivated and uninhabited. With Lieut. Hunter and a few gendarmes I climbed the ridge above the village, and walking along it for two or three miles through thick woods came to a point immediately overlooking the Greater Zab just below where the Rawanduz Chai joins it. It is here that the Zab makes its right-angled bend. On our right was the great wall of the Biau Dagh running in a northeasterly direction, until it merged into the mountains of the Barzan and Shirwan country. In front of us rose up the truncated end of a range of hills known as the Pirris Dagh, on a continuation of which we were standing; while between this and the Biau Dagh there appeared a deep depression down which the Zab flowed towards us until it finally made a big sweep, and with the added waters of the Rawanduz Chai rushed past below us, and plunged into the black gorge which leads to Bardin. On the left of the Pirris Dagh, between it and the Aqra Dagh, was a long, narrow valley coming right down to the river bank, on which was situated the deserted Zibari village of Malamus. Opposite this and just below us on our left was another picturesque valley containing the little village of Dola Tesu, the inhabitants of which we could see engaged in their daily occupations. Our view in this direction was bounded by a sheer mountain mass beyond which lay Bardin and the Dasht i Harir. We decided that a tribal force would have little difficulty in crossing the river from Malamus to Dola Tesu provided rafts were available.

While we were busy studying our surroundings one of the gendarmes rushed up to me in an excited state saying he had seen an enormous snake. We went with him and found the reptile curled up in a hollow in the ground. The gendarmes fired a volley into it and killed it; it was about 4 ft. long with a body some 3 ins. in diameter, a large flat head and black markings along its back. The noise of the firing caused considerable excitement in the village below us, and all the inhabitants collected on the rooftops and gazed in our direction. A Kurdish boy who had accompanied us shouted to them from the hillside that it was only a snake, and they returned to their several tasks.

We descended the hill and made our way back to Sawer by another path, passing en route an enormous chinar now rotting away. Its trunk must have been 10 ft. in diameter; it was hollowed and black inside, and a spring welled up from among its roots. The local inhabitants say that the chinar lives for a thousand years – for 500 years it grows, and for 500 years it is gradually consumed away by internal fires.

The village of Sawer contained some seven houses, and its mukhtar Ali Beg, the brother of Haris Agha of Biau, possessed unexpectedly delightful manners, considering the wild surroundings in which he lived. We reclined on a grassy bank in the sunshine and partook of a meal which he brought us, consisting of butter, acorn bread, lumps of fried meat, some mast and 'furu' or beestings, with an enormous bowl of 'mastao'.

We returned by the same route as we came, except for a slight detour to a village, where we wished to inquire about the crossings of the Rawanduz Chai. This stream was not fordable at this time of the year, but there is one place near Kani Wutman where the precipitous banks approach so near to each other that a bridge can be made by simply throwing a few beams across. By this route the Harki and other migratory tribes used to drive down their sheep to escape the Turkish revenue authorities.

I spent the night in the camp at Kani Wutman, and set out the following morning with Captain Hamilton for a flying visit to Rawanduz. The Gorge was magnificent in its spring garments, and in the upper part of it the slopes above and below the road were covered with masses of large scarlet tulips with spiky petals. In other places we saw what was left of great clumps of irises, a few blooms remaining to show the glory that had passed. These irises are found also in abundance in Kandinawah and are in two shades, a pale mauve and a purple, each speckled with yellow and black. Now the snows were melting the fountain of Baikal was at its finest. We found Ismail Beg and Shaikh Muhammad Agha awaiting us on the ridge above the town with cushions spread out beneath some trees and a samovar ready boiling. After half an hour's rest and some cups of tea we descended to the town, where I passed the afternoon and evening in somewhat anxious conversation with Ismail Beg and other notables.

I learnt that Nuri had left Rawanduz some days previously on a visit to certain villages in the Vale of Akoyan and the Haruti tribe, who live in the upper part of the valley that runs down towards Kani Wutman. Ismail Beg hinted that he was up to mischief, but at the time I did not believe him. I asked Bawil Agha where his son was, and he replied that he was shooting ibex on the Kurrek Dagh. The next day as I was leaving the town I saw him standing outside his father's house, looking rather shamefaced. On our return journey we took what is known as the Bejan road over the Kurrek Dagh, instead of the ordinary route through the Gorge. The first part of the ascent is very rough, the road running up a narrow gully between two of the peaks that crop out of the main range on its eastern side. The way lies over large boulders, through which runs the stream that supplies the upper part of Rawanduz with water, and is extremely difficult for animals. Emerging from this gully the path though still very steep is much smoother. Near the top were melting patches of snow, by which grew strange and delicate flowers, while here and there could be seen lines of shallow trenches which the Turks had occupied when the Russians were in Rawanduz. At the summit of the hill the road passed a thousand feet sheer above a little wild valley, across which through gaps in the drifting clouds loomed rough peaks and precipices. The descent lay through wooded country and passed by the ruined fort of Bejan, one of the many built by the Blind Pasha. Turning northwards we followed along the edge of the valley of the Alana Su, the stream which flows towards Kani Wutman and enters the

Gorge with the main road, and after passing two or three small villages finally crossed the brook and ascended to the camp.

While traversing this mountainous wooded country I was all the time imagining what we should do if attacked, and though I did not know it till some weeks later, we were in considerable peril. For the Haruti tribe, some hundred strong, were pursuing hotly on our tracks, and nearly caught us up before we reached safety. Possibly Nuri had followed us from Rawanduz and given them the word.

On the 13th I rode down to Batas, where I met Captain Littledale, also Saleh Beg, who had come to assist me with a hundred men. I accompanied him to the village of Bashur, belonging to his cousin, Obaid Beg, a sleek scoundrel who had murdered most of his own brothers in order that he might acquire their property. Hence I rode a few miles to another village in the plain called Sisawa, where I found Qadir Beg in riding boots and full war kit. He had also mobilised his men to aid me if necessary. By this time, however, news had come in that the punitive column had burnt many of the hostile villages, and the Surchi shaikhs had made good their escape to the hills. There was no longer any danger of an invasion, so that I was able to give Qadir Beg and the other chiefs permission to withdraw to their own homes. I slept that night at Bashur and returned the next day to Arbil.

On May 2nd I set out on the longest and one of the most interesting of my tours in Kurdistan, but before starting to describe it I must detail certain events that had taken place in the neighbourhood of Rawanduz since my previous visit. Almost immediately after my return to Arbil a telephone message was received from Kani Wutman to the effect that the Haruti tribe were supposed to be about to attack the camp. It appears that while I was in Rawanduz this tribe, an unimportant one, had seized and disarmed two or three gendarmes sent to collect revenue from them, and had subsequently mustered their full strength, about a hundred men, and taken up their position in some caves near the Bejan road, whence they had issued to pursue me as previously narrated.

It was necessary to maintain gendarme posts on the Rawanduz road at Dera, Babachichek, and Kani Wutman, seeing that the district was a lawless one and there was no tribal chief of sufficient standing to undertake the responsibility of protecting caravans. These gendarmes, as I have mentioned before, were an unprincipled crew, and used to inflict upon the villagers innumerable petty extortions. The people in their turn were too ignorant and too frightened to complain, and would suffer until their patience was exhausted, when some outrage would occur. The trouble among the Haruti was due in great part to the tyranny of the gendarmes, but they would never have dared to defy the Government had not encouragement been received from higher quarters.

The night after I left Rawanduz an attack was made on Fatima Khanum, who had been assisting the Government in the collection of the sheep-tax, and during the next few days the situation became very threatening. A party from the Vale of Akoyan joined the Haruti in the neighbourhood of Bejan, with Nuri at their head, and awaited a favourable opportunity to attack the military at Kani Wutman. This would have given little cause for anxiety, had I not known that the camp was situated in a dangerous position and that any slight initial success would rouse the whole country. Meanwhile Yusef Beg's brothers and some of the Balik discontents collected a force in a village on the northern edge of the Dasht i Dian and prepared to make a descent on Rawanduz. Fortunately nothing further happened. Ahmad Agha of the Shirwan sent a message to Yusuf Beg's brothers that if they moved towards Rawanduz he would descend on their rear, while Hawaiz Agha of the Haruti, learning of the dispersal of the Surchi and the destruction of their villages, disbanded his men, and released the imprisoned gendarmes, giving them their arms and a note in which he endeavoured to explain his conduct.

When the situation became normal again it was decided to withdraw the troops altogether from the Rawanduz district and to replace them by the levies, now some 200 strong, who were to be stationed in the town itself under the command of Captain Littledale. I was determined to make an endeavour to administer the area on more or less normal lines, and obtained permission from the Civil Commissioner to station Mr. Turner in Rawanduz to superintend the Customs arrangements and assist Ismail Beg in Revenue matters. Mr. Turner had previously been head-clerk at Batas, and possessed a considerable knowledge of the district and its inhabitants, besides being able to speak a little Kurdish. I was now visiting Rawanduz to install the new regime and to inquire more closely into the recent disturbances; I hoped if possible to persuade all who had been responsible to make their dakhalat and to win them over by gentle methods to the side of law and order. Under present circumstances this seemed the only course, as with the levies still untrained offensive action was out of the question. I also proposed to make a visit to the Persian frontier to enable me to determine the best methods for the collection of customs duties, which I hoped would bring in a valuable revenue, and I purposed to return through the Haruti country and the Balisan valley to Bituin and Darband, in order to meet the present A.P.O. Rania, Captain J. C. Cook, and to finish up with Koi, where Captain Bradshaw had just relieved Captain Rundle.

I set out by the main road to Shaqlawah – for I wished to learn Qadir Beg's opinions on the Rawanduz situation. The country was beautiful. The little villages in the gravelly foothills before the Bastura Chai is reached were surrounded by bright green wheat crops studded with scarlet poppies and shot beneath with the blue of a delicate campanula. Here and there were tall hollyhocks, mauve and white, and great spikes of white blossoms, something after the style of a hyacinth. We stopped for a short time on the road at Kora and drank tea in the usual spot under the mulberry tree. I have not mentioned before Mustafa Agha's coffee man Kanabi, who always served us, a cheery fellow with a round face much resembling Ali Baba in *Chu Chin Chow*. He was a well-known character everywhere, and was said to have the courage of a lion.

At Shaqlawah I had a long talk with Qadir Beg, who confirmed my suspicions that Nuri was responsible for most of the recent troubles in the Rawanduz area. He had apparently persuaded his former teacher, an aged shaikh named Kaka Amin, to call upon the surrounding tribes to rebel against the infidel Government, and the ignorant Kurds, who regarded him as a divine being, had obeyed. It was this old shaikh, too, who had afterwards stilled the tempest when he found his efforts were mistimed.

The next day accompanied by Qadir Beg's nephew, Abdur Rahman Beg, a thin man with a superior air, whom I disliked, I descended to Sisawa, and passed thence through several villages situated along the eastern edge of the plain to Batas. The country on our way was a mass of scarlet ranunculus. Since my last visit the Pasha had left and taken up his quarters with his grandson at Rawanduz, rather to the latter's annoyance, who resented the old man's thrift and wise counsel. In the afternoon I continued my journey to Kani Wutman, where I spent the night. I left early the following morning for Rawanduz via the Gorge, where the tulips had now given place to coarser summer flowers.

I had much business to conduct in the town and received numerous callers. I sent letters to Yusuf Beg's brothers, the Haruti chief, and others, requesting them to come and see me, and promising a safe conduct. Nuri was in Rawanduz when I arrived, but on my asking Bawil Agha to bring him to me I was informed that he had gone out shooting. I warned the father that I must see his son before I left for Arbil, and that if he came in to me he need have nothing to fear. I found the Pasha delighted to be back in Rawanduz, but grumbling somewhat about his son's prodigality.

The following morning I left for the Balik country, taking with me Ismail Beg, Muhammad Ali Agha, and the two Sulaiman Aghas of Balikian. Descending to the lower town we crossed the ravine by the small bridge at the bottom and followed up the left bank of the Rawanduz Chai, here an open babbling stream. The road was enclosed on the right by slopes of grey rock; while to the left along the bank of the river was a strip of irrigated fields divided by hedges and interspersed with frequent springs, round which grew thick tangled shrubs and masses of wild roses in full bloom. The air was heavy with their scent and memories of English meadows in June. From the rock on the right side of the road also three or four large springs welled out, surrounded by mosses and maiden-hair ferns. After 6 or 7 miles we turned away from the stream and climbed a very stiff ascent to the Zin or saddle of Dargala, which is some 4,800 ft. above sea-level. The road was mostly wooded except near the top where it zigzagged up red, crumbly shale bare save for patches of brilliantly coloured flowers. The descent soon brought us to Dargala, which is situated in a very strong position between this pass and a narrow gully down which the road passes to rejoin the Rawanduz Chai. Southwards a very rough road leads to Warta, and the intensely rugged country which lies eastwards of the Hindawain Dagh, while to the north the view is bounded by a steep smooth slope covered with vineyards. Dargala, once a large village, was completely destroyed by the Russians, and only some twenty houses have been rebuilt. Here Mir Muhammad Amin Beg, who, with his nephew Miro, an extraordinarily handsome boy, had accompanied us from Rawanduz, entertained us very liberally, providing an excellent dinner and accommodating us in tents on the village green, so that we escaped most of the fleas for which the village is famous. We found awaiting us there, Shaikh Muhammad Agha, with his notorious elder brother, a wild-looking villain called, like the Shaikh of the Haruti country, Kaka Amin, 'Kaka' being an honorific term meaning literally 'big brother'.

The next morning the whole party set out for Shaikh Muhammad Agha's village Walash. Leaving the high-road, which is impassable owing to the collapse of a bridge over the Rawanduz Chai, we crossed a low spur to the east of Dargala and descended to the valley of a tributary of the main river. Our path passed through delightful country between hedges and meadows gay with their spring vesture and underneath clumps of walnut trees, while beside us ran the babbling stream lined with chinars and willows. On the hillside to our right were occasional villages surrounded by vineyards. We forded the stream in the middle of a thick grove of trees, and on the further side we began to ascend. Two or three hours over rising wooded country brought us to a low pass, from which we saw in front of us Walash, picturesquely situated on the mountainside at the upper end of a little plain green with young corn. We were here about 5,000 ft. above the sea, and just at the level where the oaks and shrubs cease and the grassy upland country begins; for the hillside above the village was bare save for grass and flowers and a few patches of melting snow.

Shaikh Muhammad Agha's house was quite different from any other Kurdish dwelling I had visited. It was solidly built like an English farmhouse, and winding narrow passages led to cosy little rooms well heated by stoves or open fires. A special room was allotted to me, where one or other of the chief's three sons was in constant attendance on me. They were simple folk, the eldest somewhat shy, but the two younger joining readily in conversation; the smallest, Suayid, a boy of eleven, was by far the most quick-witted and entertaining of them.

In the afternoon I went for a short walk to look at the view. Passing through the fruit gardens I ascended a spur of the hill behind the village. Eastwards to my right was a big snow-capped barrier which formed the Persian frontier, and just within it the mighty Argot, a dome of black rock striped with snow, isolated from and overtopping the main range. In front of me lay the deep narrow valley of the Rawanduz Chai, winding amongst the hills; well-wooded country sloped down gradually towards the stream, while on the far side rose a line of snow-capped ridges and peaks separated from each other by long gullies. Below me, a mile or two beyond Walash, Mirga, the famous nest of thieves, was visible, and I began to consider how best it could be surrounded and destroyed when the levies were fit to undertake operations. The view on my left was closed by the great hog's back of the Hindawain Dagh, separated from us by the valley up which we had travelled in the morning; while behind me lay a confused mass of snow-clad mountains over 10,000 ft. in height. All around on the hillsides could be seen little Balik villages with vineyards and patches of cultivation. It is impossible to find words which may fitly describe the grandeur of this scenery. The landscape is rugged in the extreme; except for the watershed the mountains seem to obey no rule, being huddled together in wild confusion and split by great rifts into innumerable pinnacles and ridges.

I was rather disappointed in the dinner that Shaikh Muhammad Agha produced, and understood now why some of the Dizai aghas referred to Mir Muhammad Amin Beg as 'more of a man' than he. The only thing especially appetising was a dish of mushrooms, which in this part of the world always appear in the spring. The evening passed pleasantly in conversation. Suayid brought in two bear-cubs, which had lately been found in the hills, and somewhat brutally tried to make them fight; Shaikh Muhammad Agha promised to send them down to Arbil as a present to me, but a few days later they died. We talked of the surrounding mountains, especially Algurd, which my host said wandering Indians used to visit before the war, for the purpose of gathering the strange herbs that grew near its summit. He also related that beneath the snow, which has here lain for centuries, is found a weird animal that is called the snow-worm. It is about a foot long, fat and white, with no mouth, eyes, nose, or other physical features save only a stump tail. This creature when brought down to lower altitudes dies and shrivels up; its dried corpse will turn the hottest water cold in the heat of summer. Several people averred that they had seen this beast, so I suppose there must be some foundation to the story.

At Walash I found awaiting me Yusef Beg's brother, Bekr Beg, and Mulla Yusuf Agha of the Balikian tribe, a wild-looking little man with a thick black beard and tasselled cap, who was really the leader of the brothers' counsels. They made their submission to me, swearing that they raised their tribesmen with no hostile intent, but only in self-defence, fearing an attack from Ismail Beg. I accepted their excuses, and before I left Rashid Beg also arrived; all of them accompanied me back to Rawanduz to make their peace with Ismail Beg. They failed, however, to persuade Begok to come in.

The following day, May 7th, I set out with Shaikh Muhammad Agha, Ismail Beg, and others to visit Rayat and the Persian frontier. We made our way down through well-wooded country to the Rawanduz Chai, the descent being gradual except for one very steep incline known as 'The Mule Killer'. We reached the bottom of the valley by the village of Naupirdan (Between the Bridges), where we crossed a tributary of the main stream by a narrow and perilous bridge shaded by immense walnut trees. Another bridge here crosses the Rawanduz Chai, but it is in bad repair and impassable except for pedestrians. Following up the valley after three or four miles we reached the entrance of a long defile, where we were met by Ali Agha of Rayat, a quiet man with a grizzled beard, one of the most important sectional chiefs in the Balik tribe. At

ARGOT DAGH FROM THE SOUTH

(June, 1919)

the head of the defile we passed Rayat, which was mostly in ruins, and pursued our way to Ali Agha's encampment situated a mile above the village.

The sight that greeted us was most picturesque. The black tents were pitched in a small open space with groups of rough Kurds in fantastic costumes standing in front of them on the rich grass, and the whole scene was surrounded by an amphitheatre of cliffs and rocky slopes above which loomed vast snow-clad heights. Entering the guest-room I saw in the highest places two young men in the flowing 'abahs and the green head-dress which betokens the saiyid or descendant of the Prophet. They made way for me and at first I did not take kindly to them; but I soon found them to be a pair of gentlemen whose polite speech and charming manners contrasted strangly with the roughness of the Kurds amongst whom they lived. They came from the neighbouring village of Dar ul Aman. Before lunch my host brought to me the famous rewas, a herb which grows only in high altitudes, and is much esteemed by the Kurds as a digestive. It consisted of a long stalk with a curious furry exterior and a leaf at the top which was just beginning to unroll; we peeled it and ate it raw with sugar. It had a not unpleasant clean taste, and it was not till a few days later, when I met it cooked, that I discovered it was nothing more or less than rhubarb.

After lunch I set out with Ismail Beg and the others to ride the remaining 6 miles to the frontier. By a very gradual ascent over rolling grassy uplands the road approached the great gap in the watershed which is known as the Garwa Shaikh or Pass of the Shaikh. The country is bare save for a thick, fresh carpet of grass which, especially in depressions where the sun has only just melted the snow, is of the most vivid green and is interspersed thickly with tall grape hyacinths, buttercups, and squills. There were a few patches of snow still left by the side of the road. Some two miles from the actual frontier we passed a small domed tower, much ruined, which is known as the Shaikh i Balikan, and gives its name to the pass. Here lies buried some old Kurdish saint who flourished two or three centuries ago. Around the shrine is a typical disordered Muhammadan cemetery and amongst the gravestones grow thick patches of tall red tiger lilies. It is one of those places where the spirit of the Almighty seems to brood upon the earth in grand and silent majesty.

Just on the further side of the cemetery stand three or four gaunt willows, some 50 ft. tall and practically bare of leaves and branches – the only trees for miles. They once formed part of a considerable grove, but their fellows were hewn down for firewood by the armies that faced each other here. All around were traces of the conflict, lines of trenches, little huts and dug-outs made of slabs of stone, and piles of barbed wire and other materials. But the most lasting monument is the road over the pass which the Russians have made into a broad and carefully graded highway fit to take any traffic that can reach it. At the actual frontier, i.e. the watershed, the gap was a mile broad with gradual slopes on either side; a very short and easy descent led to the plain of Lahjan. I climbed a flower-covered spur on my left and looked out across level plains and steep bare hills, the home of the Mamash and Piran, towards Sauj Bulaq and Ushnu. It was with a feeling of strange delight that I gazed down upon this to me new and unexplored country of Lahjan, looking so prim and well ordered compared to the rugged tracts behind me. I longed to descend and wander among its strange tribes. Below me on my right in a well-watered plain, I could see the villages of Hassan Agha of the Piran, who a few years previously had murdered the Qaimaqam of Rania and taken refuge in this the summer home of his tribe. In front of me was just visible a black mound round which lay Paswa, the village of Qaranai Pasha, chief of the Mamash, who at present was busy collecting what he called 'customs' from all caravans that came his way. To the left, hidden behind a series of ridges, lay Ushnu, and beyond that Urmia, where even now Simko the chief of the Shikak was said to be engaged in conflict with the Persian troops. I felt like some explorer seeing for the first time an unknown continent, and it was with many regrets that I left the vision and retraced my footsteps.

It is worthy of mention that the whole of this country had been devastated by the Russians. The many villages that I could descry scattered over the plains were empty shells, and the Mamash, once a powerful tribe which boasted of 2,000 horsemen, could now scarcely muster 200 infantry. They with the neighbouring Kurdish tribes are nominally under the Persian Government; they pay, however, little or no revenue and are kept under no sort of control.

On the way back we turned aside for a special purpose to the village of Dar ul Aman, situated on the hillside just over-looking the gap on our right as we returned. Here dwelt the two Saiyids, Shaikh Obaidullah and Shaikh Ala ud Din. They were cousins, and their fathers, who had both died only two or three years previously, had settled in this spot some fifty years ago, coming originally from Lahjan, where they were held in great honour by the Mamash and other Kurdish tribes. At Dar ul Aman, which means 'The Abode of Quiet', they established a hospice and succoured many a poor traveller overcome by cold in the pass; for from December to March the whole country is snowed up. In this way they ac-quired a wide reputation for piety and good works. In 1916 they were compelled to flee by the advent of the Russians, and most of their property was destroyed. Their sons had now returned and were endeavouring in a small way to carry on the work which they had begun.

I had been requested by Shaikh Muhammad Agha to visit them in the company of Ismail Beg and Muhammad Ali Agha as a deputation on his behalf to beg from Shaikh Obaidullah the hand of his sister in marriage; for it would have been a breach of propriety for him to make the request himself. I felt much honoured at being asked to undertake a duty thus closely connected with Kurdish family life, and so far re-moved from my normal official routine. One of the Balik chief's wives had died when on a previous occasion he had visited Rawanduz to see me, and he now expressed a hope that my participation in this ceremony would be of good omen for his next venture.

We ascended by some steps to a little low-roofed room like a cottage parlour, with two little glass windows looking out towards the pass. It was heated by a large open fire, for the air up here was still very cold. Not wishing to make any *faux pas* which would spoil the proceedings, I told Muhammad Ali Agha to act as spokesman. I cannot quite remember what he said, but it was something as follows: 'Shaikh Muhammad Agha, who is chief of a large tribe and a man of considerable standing and power, has sent us to you to make a request, the nature of which is known to you; he hopes that, as the Political Officer himself has come to join in the request, you will consent and that the alliance will prove of good omen.' Shaikh Obaidullah, a young man with a refined oval face, and fair hair and moustache, replied, 'I am truly sensible of the honour that Shaikh Muhammad Agha has done to my family in making this request, for I know that he is no mean man, and is held in great repute among the tribes, and an alliance with him will be greatly esteemed by myself and my relations. There is, however, a certain condition, which is known to you. If it has been accepted I give my consent.' The condition referred to was the sum of money which Shaikh Muhammad Agha would have to pay for the girl's hand. The amount had been settled beforehand in informal conversations. A 'Fatihah', or the opening chapter of the Quran, which in some ways takes the place of the Lord's Prayer in the Muhammadan religion, was then read to seal and sanctify the betrothal. At the conclusion of the ceremony everybody muttered 'Mubarik bi', or 'May the alliance be blessed.' After partaking of tea and coffee and passing half an hour in interesting conversation, we begged permission to depart and rejoined Shaikh Muhammad Agha at Rayat.

That evening we returned through rain and cold wind to Walash, where I had a long talk with my host's mad brother Kaka Amin. He had a face not unlike Yusuf Beg's, but with a much wilder look about it, white hair and moustaches, and mad staring eyes. He ranted with a loud, harsh voice for more than an hour, explaining how, if he had looted such and such a caravan, he had only done it in just revenge for wrongs which he had previously received at the hands of its owner.

On the 8th I returned to Rawanduz, completing the journey in one day. Just two miles from the town we stopped to take tea with Muhammad Ali Agha by the spring of Zindian. Here below the road is a cave situated in a right angle formed by two sheer cliffs. From it rises a spring of icy water which flows freely throughout the year, except during the autumn, when it is intermittent, one day running completely dry and the next bursting forth with its full strength. At the mouth of the cave are seats on either side of the stream, which flows down a short, grassy slope to water-tangled gardens of pear and pomegranate. The land belongs to Muhammad Ali Agha, who lives in tents here with his family throughout the hot weather.

When I reached Rawanduz, I found that Captain Littledale had arrived with the levies and was busy pitching his tents on a hill overlooking the town. The men, Turks of Arbil and Kirkuk, Kurds from the Arbil plain and Koi, and a few Christians from Ainkawa, were all well and happy. A striking force was at last in being, though by no means trained. The old gendarmes, now called the district police, remained a separate body under the command of Lieut. R. F. Barlow.

Mr. Turner had also arrived, and I spent two or three days in making arrangements for the collection of revenue and customs and the estimation of the crops which would soon be ripe. I received several visitors including Fatima Khanum, Hawaiz Agha of the Haruti, who apologised for his behaviour, one of Muhammad Suayid Beg's relations, who alleged that his chief was too ill to ride, though he was willing to be carried down in his bed if I required his presence, and my old friends of the Shirwan, to whom I presented robes of honour, as they had greatly assisted in the saving of the situation at Rawanduz two or three months previously.

Nuri was not in Rawanduz, and Bawil Agha, when I inquired after him, said he had not returned from his shooting expedition. As he still did not come in, I left word with Captain Littledale to arrest him on the first possible opportunity.

Taking my way up the valley which runs towards the town from the south, I came to the large village of Akoyan, consisting of about a hundred houses arranged in tiers on the hillside at the mouth of a gorge between two of the peaks that crop out from the Kurrek Dagh. All around it were spread extensive gardens of fig, pomegranate, and other fruits, while above the gorge and overlooking it lay the picturesque village of Faqian. Thither we made our way through the beautiful gardens, climbing up the gully beside a tumbling stream, our path enclosed and darkened by dense walnut trees and mossy cliffs. Faqian, situated high on the hillside and surrounded by gardens and poplar plantations, is probably the most beautiful village in the district; it forms a delightful retreat in summer. Here lived Fatima Khanum, who entertained us in her new guest-house. assisted by the

Muhammad Ali Agha　　　Capt. J. Marshall, M.C.　　　Khalifa Rashid

THE SPRING OF ZINDAN

AKOYAN

greedy relations who were doing their best to deprive her of her wealth. I stayed an hour and just as I was leaving up rushed old Bawil Agha. I noticed that he had not been with the party that came to see me off; and he now said that he had been delayed by his pony not being ready, and had come to make amends. He was much surprised when he heard that I was taking my departure, and I left him standing there with a look of the greatest dismay on his face. His plans, whatever they were, had fallen through, and it was fortunate that we could not see the result of their collapse. For I felt pretty certain that he had hoped to bring Nuri to me at Faqian, and there beg my forgiveness, calculating that I should be afraid to arrest him in such a wild spot; or if it was not this, it is possible that my early departure frustrated some plot which they had made to ambush me on the road the following day.

I continued my journey over the Kurrek Dagh accompanied by Abdulla Agha of Bila, which was my next objective, ten gendarmes, and a dozen men of Ismail Beg's led by his cousin Yunis Agha. I took care to send out scouts in all directions, as I knew Nuri was lurking in these parts and might lie in wait for me. On the road a white-turbaned mulla accosted me with a message that Kaka Amin, the holy shaikh who lived in a village close at hand, wished to see me; I asked him to meet me at Bila. The ascent of the hill was not difficult, and I was surprised to find on its top a considerable depression containing a small lake. From here a long and very steep descent brought us to Bila, situated at the bottom of a narrow little valley of its own between the Kurrek Dagh and an imposing black ridge called Airon, which still retained traces of snow. The village was surrounded by rocky cliffs on all sides but the south, where it was open to the sun; it was therefore intensely hot. Abdulla Agha conducted us to his guest-room, which was situated at the top of a house of three storeys, a thing I have never seen elsewhere in a Kurdish village.

Presently Kaka Amin arrived, walking very slowly and accompanied by two mullas and a handsome, gaily-dressed youth, who I believe was his son. All bowed their head to him as he approached, and many rushed up and kissed his hands and clothes. He was indeed a venerable old man with a

benign face and forked beard a foot long. I welcomed him
warmly, thanking him for the great honour he had paid me in
thus visiting me, while he endeavoured to find out how much
I knew about his past actions. He explained to me how he
had quelled the recent disturbances and sent the Haruti back
to their homes, not mentioning that he had also called them
out. I thanked him and said that in any case bygones were
bygones with those who had come in and made their dakhalat to me. He then asked me if Nuri had come in. 'No', I replied. 'It is a pity,' he said; 'it would have been better if he
had.'

After a meal had been produced I took my departure along
a road which wound in a northerly direction through a long,
narrow gully just behind the village. The stream at our side
was lined with magnificent chinars. At the end of the gully
was an open space with a mill where I was greeted by Fatima
Khanum's brother Khurshid Beg, who had also taken part in
the recent troubles. Here we rounded the end of a hill and
turned southwards into the Haruti valley, a narrow depression between oak-covered slopes. The road ran high up along
the eastern of these passing a succession of villages each
nestling in a re-entrant in the hillside. Their inhabitants, the
men who had recently threatened Kani Wutman, were a set
of poor ignorant ill-clothed peasants. I continually stopped
and asked if they had any grievances; but they had little to
say for themselves, complaining only of oppressions and
murders at the hands of their own headmen. I stopped a
short time at Hawaiz Agha's village and talked to him; he is a
man of no personality and no importance.

At the end of the valley, the passage of which occupied
some three hours, we crossed a small ridge and found ourselves at the edge of a broad and fertile basin. We were now
in Khushnao country, which always seemed to me a haven of
peace and safety after the rugged Rawanduz hills with their
wild and ignorant inhabitants. Our road ran along the foot of
the hills, passing large and prosperous villages surrounded
by gardens, plantations, and rich pastures, while the evening
air resounded with the bleatings of many flocks. A climb in
the dark over a rocky ridge brought us to the large village of
Balisan, where with some difficulty we found our way by narrow paths among the fruit gardens to the house of Aziz Beg,

the uncle of Miran i Qadir Beg of Shaqlawah. He was a
kindly simple old man who did his best to maintain the peace
between his jealous nephews.

The following morning we proceeded down the middle of
the broad valley that leads to Bituin along the banks of the
Keshan river, which contains enough water to float down timber to the Lesser Zab. For the valley is full of villages belonging to the Pizhgali section of the Khushnao, and contains
many plantations of poplar. Our way lay over grassy
meadows thick with flowers; I noticed especially patches of
tall purple orchids. About noon we emerged on to the northern edge of Bituin, near the spring of Serchinar, where the
water gushes out from the rock at the foot of a spur, and
flows away a broad stream amongst reeds and sedges. The
plain was covered with thick grass that reached up to my
pony's ears; flowers, especially hollyhocks, abounded and the
air was permeated with the sweet scent of hay and clover.
The flies were a plague, our animals being tormented by huge
gadflies. I lunched with Kaka Hamza, a cousin of Sawar
Agha's, who was encamped in his black tents near the village
of Girda Tilleh. He was wearing the broad, flat head-dress,
thick twisted waistband, and enormous trousers that are
characteristic of his tribe, for the Piran affect a richer and
more exaggerated costume than any other Kurds I have met.
He accompanied me in the long and weary ride across the
plain to Darband, where I spent the night with the A.P.O.,
Captain Cook, being the first officer he had entertained for
five months. Captain Barker, before he left, had built a house
here just below the defile overlooking the river, and had
transferred to it his headquarters from the unhealthy rice
swamps of Rania. Levies were established in the fort, which
had been repaired, and great efforts were being made to re-
populate the ruined village.

I had hoped to see Babekr Agha again, but found that he
was away on a journey, so I departed the following morning
for Koi, accompanied by Kaka Hamza. While crossing Bituin
I was met by Mam Qaranai, who was acting as chief in Sawar
Agha's place, with a party of Piran aghas and retainers and a
man piping away on the zurnai. They were all unarmed,
having vowed never to carry arms in public until their
beloved chief should return to them; I learnt also that the

guest-house at Sarkhuma had remained closed ever since his arrest. I was entertained to lunch by Sawar Agha's brother who, with the inhabitants of Sarkhuma, was encamped in a pleasant spot below the village just by the junction of the two rivers. Here we sat in the shade of tents watching the children bathing and bare-legged Kurds piloting logs down the stream.

After the meal we continued our way to Koi, passing 'the Bishop's' retreat at Chinarok, which was now at its best surrounded by wild roses, green shrubs, and all sorts of flowers. I spent the night at Koi with Captain Bradshaw, leaving for Arbil early the following morning. The little valleys of the red sandstone country were still thick with flowers, especially hollyhocks and a flower like a hyacinth with innumerable pale green flowers and a feathery purple tuft at the top.

On approaching Arbil I was surprised to see the entire population encamped round the outskirts of the town, the richest families in tents, and others in shelters constructed of blankets or wicker-work screens. The reason for this exodus was an earthquake which had taken place during my absence, and of which I had only heard the barest outlines over the telephone.

The first shock had been felt at 10 p.m. on the night of the 8th. It was very slight, but was succeeded within a quarter of an hour by two more shocks of greater violence. Little damage was done, but the people became considerably alarmed, and some madman stood up and announced that he had dreamt that there were to be two more shocks, and that with the last the world would come to an end.

Nothing happened for three or four days, and the alarm began to subside, when suddenly on the night of the 12th–13th, shortly after midnight, came a much more serious shock than any of those which had gone before. Ten houses collapsed and a very large number were damaged; two men were killed and several injured. The terrified inhabitants fled from the town and passed several days and nights in constant prayer. Then, as nothing further occurred beyond one or two very slight shocks that were almost imperceptible, they began to return to their houses and repair the damage that had been caused.

It is extraordinary that this earthquake was absolutely local in its effect. On the 8th I noticed a faint tremor at Rawanduz, but the biggest shock which occurred on the night of the 12th–13th was not felt at Darband or Koi except by a very few who happened to be awake. The towns of Kirkuk and Mosul were unaffected, while the villages within a few miles of Arbil only experienced a very slight motion. According to the inhabitants no shocks of such severity were known ever previously to have occurred in Arbil or its neighbour-hood.

CHAPTER XVI

NURI: THE DEATH OF TWO GREAT MEN

ALMOST IMMEDIATELY AFTER my departure Nuri returned to Rawanduz. Captain Littledale did not interfere with him for a few days in order to allay his suspicions; he even professed friendship for him and took tea with him on one occasion. On the 18th he put his plans into execution. Nuri was invited to come and view the camp; the young man unsuspectingly complied, and when he reached the top of the hill suddenly found himself seized and bound. A shot was then fired, at which signal two parties who were in readiness proceeded to the houses of Nuri and Bawil Agha and seized all rifles, ammunition, and correspondence they could find. Sixteen rifles were forthcoming with 2,000 rounds, and amongst the letters was an incriminating document written by Shaikh Obaidullah of the Surchi, and addressed to the aged Shaikh Kaka Amin. Nuri was despatched to Arbil with a small but trusty escort, and there imprisoned, while Bawil Agha, who was not arrested, was ordered to follow him. The Civil Commissioner wired his congratulations on the arrest, and I began to feel that the position at Rawanduz was now secure.

On June 6th we received information of the outbreak at Tel Afar, a town situated some 50 miles west of Mosul. A party of Arab tribesmen led by Sharifian officers had attacked the town and assisted by the inhabitants besieged the Government offices and murdered the A.P.O., Major J. E. Barlow, D.S.O., M.C., the gendarme officer, Lieut. B. Stuart, D.S.O., and two British subordinate officials. General disorder followed throughout the Arab portions of the Mosul district, and raiding parties visited even the Quwair–Mosul Road. Timely action by the troops quelled the disturbances.

This news caused considerable excitement in Arbil, and from now onwards anti-British propaganda increased daily in violence, notorious malcontents preached open sedition in the coffee-shops, and letters purporting to come from the Sherif of Mecca and others circulated amongst the ill-disposed notables and chiefs, such as Ahmad Pasha and Hajji Pir Daoud Agha. The Surchi, too, were active, flooding Koi and Shaqlawah and the neighbourhood of Rawanduz with letters supposed to come from the Wali of Van and similar personages. This propaganda, which issued both from Syria and Anatolia, had been secretly at work for months, but only now that large numbers of troops had been withdrawn and the Government's prestige was on the wane did it come to the surface. I had long known the identity of the principal agitators in Arbil, and I felt that to take any action against them at present would only increase their importance in the eyes of the populace; as it was, their tales so often proved false, that they merely covered themselves with ridicule; for the people at large in this area were, and remained, well disposed to the Government.

During the greater part of June and July I was busy with the estimations of crops in the Arbil District. The revenue from the wheat and barley was so valuable, and so great a loss had occurred in the previous year from the corruption and timidity of the officials, that I determined to tour widely and where possible check the results in person with the assistance of two reliable estimators. I visited over seventy villages during the barley harvest and as many for the wheat. The work was extremely tiring, and the heat intense.

My first tour took place during the Muhammadan month of Ramazan, when all the Kurds of any standing were fasting. The peasant is only a peasant, and it does not seem to matter whether he fasts or not; in any case he cannot do so, as he is at work all day in the fields. The chiefs, on the other hand, pass as much of the day as is possible in sleep; towards evening they come into the guest-room with drawn faces, and eye a bowl of water or 'mastao' which is placed before them, anxiously awaiting the muezzin's cry which announces sunset and the termination of their fast. At his first words they drink a small quantity and then betake themselves to prayer, after which they prepare for their meal. I have seen some break their fast with a cigarette, an extraordinary feat after some sixteen hours without water. Though there are some delinquents who secretly quench their thirsts, the majority of Kurds, who can afford to pass the days in idleness, keep the fast with the greatest strictness. Ramazan fortunately made no difference to the hospitality which was everywhere shown me both by day and night.

My tours were confined to the Dizai country, and I became very familiar with all the aghas, old and young, big and small. The more I came to know them the more favourably did they compare with the rough and savage chiefs of the hill country. I was by this time acquainted with all their relationships and petty quarrels and ambitions, and almost began to consider myself as one of the tribe. There is no guest whom the Kurd appreciates more than one who is 'Sharazai' or full of local knowledge, and can talk to him about his own little affairs and enterprises which interest him far more than the wonders of the outside world. They would often ask me what England was like, and where I lived and what relations I had alive; they took great interest when I talked of the crops and cattle at home, and also of marriage customs, but when I told them of the size and population of London and the wonders of modern science they gaped and passed on to other subjects. Tribal politics were usually the main theme of conversation, for there is nothing the Kurd loves to discuss more.

At every village the old farmers would gather round us as we judged the heaps, explaining how poor the grain was and how long the straw, and enumerating all the pests which had attacked their unfortunate crops. However light our estimation, they would ask us to come and thresh the heap and offer to give us the whole of the grain if it proved to be more than half what we said. Though of course they groused they were very good-natured, and when the business was done would treat us with the greatest friendliness and hospitality, all except a few grizzled misers who would continue to mutter about the severity of our estimations until we left the village.

I saw Ibrahim Agha at Makhmur nearly every week during these two months, usually taking with me Captain H. Williamson, who, in March, had taken over the duties of Civil Surgeon at Arbil. The old chief had been taken ill early in April, shortly after his return from a journey which we had

made together to Baghdad. An abscess in the lung was diag-
nosed, and although everything possible was done to preserve
his life, and he seemed at times to be recovering, he became
weaker and weaker. On June 15th I visited him when he was
very bad indeed; he was no longer in the guest-house, but in
his private quarters, at night in a tent in the courtyard, and
by day in a small room full of treasured ornaments and
knick-knacks. Whenever I went to see him he would stretch
out his feeble hands and hold tight on to one of mine, looking
at me with his fevered eyes now deep set in his shrunken
face. While he could he would endeavour to sit up to receive
me, supported by Kurshid Agha or another of his relations. I
would sit down on a cushion by his side, and if in talking to
him I leant forward or appeared to be in a strained position,
he would interrupt me saying slowly in a persuasive voice, a
sweet smile spread over his noble features, 'Istarahat,
Istarahat'. 'Take your ease, take your ease.' I shall never forget my interviews with the dear old man for whom I had such
a deep affection, he seemed to love to cling to my hand and to
talk to me, and I believe he thought that if anybody could
save him, I could. He insisted on my coming to see him as
often as possible, and complained if I was away more than a
week.

On this occasion, June 15th, he was very weak and could
hardly talk. When I came to him he ordered tea and coffee to
be brought and then sent everybody out of the room; after
clinging to my hand for some time he said, 'I may live for a
few days or a few weeks, but I know I am going to die. My
call has come. My brother, Khurshid Agha, will sit in my
place, and I have only one request to make to you. I pray you
to be as good to him as you have been to me, that you will
care for him as you have cared for me, and show him even
greater favours.' He then continued, 'How I long to live. If I
live I will do something so great for you, that all the world
shall wonder.' He seemed to faint before I could make a reply,
and overcome with sorrow I left the room. That night he became worse and the house was full of wailing; in the morning
he was speechless, but recognised me when I came to see
him.

However, the end was not yet. He rallied, and I paid him
several more visits, during some of which he was strong

enough to discuss tribal matters and the political situation; but he would always cling hold of me and gaze at me with the same yearning eyes full of a longing for life. During one of these visits he spoke of a letter he had written on Nuri's behalf, which by the way I never saw, saying that he made no request, but merely suggested that if I thought it possible I might permit the young man to remain at liberty in Arbil on security. It would have been well had I taken his advice.

Ibrahim Agha always had deeply at heart the interests of his friends and tenants, begging me to lower the assessment of such and such a man's crops, which had been over-estimated, or to appoint some penurious but honest acquaintance of his to a post that was vacant, and it was rarely that I could refuse his requests, for he was wise enough not to ask anything that was too difficult for me to perform.

Khurshid Agha remained at Makhmur during the whole of his brother's illness, and did the duties of host when I was there. The dour old man was more than ever depressed and pessimistic, though he always had a kindly smile for me when I arrived. He was convinced that our visit to Baghdad was the cause of his brother's malady. He was deeply attached to Ibrahim Agha and spent the greater part of his time in watching by him and praying for his safety. He eventually went down with a heavy fever and lay in bed by his brother's side, looking the more ill of the two.

Three or four other relations were generally present, and sometimes when the dying chief was in an unusually grave condition twenty or thirty aghas would assemble round him, including his son and all his brothers, nephews, and cousins. Rahman Agha was often there with the youngest brother Muhammad Amin Agha, a handsome, finely built man of thirty. Chief amongst the more distant relations were Hussain i Mulla and Jukil Agha. The former, a bucolic gentleman of sixty with a red face and jovial manners, had in Turkish times borne a bad character for lawlessness. From now onwards he was one of my most ardent supporters. Jukil Agha was a pleasant man without sufficient personality to play an important part in tribal affairs; he had a cheery little son of ten called simply Agha, who was old Ibrahim Agha's favourite, and one day on my arrival at Makhmur greeted me, to my great surprise, with a poem of welcome in Persian of his own composition.

On June 29th I formally tried Nuri on a charge of fomenting trouble and conspiring against the Government. Ismail Beg sent down two witnesses from Rawanduz, one of them Khurshid Beg, the brother of Fatima Khanum, who had actually taken part in the rising. Nuri made a spirited defence, detailing his whole conduct since the coming of the British Government, and skilfully explaining away the charges that were made against him. He presented a fine upright figure with flashing eyes, and had I not from personal experience known the part he had played, his words would have convinced me. He only quailed when I produced the letter from Shaikh Obaidullah found in his house. I sentenced him to five years' imprisonment, and in an evil moment decided to despatch him to Kirkuk, instead of Mosul, where prisoners were usually sent, arguing that Sulaiman Beg and his friends in that town might by some means devise his escape. Mosul, further, was the centre of the propaganda amongst the Kurds in the Aqra and Rawanduz districts. As had been the case when he was despatched from Rawanduz, I preferred to send him swiftly and secretly with a small and trusty escort rather than with a big cavalcade. I chose an Arab Ombashi, or corporal, of the gendarmes, called Yunis, whom I knew well to be most trustworthy and brave as a lion, and left it to Saiyid Ali to select six other men to accompany him. On the evening of the 30th I received news of his safe arrival at Kirkuk, and ceased to be anxious about him. I triumphantly sent word to Ismail Beg, at Rawanduz, to post notices making public his sentence and the crimes which led to it.

On July 7th I returned in the evening from a visit to Ibrahim Agha, at Makhmur, to find awaiting me the bitter and almost incredible news that Nuri had escaped on the road between Kirkuk and the railhead at Kingarban. I have rarely, if ever, been so disturbed, and I paced up and down the room for nearly an hour in my vexation. The next morning I visited Kirkuk to find out how it happened and, if possible, to take steps for the prisoner's recapture.

Nuri had arrived safely in Kirkuk, and after being detained there three days had been sent on with the same es-

cort to the railhead at Kingarban, whence he was to proceed
by train to Baghdad. Yunis Ombashi and his men had been
alert enough during the journey from Arbil to Kirkuk, but
must have somewhat relaxed their vigilance during their
detention in the latter place and the subsequent days spent
on the seventy-mile road to Kingarban. The result was that
either Nuri himself or somebody from outside succeeded in
bribing or persuading two of the gendarmes to assist in his
escape. About an hour after sunset, on July 6th, when the
party was only a few miles from the railhead, the Ombashi,
who was riding on ahead, was suddenly shot at from behind
by the two gendarmes who were beside the prisoner; his
horse was killed and he himself was wounded through the
stomach. The conspirators then seized the prisoner and made
off with him into the low hills on the east of the road; Yunis
pursued them until he sank overcome by his wound, while
the other gendarmes, who may or may not have been in the
plot, for some time stood gazing and then fired wildly and in-
effectually in the direction of the fugitives, making no attempt to pursue. Yunis was taken into a hospital at Kifri,
where he reported the affair to the authorities, and the other
gendarmes were arrested. Nuri and his companions made
good their escape, and though there were many rumours,
nothing definite was heard of them for some weeks.

The wire announcing the escape had arrived while I was
at Makhmur, and Captain Dickinson had promptly imprisoned Bawil Agha. On my return I had telephoned to Ismail
Beg instructing him to watch Nuri's brothers and, if possible,
detain them in Rawanduz on security. This order was made
the excuse for a cold-blooded murder. On July 9th it was announced to me that the four brothers had attempted to leave
the town, and being followed by Ismail Beg's men had opened
fire on their pursuers. The latter had returned it and killed
two of them, while the other two made good their escape. I
was compelled by circumstances to accept this story, though
the popular version says that Ismail Beg's men, whether at
the orders of their master himself, or, as is possible, at the
bidding of some of his relations, had come upon the brothers
unarmed while they were tending the channel that brings
water to the town and attempted to shoot them all down in
cold blood.

Before this incident, though extremely annoyed by Nuri's escape, I had not feared any serious consequences. He had not a large following either amongst the people or the tribes, and I thought it probable he would fly to Persia or Turkish territory until a suitable opportunity offered itself for his return. Now, however, the matter was deeply changed. I knew Nuri would never rest until he had avenged his brothers' blood, and I felt that such an awful deed was bound to bring Nemesis upon its authors. Further, the incident did much to alienate popular sympathy from Ismail Beg, who previously had enjoyed a wide support in the town and amongst the surrounding tribes. To make him even more unpopular it was alleged that his men had brutally killed an infant son of Nuri's while they were searching his house; in reality the child had died of fever. From this time onwards both literally and metaphorically dark clouds began to gather over the Kurdish hills.

It was a month before I was able to visit Rawanduz and ascertain the real facts of the murders, and by that time the situation through Mesopotamia was so critical, that I was unable to take any action which might offend our only real friends in Rawanduz, Ismail Beg and his grandfather.

The day after the news of the murders was received I released Bawil Agha from prison and informed him of the death of his sons. The poor old man went mad with rage and grief, saying he had seen the whole thing in a dream the night before it happened, cursing Ismail Beg and calling upon me to avenge him. For several days he wandered round the town like one distraught, stopping all and sundry and bewailing his lot.

On July 11th I set out on another visit to Koi. The evening before I left Hama Agha gave a great dinner party, which was attended by Captain Bradshaw and myself and all the notables and leading officials. Eight great piles of rice with fifty or sixty smaller dishes were spread out for us down the centre of a dais under a big mulberry tree beside a tank of water. This was the last time I was to partake of the old man's lavish hospitality. He had been ill for some time, but now appeared much better; after the meal he smiled at us benignly, and was really quite lively, joining constantly in the conversation.

The following morning, before my departure, I went to say good-bye to him. He was sitting, as was his custom in the hot weather, on a raised ledge inside the archway that led to his guest-house. 'Is all well', I asked him, 'in Koi? Is there anything that is likely to cause trouble?' 'There are some things – ', he said, and then broke off with a childlike smile. 'What things?' I asked him repeatedly; but he kept on refusing to tell me, still smiling. Then, 'Next time will do,' he said, 'next time.' And I was compelled to desist from my inquiries, and to say good-bye. There was no 'next time'.

On August 1st I received a private wire from Jamil Agha of Koi asking urgently for a doctor from Baghdad to attend Hama Agha, and the following day the news arrived that the old man was dead. He was a great loss, and if only he had lived two months longer we should have been spared much trouble and anxiety . For there was none to succeed him, and after his death Koi was left like Rawanduz with a set of intriguing aghas in which none predominated, a state of affairs full of danger to an A.P.O. who has not at hand a force sufficient to oppose all possible combinations. Hama Agha, though for the greater part of his life he had been a man of blood, and it was commonly said that when he perished hundreds would perish with him, meaning that his death would not be peaceful, had since the coming of the British been always on the side of law and order and an uncompromising supporter of the Government. It was chiefly he who had saved the situation in Koi in the blackest days of Shaikh Mahmud's revolt. He was a dear old man, a typical benign patriarch, and when I saw him I always thought of the King in the song in 'Pippa Passes' with the

'. . . old smiling eyes
Where the very blue had turned to white.'

At the same time news came in that Ibrahim Agha's last moments were at hand. I felt that it was best now to leave him to his relations and women-folk. He died on August 4th. He had been ill so long and so often on the brink, that his end was really a happy release; we had mourned him as lost weeks earlier. With him passed a historic figure, the founder

of Makhmur and paramount chief of the great Dizai tribe for
thirty-seven years. He was a clever diplomat and a man who
really loved and was loved by his people. On the day he first
ascended my steps as I was sitting on the roof in my house at
Arbil I conceived a great regard for him, which quickly ri-
pened into a personal friendship; he I think returned my affection, and it is probable that this attachment counted for
more with him and his family than thousands of arguments
for or against the Government.

I set off on August 6th with Ahmad Effendi to attend his
'tazia'. For in Kurdistan when a chief or important man dies
his successor and relations are 'at home' often for several
weeks to all the deceased man's friends and neighbours, who
come to condole with the bereaved and to read a 'Fatihah' for
the repose of the departed. On arriving at Makhmur I saw a
black banner set in the courtyard of the dead chief's house, at
the door of which I was greeted by Khurshid Agha and a host
of other relations. I was conducted to the guest-room, where
we all sat round for a long time in silence. A 'Fatihah' was
read, and then Ahmad Effendi and myself started to express
our sorrow, whilst Khurshid Agha would interject such remarks as 'It is the will of God' or 'It is the fate of all
mankind.' The Kurds have a beautiful expression when they
wish to imply that a man is dead; they say, 'He has performed
the will of God.' Next we praised the dead man's virtues in
detail; and finally, as is the custom, thanked God that he had
left so many fine men behind him, expressing a hope that, if
it were possible, they would excel the late chief in honour and
glory. A simple lunch was now served, and, our personal respects having been paid, I still had an official duty to perform. For a successor had to be appointed to Ibrahim Agha,
and I intimated to his relations that whomever they should
choose I would approve. Since his death they had spent
several hours in conclave discussing this subject, and they
now, through Ahmad Effendi, informed me of their decision,
which was that Khurshid Agha should succeed as official
chief of the tribe and reside at Makhmur, while Mushir Agha,
who was too young for such serious duties, was to take
charge of his father's household and to be the leader of the
tribe in war. I noticed that he was seated beside and just
below Khurshid Agha, while all the relations, including his

uncle, either sat below him or remained standing, and I gathered that he was thus selected as heir presumptive to Khurshid Agha. As Hussain i Mulla said, he was not yet 'man' enough to perform the duties of chief. He gazed at me fixedly the whole time I was in the guest-room with pathetic and inquiring eyes, and I believe he hoped I should install him in his father's place. Before I had always looked upon him as a reckless young blood; from this day onwards he became a man.

I now made a speech formally confirming Khurshid Agha as his brother's successor, while Ahmad Effendi placed over his shoulders the 'abah or ceremonial robe which we had brought with us for the occasion. I assured the new chief that as long as he remained loyal to me, I would regard him with the same devotion and treat him with the same favour as I had shown to his predecessor. After wishing him every success in the future, I turned to Mushir and expressing sympathy with him in his bereavement urged him to follow in his father's footsteps and aspire to become a man after his kind. As Khurshid Agha was old and in bad health, and always objected to publicity, I suggested that he should assist him in every possible way, and go to and from Arbil, whenever occasion demanded, as his representative. I finally expressed a hope that the whole family of Baiz would continue to prosper and remain firm in their loyalty to the Government.

On the conclusion of my speech all the relations came before me in a body, and Hussain i Mulla, who from now onwards was the most active leader of the party, taking upon himself the duties of spokesman, conveyed to me the thanks of the whole family for the way in which I had complied with their wishes and invested Khurshid Agha with his late brother's appointments. He then referred to the care and devotion which I had always shown to Ibrahim Agha, especially in his illness, and promised to me the whole family's undying gratitude and their support in any danger or difficulty. After this the assembly seemed for a time to forget the sorrowful past and talked gaily of the future, Khurshid Agha, all smiling and radiant with tears in his eyes, thanking me for the favours I had bestowed upon him.

I did not know then, but learnt later from Khurshid Agha's own lips, that Ibrahim Agha shortly before he died

had solemnly committed me to his brother's charge, and enjoined upon the whole family that as long as I was in Arbil
they should serve and protect me as though I were their own
tribal chief.

CHAPTER XVII

THE BEGINNING OF THE TROUBLE

ON AUGUST 4TH, Ahmad Beg Zarari came in with letters from the Aqra Surchi, in which they asked to be allowed to make their submission. They were not in my division, and I was unable to deal with them without the permission of the Political Officer Mosul, Lieut.-Colonel Nalder. I was particularly anxious that they should be allowed to come in; though I did not fear an actual invasion in force on their part; while they remained in revolt they were an asylum for refugees from the Rawanduz district such as Nuri and Hamada Shin, and a centre of intrigue and propaganda which was always liable to disturb the Surchi of the Dasht i Harir and malcontents like Yusuf Beg's brothers. Further, the river was now low, and during the last few weeks raiding parties from the Aqra Surchi had several times attacked caravans in the neighbourhood of Duwin and Babachichek, so much so that the main road was now hardly ever used. The attitude of this tribe kept Captain Littledale in Rawanduz and myself in Arbil in a state of continual nervous apprehension, and especially with the unrest that was now spreading through this country I would have given a great deal to see them pacified, 'Dis aliter visum.'

At this time efforts were being made to repatriate via Aqra a very large number of Christian refugees from Urmia and the Tiyari country. The men, an ill-disciplined rabble, had been armed and were now encamped not far from the Surchi country. It was believed that the tribe was at our mercy, and that in any case if we granted them terms we could not guarantee them from the ravages of the refugees. There was also some idea of evicting the Surchi and permanently settling the Christians in their country. Permission to negotiate was therefore refused.

On August 8th I set out on a long-deferred visit to Rawanduz, accompanied by Major C. C. Marshall, D.S.O., who was
on a short visit to Arbil to acquire a knowledge of local conditions, and Lieut. H. E. Bois, who had been sent up to command the new squadron of levies which was in the process of
being raised. I had proposed taking only half a dozen gendarmes as escort, but the previous day Ahmad Effendi had
said to me, 'Why not ask Mustafa Agha to come with you?'
'Why,' I said, 'do you think there is any danger on the road?'
'No,' he replied; 'but you never know what may happen, and
it would be safer to take him.' I therefore wrote to him. After
providing us with an excellent lunch as usual under the mulberry tree at Kora he joined us with four men, viz. his coffee
man, Kanabi, the aged mukhtar Garrawi Chokha Abdulla, a
young cousin of his own also called Abdulla, and a retainer of
his brother's by name Majid. In the evening, after a furious
gallop across the plain, we reached Batas, whither Yahya Beg
had two or three months previously transferred his headquarters from Dera. All night a wild reshabah or black wind
blew down from the mountains and compelled us to sleep indoors.

The following day we made our way to Rawanduz through
the Gorge, at the mouth of which we were met by a dozen of
Ismail Beg's men. On the ridge we were welcomed as usual
by Ismail Beg and Shaikh Muhammad Agha.

We found the atmosphere heavily charged. The people
gazed at us curiously and intently as we passed and all wore
an air of expectancy and apprehension, as though some great
upheaval were at hand. On two occasions within the last few
days mysterious figures in the dark had fired shots into the
Levy camp. All the notables had rushed up to Captain Littledale with offers of assistance, but the assailants, whoever
they were, were few in number and soon disappeared into the
hills. Many conjectures were made as to their identity: some
said Nuri or his brothers, some the Surchi, while the most
popular interpretation was that Ismail Beg had arranged the
whole affair to deter me from making any decrease in the
garrison, and to spur me into more vigorous action against
the whole family of Bawil Agha.

Meanwhile the air was full of rumours about Nuri, who
was alleged to have returned. It was said that he had visited

his family in the town a night or two previously, and was now
hiding in a village close by. On the day of my arrival the
channel which supplies the town with drinking water was
cut. The party who went out to repair it said the breach was
the work of wild pig; but most people saw in it, and saw truly,
the hand of Nuri.

The escaped prisoner had passed through many vicissi-
tudes. Yunis Ombashi swore that he had wounded him, and
in any case he and his companions were deprived of their
clothes and arms by the Hamawand, through whose country
they passed. After some weeks they had managed to reach
Baitwata, the residence of Ahmad Beg, chief of the Pizhgali
section of the Khushnao, and join the two surviving brothers.
From here they had proceeded to the village of the old
Shaikh, Kaka Amin, and were now believed to be with the
latter's brother, the Shaikh of Sellan, in the vale of Akoyan.

Personally though I, too, was filled with a certain nervousness, I did not think the situation was serious. The most
Nuri could do was to collect a small party of men to fire into
the Levy camp or attack convoys in the Gorge. His personal
following was not large, and he had not enough money or influence to raise the surrounding tribes who at present were
peacefully pursuing their normal avocations. Yusuf Beg's
brothers had been quiet for several months, and in any case
were held in check by Ahmad Agha of the Shirwan, while
Shaikh Muhammad Agha's hold over the Balik country
seemed stronger than ever. I calculated that the Aqra Surchi
would be far too much frightened of the refugees to dream of
interfering on my side of the river, and I looked forward to a
long period of security, Nuri being the only fly – and that a
small one – in the ointment.

There was one other thing, however, that caused me some
anxiety. Ismail Beg was becoming daily more unpopular and
less fitted to occupy the position of governor. He was haunted
by fear of the assassin and could rarely be persuaded to leave
his house; except for Muhammad Ali Agha he suspected all
men of plotting against him; and after seeing the fate of
Nuri's brothers those whom he suspected had good reason to
fear and hate him. I think his mother was largely responsible
for his actions, for in his conversations with me he appeared
the same unspoilt unsophisticated boy that I had previously

known. The old Pasha, who had been ill, was now completely recovered, and by his tact and diplomacy did something to make up for his grandson's foolish policy.

Thanks to the unremitting efforts of Captain Littledale and Captain Hutchinson the levies were now a smart body of men, and their training had progressed considerably. I watched them on parade one morning, when besides ordinary drill they took part in physical exercise and boxing, and I was much struck by their improved training and physique and good spirits. Nearly all the men were young, and a real *esprit de corps* was beginning to show itself.

We debated much how the levies were to be sheltered during the winter. Plans had been made for a building to be erected on the site of the old Turkish barracks, which lay eastwards of the lower town on a level space between the Persian road and the Rawanduz Chai. Many delays had occurred and we were already thinking of abandoning the scheme when Hajji Nauras offered to sell his house to us for a very moderate sum. Though situated in the middle of the town and possessing an uncertain water supply this building would provide excellent accommodation, and we readily accepted the offer, hoping it would be possible to build proper barracks the following year, when the place could be used for Government offices.

I was much puzzled, however, by the motives which prompted Hajji Nauras to make the offer. He was certainly not in need of money, and I was half inclined to believe that like a rat he was leaving the sinking ship. He had long conversations with me in which he complained at great length of Ismail Beg's suspicions, which made him fear for his own and his family's safety, and announced his intention, if matters did not improve, of leaving for the Balik country or Persia. His attitude the whole time was very nervous and shifty, and he embarrassed me by asking me to lunch with him on the 12th; for I proposed that morning to leave Rawanduz, but wished to keep my departure secret lest enemies might lie in wait for me on the road. I gave a hesitating answer, saying I would let him know for certain later whether I would come or not. This was sufficient to provide him with the information he required.

ENTRANCE TO THE GORGE

From the Rawanduz end

On the night of the 11th all the notables and chiefs present in Rawanduz were invited to dinner on the roof of Ismail Beg's house. After the usual excellent meal we all sat round on benches and chatted. Before the guests departed I made a speech, commenting on the peace and quiet which had reigned for the past few months, and urging those who were present not to put any credence in the exaggerated rumours from the south that were beginning to circulate. I assured them that despite reports to the contrary there was not the slightest intention of our evacuating Rawanduz, either now or at any time in the near future.

The next morning we departed at 4.30 a.m., Ismail Beg and Shaikh Muhammad Agha, whom alone we had informed of our intentions, riding out as far as the ridge to see us on our way. Before saying good-bye Ismail Beg offered to send a party of his men with me to scout through the Gorge; but I refused, not wishing to give him trouble and thinking that as we had started off so early and so secretly we were unlikely to meet with any trouble.

I rode on ahead down the Gorge with Mustafa Agha and a boss-eyed man called Ali Effendi. With us were Kanabi, Chokha Abdulla, and Majid, with two or three gendarmes, while Major Marshall, Lieut. Bois, and the rest of the party came on more slowly and were soon quite a mile behind us. On the way we passed two or three men coming from the opposite direction, including an Arbil merchant called Saiyid Abdulla Effendi; all eyed us closely but said nothing and passed on.

When we had descended from the upper part of the Gorge, where the road is open, to the close country which begins three or four miles from its mouth, I noticed that Mustafa Agha sent his three men galloping on ahead, and looked round anxiously for the fourth, whom Major Marshall had detained. As he could not find him he signalled to one of the gendarmes to ride on also. For a quarter of an hour we pursued our way closely engaged in conversation until we reached a small opening where the road passes through a patch of mash. A Kurdish boy from the Serchia country was here at work tending the water channels. Suddenly we heard two shots in quick succession just ahead of us. Mustafa Agha stopped dead and pricked up his ears. 'It is probably only the

men on ahead shooting at game', I said. 'No,' replied Mustafa
Agha; 'it is an ambush.' He told me to stay behind while he
rode on ahead and made inquiries; but I had no wish to be
left alone in this death-trap and insisted on accompanying
him. We rode on slowly for two or three hundred yards while
all was deathly still until we reached a point in the road
where a large rock blocked the view ahead. We stopped a
minute and listened and were just about to peer cautiously
round when the gendarme, who had ridden on, ran back on
foot into us panic-stricken. He hurriedly cried out that one of
Mustafa Agha's men had been killed and the other two taken
prisoner; and that he himself had only escaped by jumping
off his mare and running back under cover. There were at
least seventy men, he averred, lying in wait by the roadside.

With two other gendarmes that had by now ridden up we
had only four armed men, while Major Marshall, who was a
long way behind, had about the same number. With such a
small party it was vain attempting to force our way through
this narrow passage thick with trees and enormous rocks,
where a handful of men could hold up an army. I therefore
despatched a gendarme to ride back as fast as he could to
Rawanduz with a note to Captain Littledale, informing him
of what had happened, and asking him to despatch a force of
levies to help us through. My little grey pony must have
scented the danger, for as soon as I turned his head he tried
to gallop back. I kept him, however, at a slow trot, fearing
that another party might be on the road in our rear; we soon
met Major Marshall and Lieut. Bois, who turned back with
us. With all its wild beauty and magnificent scenery the
Gorge now seemed like one dark endless dungeon, with unknown enemies lurking in every corner. Its grand cliffs became unscalable prison walls, its majestic chasm a dark pit
for the destruction of the doomed. As soon as we were clear of
the close country and had climbed the first steep ascent we
halted and held a council of war. We decided to ride back at
any rate as far as the site of the Russian outpost at the
highest part of the Gorge, and there await reinforcements.
On our way I thought I noticed a figure in a kneeling position
on a slope across the ravine, and soon after we passed by we
heard two shots, which we interpreted, probably correctly, as

a signal to the party in ambush that their prey had escaped them.

We waited at the Russian outpost for some time, but as the sun grew hot and our water gave out we decided to return as far as the springs of Baikal. No sooner had we reached this delightful spot and refreshed ourselves than Ismail Beg appeared with the other notables of Rawanduz and their retainers; Hajji Nauras alone was conspicuous by his absence. Shortly afterwards Captain Littledale, armed to the teeth, arrived on his old mare full tilt over the rough ground. Then came groups of levies running hard and streaming with sweat, but obviously eager for a scrap. When some seventy had arrived, Littledale took fifty and proceeded down the Gorge, leaving twenty to come on with us when we should have had the meal which Ismail Beg had sent some of his men to fetch for us.

We spent two or three hours at Baikal, wondering who our assailants might be. Most were inclined to suspect Nuri; but I, refusing to allow myself to be haunted by this bugbear, and being exceedingly sceptical of the rumours that he had returned, was of the opinion that the leader of the enterprise was Begok, the brother of Yusef Beg, who had never forgiven me. The belief was strengthened by the consideration that it was his father-in-law, Nauras, who had supplied information as to the date and hour of our departure from Rawanduz. One or two solitary Kurds coming up the Gorge could give us little news beyond confirming what the gendarme had already told us.

After partaking of some lunch we said good-bye to Ismail Beg and the other notables, thanking them for coming to our assistance, and rode once more down the Gorge. On the way we met the malign hunchback Shaukat Effendi of Bardin and Hassan Agha the mukhtar of Batas riding up to meet us; they informed us that it was the coffee man, Kanabi, who had been killed, and that the other two men, after being plundered and beaten, had been released and were now in Kani Wutman. Word had been sent by telephone from Rawanduz to Yahya Beg at Batas, and all the tribesmen from Serchia and the Dasht i Harir were assembled at the mouth of the Gorge to assist us should necessity arise. We passed through the patch of mash where we had heard the shot, and soon reached the rock which a few hours previously had alone stood between us and death. Some fifty yards beyond the road runs down to the edge of the stream, where there is a little beach, a favourite spot for watering animals. On the further side of the stream is a patch of young willows. Passing the beach the road turns to the left, running along a sort of causeway beneath an enormous rock. It was here that our assailants had hoped to trap us, where the great wall of rock cut off all hope of escape; and on the little white beach a dark stain marked where Kanabi had breathed his last.

From here onwards we found the road picketed by groups of levies, and we soon reached the end of the Gorge. I cannot describe to the reader our feelings at breathing once again the fresh air and seeing before us the little sunlit plain of Khalifan and the surrounding hills. We entered the Gorge soon after 5 a.m., and it was now close upon 5 p.m. We had been shut up in it like flies in a trap for nearly twelve hours, and had three times traversed practically its whole length. It was the last journey I was to make through it – at any rate for some time, for I do not despair of revisiting this country.

Littledale met us just outside the Gorge, for he and his levies had pushed through without encountering any opposition. A party of some fifty Surchi from the Dasht i Harir also greeted me with congratulations on my escape and offers of assistance. Climbing up to Kani Wutman we found Chokha Abdulla looking very sorry for himself in some rough peasant's clothes, the young boy Majid attired only in his undershirt and white drawers with his gay silken coat gone, and the dead body of Kanabi. We heard now the details of their encounter. Kanabi, riding on ahead, had arrived at the little white beach where we saw his blood and, dismounting to drink some water, saw in the willows in front of him a party of armed men. They immediately cried out to him saying, 'Pass on ahead. We do not wish to trouble you, we are waiting only for the hakim [Political Officer].' With the answer, 'I am the hakim's man', Kanabi seized his rifle and fired at them. An answering shot laid him low. Meanwhile some of them rushed out and seized Chokha Abdulla and Majid, stripping them of their arms and outer garments and taking their ponies. They then questioned the old chokha, saying, 'Where is the hakim?' 'He left Rawanduz this morning', he replied, 'with Shaikh Muhammad Agha to visit the Balik country.' 'It is a lie,' they replied; 'we have received word from Rawanduz that he was leaving this morning by this road for Arbil.' 'I tell you,' he insisted, 'he travelled in the other direction.' And they beat him for half an hour, but he would not give us away. After waiting for some two hours in all the party that was lying in wait withdrew, releasing their prisoners, who obtained help and conveyed the dead body of Kanabi to Kani Wutman.

When questioned as to the numbers of the assailants Chokha Abdulla said there were at least thirty, and might be sixty. He was unable to recognise anybody, and the description he gave of the leader of the party only increased the number of conjectures. Knowing how prone a Kurd is to exaggerate where numbers are concerned, I calculated the strength of the party at from fifteen to twenty, and I still clung to the idea that my assailant was Begok.

Subsequent inquiries showed that the chief participator in this ambush was none other than the man who, I suspect, had already once tried to assassinate me through my bedroom window, Khidhr the son of Hamada Shin. He was accompanied by some thirty men, while Nuri was waiting with a similar number on the heights just above ready to assist him. After his night visit to Rawanduz, Nuri had made his way to Biau, where Haris Agha had supplied him with arms, and had then crossed the river and taken refuge with the Aqra Surchi. Almost immediately he and Khidhr had returned with their personal following and some twenty of the Surchi. Marching through Serchia they forcibly enlisted a few men on their way and crossed the Rawanduz Chai to Biau, where Haris Agha aided them with food and a small contingent to swell their force. On the morning I left Rawanduz they proceeded to the village of Sirishma, whence they were able by a narrow path to descend into the Gorge on its north side just a mile above its commencement. The two or three travellers who met us on our first journey down, and the boy working on the mash patch, had been detained and made to swear on the peril of their lives that they would not reveal the presence of the ambush. Only the forethought of Mustafa Agha and the bravery and loyalty of his men saved me from certain death; and if I had ridden on a few steps past the rock which hid us from view it is probable that their efforts would have been in vain.

Mustafa Agha, mild and pious man though he usually appeared, was noted for his pertinacity in revenge. His tribal spirit roused by these events, he refused to bury the dead body on the spot, but obtained an animal and sent it back to his village through the Khushnao country as an incitement to the tribes to avenge the deed. For Kanabi, or 'Ali Baba', as we called him, was no mean man, and there probably was not a braver spirit in the whole Khushnao country. When small he had fallen from a walnut tree and torn his right eye-lid, and the eyelash had re-set crookedly. I can still picture his plump, good-natured face and his curious scar as he used to serve us so often with coffee beneath the mulberry tree at Kora.

We returned to Batas, stopping on the way at the tea-shop just below Hamada Shin's village of Kalikin. Here Yahya Beg and all the Surchi chiefs of the Dasht i Harir had assembled to meet me and congratulate me. They were accompanied by large numbers of armed men, who, I suspect, had been mobilised since the early morning ready to attack Rawanduz or Batas if I had been killed, or to offer me assistance if I escaped. We reached our destination an hour after sunset, and were glad to retire to bed.

The next day Major Marshall and Lieut. Bois returned to Arbil, while I remained at Batas to continue inquiries and institute a campaign against my assailants. I telephoned to Arbil for Saiyid Ali with a party of gendarmes and mounted levies to be sent up to me, and in the evening rode up to Shaqlawah with Mustafa Agha to enlist the help of Qadir Beg. A large party came out to meet me and congratulate me, and Qadir Beg, without being asked, volunteered to raise the whole of the Khushnao to avenge me. I requested him, however, only to provide me with a few trusted men, as I wished to carry out a raid upon Hamada Shin and Nuri, and had no idea of making a general attack upon the hostile shaikhs.

It was on this day, the 13th, that I first obtained news of tribal risings round Baqubah. Ever since the beginning of July we had been receiving almost daily telegrams concerning the disturbances which had broken out on the Euphrates. Though extremely serious they sounded very remote, and did not cause me much anxiety; now the trouble had come east of the Tigris, and it was necessary for me seriously to consider the position in Arbil, which since August 1st had been left without any troops.

On the 14th I returned to Batas to continue my investigations. Saiyid Ali having arrived I despatched him to Serchia to collect information and make all necessary arrests. He returned in the evening with the mukhtar of Sirishama, the boy who had been in the mash patch, and two or three others, who revealed the identity of my assailants. Nuri and Khidhr and their men had returned across the Serchia country with the booty and crossed the river above Bardin. They were now believed to be encamped on top of the hill overlooking the Zab gorge. Haris Agha's men had returned to Biau. Releasing the boy, I sent the others down as prisoners to Arbil and despatched Saiyid Ali with his men to round up Haris Agha. During the day Littledale rang me up to say that Hajji Nauras had fled from Rawanduz towards the Balik country. Efforts were made to bring him back, but he took refuge with Shaikh Muhammad Agha at Walash, where he was allowed to stay.

On the 15th I returned to Arbil via Kora, riding the whole forty miles. I rested during the heat of the day at Kora, where I learnt that Chokha Abdulla had been carried to his village, dying of shame and his injuries. On reaching Arbil I despatched an Arab doctor to attend him. He reported that the old man's condition was not serious, but that he had complained, 'How can I continue loyal to the hakim while I have no rifle and no pony?' I sent him a rifle immediately, and took steps later to compensate him for the loss of his animal.

The next thing I did after my return was to inquire for Bawil Agha, when I learnt that he had fled from the town the previous day. Though annoyed at his escape, I was glad that the poor old man would now be able to ease his aching heart with the sight of his family and his beloved Nuri.

I found the situation in Arbil far from satisfactory. The air was full of rumours of disturbances in Kirkuk and a big revolutionary outbreak was supposed to be imminent there. Sedition mongers were busy in the coffee-shops, inciting the people to rise and defy the Government. Hajji Rashid Agha had appointed a new set of officials to replace mine, most of them scoundrels whom the people would not have tolerated for a week. He had attracted Saiyid Abdulla Agha to his side by offering him the post of Governor. He could do little without tribal support, but Ahmad Pasha and Hajji Pir Daoud had always been his clients, and these two now paid a visit to Jamil Agha at Buhirka, where they formed a conspiracy. I do not think they made any definite plans, but simply agreed to act together in opposition to the Government, secretly for the present and openly whenever an opportunity appeared. As long as nothing serious happened in Kirkuk or Mosul I felt pretty secure.

This day, August 15th, was a Sunday, which with Friday was observed as a half-holiday in my office. That morning Hajji Rashid Agha had sent for the Qazi and said to him, 'Are you working all day today?' 'No,' he replied; 'it is Sunday, and we leave off at noon.' 'Why should you leave off at noon on Sunday, which is not a Muhammadan festival? I am Governor now. Go and tell the officials that they are to work all day, and not leave the office at noon.' 'Well,' replied the Qazi, 'if those are your wishes, you had better go and stand at the top of the steps yourself and prevent them descending when the time is up. I am not going to take any action.'

That evening over the telephone I received good news from Saiyid Ali at Batas that he had captured Haris Agha and seized several rifles. With only twenty men he had crossed the Rawanduz Chai and surrounded the Biau chief's house. He was asleep, and when he came out to see what was the matter he was seized and bound with two or three of his followers and hastily carried off. I told Saiyid Ali to send the prisoners into Arbil, and directed him to stay at Batas and collect men from Qadir Beg and Mustafa Agha to make a raid upon Nuri. Owing to Hama Agha's death it was essential that I should visit Koi, and I left him to make such arrangements as he could.

On the morning of the 16th an anonymous notice appeared in the town calling upon all good Muhammadans to revolt against the infidel Government, and giving notice of a big Maulud, a sort of politico-religious meeting, to be held shortly in a mosque at Kirkuk, which several thousand of the faithful would attend armed. I now determined to make some arrests, but, if possible, wished to associate the notables of the town with me in my action. I therefore summoned them all, except Hajji Rashid Agha, to a conference. After thanking them for the congratulations which they offered me on my escape in the Gorge, I referred to the disturbances in the south and the seditious meetings that were being held in the town. I then asked them if they did not think it would be for the good of the community at large if the worst of the agitators were imprisoned or expelled. Though most of them would have said 'Yes', if in private conversation with me, all were now afraid to speak except Ali Pasha, who gave a grudging assent, presumably to hide his strong anti-Government sentiments, and Saiyid Abdulla Pasha, who suggested that it would be sufficient to warn them.

The meeting broke up, and I immediately had four of the worst agitators arrested. Two of them I imprisoned and two were conducted out of the town. This action had an excellent effect; Hajji Rashid Agha retired to his village on the Quwair road, complaining that Arbil was unhealthy at this time of year, and there was no more seditious talk in the coffee-shops. Largely owing to reports of debates in Parliament which now reached the country, there was a very widespread belief among the people that we were about to evacuate. It was this belief that encouraged tribes and communities hitherto friendly to join the insurgents, and the stronger it grew, the more unsafe did the life of all Political Officers become. Hitherto I had always considered an escort of two or three gendarmes sufficient and never went about armed. Now my friends warned me to be always on the look-out for the assassin. There were several people, about whom I knew too much for their peace of mind, who would have seized any opportunity that offered to rid themselves of me. I therefore, even when moving from my house to my office, was accompanied by at least six gendarmes and always carried a pistol in my pocket. Further, having now good reason to distrust the gendarmes, I asked Khurshid Agha to send me his son's famous paid brigand, Simo Qala, and five stout men to be my constant bodyguard.

On the evening of the 16th I received a telegram in cypher from the Civil Commissioner, the substance of which was something as follows: 'The Political Officer at Khanaqin has had his house and office burnt and is expected to fly the town. The situation on the Diala is very grave. Military detachments have been surrounded, bridges destroyed, and the railway damaged. Baqubah town has been sacked, and the refugee camp attacked. Communications are not likely to be restored for some time as no troops are available. Colonel Leachman has been murdered and the Dulaim Division is in an uproar. If you have trouble we cannot help you with a single aeroplane. Make use of any pretext you can to evacuate all personnel you can spare.' Despite this alarming news I felt confident that nothing really serious would happen in the Arbil Division. In the plains the situation was controlled by the Baiz section of the Dizai, whom I could trust; firm in my conviction that the Surchi were held by the refugees, I decided there was no necessity to evacuate Rawanduz and destroy the fruits of my eight months' labour, in the course of which I had run so many risks. I started, however, slowly to send into Mosul and Kirkuk all surplus cash and British and Indian personnel whose services were not absolutely essential.

The Rais Baladiyah, Ahmad Effendi, was, as usual, my chief adviser in all my difficulties. I lunched with him on the 17th, when he arranged for his father-in-law, Shaikh Maruf, to see that I reached Koi in safety; for I was leaving for that place the next day, it being absolutely necessary that I should judge for myself the exact effect of Hama Agha's death upon the situation. Before I left I had a long talk with Saiyid Ali upon the telephone, and found to my chagrin that the plans for the raid on Nuri had made little progress. I again urged upon him that I did not wish to undertake big tribal operations, and warned him that everything should be finished before the 'Id, which was due on the 25th, when the tribesmen would certainly refuse to undertake any expedition.

I spent the night of the 18th at Alaja with Shaikh Maruf, whom I found very friendly and well disposed. He is a nice talkative old man and a cheery optimist, much given to elaborate religious devotions. A party of his sons and cousins accompanied me the following day to Koi. We halted on the way to have lunch with Karim Agha at the headquarters of his district, Gomashin. He was busy collecting revenue, and reported that everywhere law and order reigned, the only man who was giving him any trouble being Shaikh Muhammad Agha of the Girdi, usually known from his character and appearance as 'The Villain'.

I found Bradshaw quite happy about the situation, although news had just come in that Kifri was in the hands of the tribes and the A.P.O., Captain G. H. Salmon, a prisoner. The only difficulty at present was a dispute amongst Hama Agha's relations as to the possession of his property. His nephew, a red-nosed doddering old man of eighty, called Rasul Agha, with a reputation for being 'Shaitan', or a 'cunning devil', had come in from the Rania district and insisted on being present during the old man's last hours. Subsequently to his death he had refused to go away, and not only claimed the headship of the Ghafuri family, which was conceded to him, but also a large part of Hama Agha's property from which, he alleged, he had been unjustly excluded for many years. He claimed certain shops and the old man's own guest-house, which he said should have passed to his father on the death of his great-grandfather, which had occurred more than a century ago.

I heard both sides of the case, and found that 'The Bishop' and all the notables were united in a wish to rid Koi of this objectionable old man as quickly as possible. They had succeeded in evicting him from Hama Agha's guest-house, but he had established himself elsewhere. He had allied himself to his hereditary enemy, Abdulla Agha, who in May had been allowed to return from Baghdad, and the more Government prestige declined with the bad news that came in, so much the more did the guest-houses of these two become thronged with visitors.

Though there was no immediate danger, it was pretty certain that if the country round became disturbed these two would assert themselves, for though unpopular they were the two most capable men in the town. Jamil Agha, a good and honest man and a well-wisher of the Government had not enough moral character to face a storm. Almost immediately after Hama Agha's death he had been formally appointed to succeed him as Governor, lest Abdulla Agha might aspire to the position, and Rasul Agha together with all the other Ghafuri aghas was now claiming the right to be appointed his assistant, in order that their faction might be represented, forgetting that Hama Agha's age and infirmities necessitated an assistant, whereas Jamil Agha was quite capable of performing his duties unaided. I encouraged them, however, by the assurance that their claims would be considered when they had settled their family differences.

Hama Agha's nephew, the sheep-faced Mulla Ahmad Agha, and grand-nephew, the overgrown weakling, Mulla Hawaiz, had succeeded in establishing themselves firmly in the old man's guest-house, and obtaining possession of his fat little eight-year-old son Muhammad Ziad, whom they paraded everywhere as the head of the family and true successor of their grand old man. By this stroke they really defeated Rasul Agha. If either of them had possessed any presence or intelligence they could have made themselves masters of the situation, for they were wealthier and commanded a greater following than any other of the notables. Poor creatures though they were, they carried on Hama Agha's tradition and remained firm in their loyalty to the Government in its most stormy days.

The next morning I attended the 'tazia' of Hama Agha. All his relations and the notables were present except Abdulla Agha, and we sat in the archway of the guest-house where I had had my last interview with the old man. His son, a handsome but rather bloated child, occupied a seat of honour and was treated as a little prince. As was the custom I expressed my sympathy with the relations in their loss, and praised the deceased's virtues; but those present did not seem to appreciate this topic, possibly because they were tired of condolences, but more probably because they were glad to see the old man go, and the conversation quickly turned to politics. After making a speech on the general situation, I bade farewell to them, and at 2 p.m. started out with Captain Bradshaw for Batas, where I felt my presence was urgently needed.

We travelled by a route I have previously described past the stream of Jali and along the eastern slope of the Safin Dagh through Nazanin to Iran. This is, I think, the most beautiful road I ever traversed in Kurdistan, for after Jali the whole path runs continually between brambles, reeds, and flowers, the sweet-scented wild mint everywhere perfuming the air. We passed many patches of tobacco, where women were busy picking the leaves, which in the villages we saw skewered and drying on the roofs. We reached Iran just after sunset, and were entertained on a house-top by the mukhtar, Ali Beg, who, though he provided us with a poor meal – travellers often complained of inhospitality at this village – seemed most pleased to see us, and treated us with the greatest courtesy. Here we learnt that Qadir Beg was busy collecting a large force of tribesmen to fight the Surchi, and that we should probably find him at Batas the next day.

When we set out again, therefore, we left the main Shaqlawah road and made our way through the Vale of Baraka towards the Dasht i Harir. The country was beautiful in the extreme and very wild. At the village of Baraka we were entertained by the mukhtar, Mam Kak, a rough, jovial old man, who in a record time produced a meal which we ate beside a spring overshadowed by willows. He told us that all the ablebodied men of the village had taken their arms and left for Batas at the bidding of Qadir Beg. He showed the greatest friendliness towards us, and in none of the villages through which we passed did the raising of this force on my behalf seem to have caused any resentment.

On reaching Batas I was surprised to find neither Qadir Beg nor Saiyid Ali. The former had not yet arrived, while the latter, according to Yahya Beg, had collected all the Surchi of the Dasht i Harir and taken them across the river to attack their brethren on the further bank, leaving word for Qadir Beg to follow him as soon as possible. I was much disturbed. In the first place, it became evident that instead of a raid preparations were being made for tribal operations on a large scale; secondly, it was certain that Nuri and the Aqra Surchi had long ago had news of our plans and accordingly were prepared for resistance; thirdly, the 'Id was at hand, and as far as I could see was likely to prevent anything being done at all; and fourthly, if Saiyid Ali had really led the Surchi across the river to attack their brethren he was as good as dead by now. So anxious was I on this last point that I determined to ride that night to Bardin. My escort was too tired to go further, and I only had with me a small contingent of men who had come in from Baraka and the neighbouring villages, and Obaid Beg of Bashur, with two or three of his followers. The latter, the sleek cousin of Saleh Beg, whom he had recently taken an oath to murder should he occupy a certain village, volunteered to accompany me; but the men of Baraka, when I suggested they should find me an escort, began to growl and murmur. Their leader, Mam Kak's son, eventually made them march, but their attitude was such that I dismissed them and sent them back. I rode on through the dark accompanied only by Obaid Beg, an extremely untrustworthy gentleman, his brother, and two gendarmes. It was not a pleasant experience, for I was tired and the road was so rocky that we could only ride at a slow walk. We carefully avoided all villages, and it was midnight before we reached our destination. We only encountered one man on the road, who was terrified when we stopped him and asked his business; he said he was one of Shaukat Effendi's men, and was on his way to Rawanduz to buy sugar, but when we arrived at Bardin the malign hunchback said he had sent forth no man.

To my great relief I found that Saiyid Ali had not crossed the river. He was now bivouacked with some fifty gendarmes and levies and a hundred of the Surchi, whom he had collected chiefly by threats. All their chiefs were there, including Ali Beg, Taj ud Din Agha, and Aziz Agha, while Shaukat Effendi was doing his best to entertain his unwelcome guests. I slept that night just beside Saiyid Ali, while all the Surchi chiefs sat in a circle whispering together a few yards away. They must have been cowed by Saiyid Ali's masterful spirit and the presence of the gendarmes, most of whom would have run away if there had been any trouble; or possibly my arrival took them by surprise, and their slow wits had not time to decide before the morning whether it was convenient to murder me or not.

I was glad to find that Saiyid Ali had realised, too, that these gentlemen were far more likely to fight against us than with us, and I told him to stay at Bardin and watch them carefully. The news from the further bank was that Nuri and Hamada Shin had joined Shaikh Obaidullah at Bajil, where a large force was prepared to resist us. Early in the morning I left Bardin and returned to Batas, to find that there was still no sign of Qadir Beg; about 10 a.m., however, he arrived with Mustafa Agha, Saleh Beg, Rashid Beg, and a large number of minor chiefs followed by contingents of tribesmen, who continued to stream in all day.

All the chiefs, some seventeen in number, came and sat round me in Yahya Beg's room. We talked vaguely about the proposed operation, and after a few minutes Qadir Beg said that he and the other three big chiefs would like to hold a private conference with me. I therefore adjourned with them to the office, at the head of which I sat with a little table before me, while they ranged themselves on benches along the side of the room to my right. Qadir Beg's eyes were nearly bulging out of his head, Rashid Beg and Saleh Beg appeared ashamed and sullen, and were unable to look me in the face, while Mustafa Agha wore a worried look and watched me the whole time with the greatest anxiety. Qadir Beg then began a long rigmarole in which he said that he and his brother chiefs, who were always ready to obey my slightest command, had raised a large force of 400 men, but in doing so had encountered the opposition of the mullas, who declared that it was unlawful for Muhammadans to fight Muhammadans at the bidding of a Christian Government, and more especially was it shameful for them on the 'Id i Qurban, the festival of sacrifice, to offer up to God the blood of the faithful in the place of that of the ordained sacrificial victims. He and his brother chiefs had, he alleged, beaten and imprisoned several of the mullas, and they were willing even though it was contrary to the law of their religion and the decrees of their spiritual authorities to obey my bidding. They would become infidels for my sake. But they could not answer for their men. They were ready, if I gave the word, to lead them across the river, but would they fight on the further side with the threat of hell-fire before them? They were afraid of some disaster which would shame them and their tribe for ever in my eyes. My heart sank within me at his words, not from any disappointment – for I was only too glad to avoid operations on the scale for which Qadir Beg had prepared, and had suspected for some days that the 'Id would prove a stumbling-block – but because I felt instinctively there was treachery at work. His bulging eyes and the shamefaced looks of his companions told their tale. I asked him what course he suggested we should adopt to save our faces. He then undertook to make an announcement to the assembled tribes that I was unwilling to keep them from their homes during their great festival, and that I had given orders for the dispersal of the force and the postponement of the operations. He warned me of the doubtful attitude of the Dasht i Harir Surchi, especially Ali Beg and Shaukat Effendi, and suggested that I should order their chiefs to Batas and explain my intentions. He further promised to invite them all to Shaqlawah for the 'Id, and undertook to be responsible for their behaviour. His force, which now numbered some 400, was not to be disbanded till the following day, in order to give me time to summon the Surchi chiefs, and take measures to prevent an outbreak among them. I accepted his proposals, and he and his companions now left me pondering on the awkward situation. Mustafa Agha managed to see me alone; he would give me no information, but warned me to leave with him for Arbil very early the next morning. I had proposed making a flying visit to Rawanduz to reassure myself of the situation there, but he would not hear of the idea, and taking into consideration that if anything did happen to me the whole division would probably be in an uproar, I determined that it would be wiser to return to my headquarters. I sent word to Saiyid Ali to come in immediately to Batas, bringing with him all the Surchi aghas he could collect.

I now seriously considered the evacuation of Rawanduz or, at any rate, the withdrawal of the greater part of the levies to Batas. Captain Littledale was much surprised when I made the suggestion over the telephone to him, and firmly convinced that the Aqra Surchi could not make an attack in force, and resolved that whatever happened it should not be said that fear of Nuri had twice caused the British to fly from Rawanduz without a struggle, I made up my mind to stand firm. Littledale now asked if he might come into Arbil, which he had to visit monthly for the purpose of seeing to the affairs of the levy depot and the new squadron. After considerable hesitation I granted him permission, calculating that during the 'Id and the few days following any hostile movement would be unlikely and that he would be able to return before the situation developed.

I lunched in Yahya Beg's house, and was afterwards resting alone in my room when I heard a great commotion below. Opening the door I perceived that the house was full of smoke, and it appeared that some straw in a room below had caught fire. I descended hastily and found the house surrounded by a mob of shouting tribesmen; fortunately Qadir Beg appeared on the scene, and between us we managed to keep the crowd under control; the conflagration was quickly extinguished, and I returned to my room. Mustafa Agha informed me later that the straw had been deliberately set on fire in the hope that if I did not perish in the burning house there would at any rate be a chance of disposing of me in the tumult that was bound to follow.

Shortly after this incident, to my great relief, my Dizai bodyguard arrived led by Simo Qala. He was an officious little fellow, and immediately started talking at a tremendous pace in a hoarse whisper. 'Alu told me you specially asked for me, so, of course, I left my work and came. Even though I were to lose hundreds of pounds I would come at your bidding. You should have seen the sensation we caused when we rode into Arbil; Ali Pasha and Hajji Rashid Agha trembled, I can tell you. We'll teach them something. But what are you doing here? Do not trust the tribes. Go back to Arbil as quickly as you can. Do not trust the tribes, I say, do not trust the tribes.' I let him talk, and assured him that I proposed leaving Batas as soon as I possibly could.

I spent some time in pondering over Qadir Beg's attitude. As I suspected, he was on the horns of one of his frequent dilemmas. Rashid Beg, Saleh Beg, and his clerk, Ahmad Midhat, had for several days been regaling him with tales of British disasters in the south, and had finally succeeded in persuading him that he was backing the wrong horse. On my visit to Shaqlawah his offers of assistance had been sincere, but the tales that had been poured into his ears since then had made him delay his preparations until the 'Id gave a good excuse for backing out of his promise. He was still, however, influenced by a certain attachment to myself and to the Government, which had raised him to his present prominent position, while his jealous brother and former friend in league with his confidential clerk, the poisonous scoundrel Ahmad Midhat Effendi, did their best to compromise him, arguing that either the Government to which he owed his position would fall, or else, if it appeared likely to survive, they would be able to ingratiate themselves with it by betraying him. Letters were actually written by Ahmad Midhat to the Surchi shaikhs at Bajil in the name of Qadir Beg, promising to attack me in the rear as soon as I crossed the river. In this way Qadir Beg was gradually committed to an anti-Government policy, Mustafa Agha alone warning him of his folly.

Saiyid Ali arrived about 9 p.m. with two or three of the Surchi chiefs, but not Ali Beg or Shaukat Effendi, who had made their excuses. Soon after their arrival I received a telephone message from Captain Littledale to say that Nuri was on our side of the river. That morning he had looted the postman in the Gorge; he had later ensconced himself in a village just outside the town where he had been secretly joined by his own and his father's womenfolk. He was now supposed to be on his way back over the Kurrek Dagh with a long caravan. On hearing the news Saiyid Ali immediately hurried back to Bardin to collect a party of gendarmes and attempt to intercept him. My hopes ran high, but there was really little chance of success, for the whole countryside would aid one who was thus risking his life for the sake of his womenfolk.

I said little to the Surchi chiefs that evening, and slept on the roof with my bodyguard round me and the Khushnao chiefs a few paces away. During the night the clouds gathered and all the stars were darkened; a howling wind rose which threatened to blow our beds off the roof. Then came thunder and lightning and a heavy burst of rain, a strange disturbance for this time of year. We were all compelled to hurry downstairs and remake our beds in the hot room below.

The next morning dawned heavy and sultry with great black clouds over the Harir Dagh. The elements seemed to betoken some catastrophe. At a very early hour I summoned the Surchi aghas, told them that out of respect for their festival I had decided to postpone operations, and urged them to accept the advice of Qadir Beg, who had accepted responsibility for maintaining law and order throughout the Dasht i Harir. I then set out across the plain with Mustafa Agha and my bodyguard, and I could not help feeling that I was bidding a long farewell to Batas, and that some disaster was imminent. One of Mustafa Agha's men acted as guide and took us by a strange and devious path that avoided Obaid Beg's village and crossed the Babachichek range far to the north of the usual route, descending to Pilinga, a village several miles below Mawaran in the valley of the Shaqlawah river.

Mustafa Agha kept on saying to his guide, 'Why do you take us by this road? It is much longer and rougher'; but all the while we pushed on, cantering wherever possible and maintaining a pace altogether unusual for a journey of this kind. At Pilinga we rested in the porch of a rude hovel where a woman brought us a basket of purple grapes picked from a vineyard close at hand; our stay was brief, and afterwards we rode on faster than ever, not resting until we reached Kora. I realise now that the rebukes Mustafa Agha showered upon his guides were but feigned; he was hurrying me away by an unfrequented route from the dangers that now lurked everywhere in these hills.

I remained some hours in Kora, resting in the archway on top of the hill beside the guest-house. A wonderful meal was produced with 'mastao' full of lumps of snow. Chokka Abdulla was there to greet me, recovering now from his injuries, and Kanabi's brother was also brought to me swearing to revenge his loss. After thanking Mustafa Agha for all the devotion he had shown towards me I departed with a large escort over the hill to the Bastura Chai where my car awaited me. This was my last journey among my beloved Kurdish hills, so magnificent and full of beauty, yet so often the lurking place of murder and sudden death.

CHAPTER XVIII

THE STORM BURSTS

EVERYTHING REMAINED QUIET in Arbil and the 'Id was
one of the gayest and most joyous ever known. Never had the
town appeared so peaceful and so prosperous; the streets
were full of the laughter and shouting of children, and there
could be no doubt that the people at large were happy and
contented. On the first day, August 25th, all the notables and
officials came to my office, as was the custom, and the following day I returned their calls, purposely omitting Hajji
Rashid Agha. As a result of this he and his guest-house were
boycotted for several days, and he was humiliated into begging for an interview with me. He protested his loyalty, and I
told him he would probably soon have an opportunity to
prove it and by his acts I should judge him. On the afternoon
of the second day of the festival I paid a long call on the
saintly shaikh, Mustafa Effendi, who questioned me much
concerning the Christian religion. He asked me if possible to
supply him with the Gospel in any language he could read,
and the next day I sent him an Arabic Bible which I happened to possess.

Meanwhile I received news from Saiyid Ali that he had
reached Khalifan to find that Nuri had already passed that
village; he pursued him through the Serchia country without
success, and it appears that the caravan crossed the Zab just
below the junction of the Rawanduz Chai, near Sawer, while
a large party of the Surchi threatened to attack the post at
Bardin in order to prevent patrols being sent out in that
direction. I ordered Saiyid Ali to return to Arbil, leaving a
strong post of gendarmes and levies to watch the crossing at
Bardin. On the 25th, Captain Littledale arrived; he had followed on Nuri's tracks across the Kurrek Dagh and just
missed him by a few hours.

On the 27th I was informed by the telegraph master that communication with Batas was interrupted. I suspected that some raiding party had cut the wire, and sent out a few gendarmes with a man to repair it. On the evening of the 28th I returned from a visit to Makhmur to learn that the previous morning the Surchi with Nuri and Hamada Shin had crossed the river a hundred strong, and had been joined by the whole of their fellow tribesmen of the Dasht i Harir. They had captured, destroyed, or expelled the gendarme posts at Bardin, Batas, and Babachichek, and were now marching on Rawanduz.

The trouble started with the action of Ali Beg of Khurra, who early on the 27th surrounded and disarmed the gendarme post at Babachichek and destroyed a considerable length of the telephone line. He then sent word to the Surchi, who were waiting prepared on the other bank, and they, crossing the river in force, laid siege to the post at Bardin. Several gendarmes were killed and many captured, while two or three succeeded in escaping and conveying the news to Yahya Beg at Batas, who was just able to inform Captain Hutchinson at Rawanduz before the line between the two places was cut. Then seizing all the Government money he fled with a few gendarmes to the Khushnao village of Sisawa, which he just managed to reach in safety. The insurgents occupied Batas, looting the Government offices and the Pasha's house. Qadir Beg took no action whatever.

I had a long talk with Captain Littledale, and it was arranged that he should collect all the men available and leave as soon as possible with Saiyid Ali for Shaqlawah, where he was to obtain help from Qadir Beg. If he was strong enough he was then to attack Batas and to try and fight his way through to Rawanduz. He left before dawn on the 29th with Sergeant-Major Kennard, Saiyid Ali, and two junior officers, Hamid Effendi and Darwish Effendi, and about 100 men, of whom forty were mounted, nearly all of them raw recruits. It was a forlorn hope, but knowing Captain Littledale's courage and character, I did not despair of his success.

I passed the three days from the 29th to the 31st in a state of the greatest suspense. All was quiet in Arbil; though Hajji Rashid Agha, the opposition Dizai chiefs and Jamil Agha of the Girdi, were still busy holding conferences and intriguing. Fearing a possible *coup d'état* I sent a message to Khurshid Agha, asking him to come into Arbil with his following to support me.

All this time the poor Christians of Ainkawa lived in a state of terror and kept begging me for rifles, which if I had given them they would probably have sold to the tribesmen on the first opportunity. The Mutran or Metropolitan of Kirkuk, Istefan, was staying there at that time, and on the 29th invited me to dinner. I rode out with Lieut. Bois and my Dizai escort; the old man in his purple robes came out to meet us, and we dined on the roof of his private room which adjoined the church. These people were sincerely to be pitied, and Ahmad Effendi kept on saying how his heart ached for them, for if any general tribal uprising took place a brutal raid on their village was a certainty.

Ever since the news of the Surchi invasion had reached Arbil I had been sending wires begging for aeroplanes and action either by the military or the refugees in the Surchi country north of the Zab to compel those who had crossed the river to return. No aeroplanes were available, the military position in Mosul was such that not a man could be spared, while there were so many obstacles to action on the part of the refugees that nothing was done. For a fortnight the Surchi shaikhs of the Aqra district were able to devote their whole strength and undivided efforts to the destruction of Government authority in the Arbil Division.

On the 31st, while we were at dinner on the roof, we heard someone galloping furiously towards the house, and in a minute Captain Littledale, much bedraggled, came rushing up the stairs. His first words were that the whole of the Khushnao had risen against us, and that he had barely escaped with a handful of his men. The details of the disaster were as follows:

Captain Littledale reached Shaqlawah on the 29th to find Qadir Beg in a state of great agitation with his eyes bulging out further than ever. He promised Captain Littledale to assist him in evicting the Surchi from Batas, but asked for time to collect his men, saying that he would be ready the following morning. The next day came and Qadir Beg begged for operations to be postponed till the evening. The whole party now moved down to Sisawa at the southern end of the Dasht

i Harir and about eight miles from Batas. Here all the
Khushnao chiefs were collected together with Mustafa Agha
of Kora; they sat in conference practically the whole day and
many heated discussions took place. Evening came and Qadir
Beg requested a further postponement. Captain Littledale
could now see by his attitude and that of his brother chiefs
that they were contemplating treachery, and he decided that
the only thing to do was to attack at once, especially as according to his information there was only Bawil Agha in
Batas with about forty men, the rest of the insurgents having
moved up towards Rawanduz.

He therefore ordered his men to prepare to march. Qadir
Beg now clung to him and besought him not to attack till the
next day when he would assist him with 400 men, and just as
he was about to depart Saleh Beg rushed up to him and
kissed him on each cheek, imploring him to abandon his intention. Whether this was remorse or a piece of pure humbug
I have never been able to decide. Captain Littledale, however,
had made up his mind and remained firm. He set out, with
Rashid Beg's nephew, Abdur Rahman Beg, following just behind with a few retainers. Halfway to Batas they met coming
from that village Azo, the headman of Mawaran. As he could
give little explanation of what he had been doing there Saiyid
Ali threatened him and made him accompany the party. The
force numbered about forty mounted and sixty foot. A mile
from their objective the former were made to dismount and
the ponies were left with a few men under Sergeant-Major
Kennard. It was now noticed that a beacon had been lit on
the crest of the Harir Dagh, obviously a signal to Shaikh
Mazo, Nuri, and the other insurgents who were supposed to
be near Kani Wutman. Two parties were formed, one to attack Batas from above and one from below. Captain Littledale accompanied the latter, which within a short distance
of the village suddenly encountered very heavy fire; for
Shaikh Obaidullah himself had just arrived with a hundred
men to reinforce Bawil Agha. The raw levies immediately
turned and fled, Saiyid Ali Effendi and three or four veterans
alone remaining with Captain Littledale. These, though attacked by vastly superior numbers, managed to hold their
own and cover the retreat of their men to the point at which
the ponies were held. Here too, the second party retired and

the whole force rallied. The men recovered their spirits, and Littledale was about to make another assault with his whole strength, when he found himself heavily attacked in the rear by, as he presumed, the Kushnao. There was nothing left for him to do but to make his way back across the hills to Arbil. Forming up his men he withdrew across the plain while the whole country resounded with the noise of rifle fire, and the night was illumined by signal fires from every height. A volley greeted the beaten force from every village on its way, and when they entered the hills every corner and depression seemed to be alive with armed men. Providence or the darkness protected them and the morning found them approaching Kora. Majid Agha, Mustafa Agha's brother, met them on the road and asked them to come in for rest and refreshment; but they counted him an enemy, and pushed on all the faster. Not until they had crossed the Bastura Chai and descended to the plains did they take any rest.

Altogether out of the hundred who set out some sixty or seventy came through, of whom thirty-six were mounted. Only four ponies were lost. Of the remaining men, some were detained by Qadir Beg, and some stripped by the insurgents and released. A few were killed. Four men took refuge with Azo of Mawaran. He served them with tea and then suddenly attacked them, killing three, while the fourth escaped wounded to tell the tale. Hamid Effendi, one of the officers, was wounded in the attack on Batas and fell into the hands of Shaikh Obaidullah; here he was killed in cold blood, it is said by being hurled down from the roof of a house on to the stones below. This vengeance was demanded by the relations of some woman he had wronged, when he had previously been stationed in the village as a gendarme officer.

Captain Littledale was awarded the M.C. and Saiyid Ali the Military Medal for their behaviour on this night. To lead such a forlorn hope required the greatest bravery; and it was owing to their courage and endurance under the greatest difficulties that such a large proportion of the force returned in safety. Sergeant-Major Kennard's steadiness was of the greatest value to Captain Littledale, while Darwish Effendi, who was one of the two officers found hiding under the seat at the time of the murder of Sergeant Methuen, displayed unexpected coolness and presence of mind, and was most active in encouraging the men to keep together and avoid panic.

On hearing the result of this affair I realised that a serious crisis was at hand. The wavering Qadir Beg had willy-nilly been committed by his relations to an anti-Government policy, and the whole Khushnao were therefore in a state of revolt. Rawandus was now doomed – in fact it had already fallen – and my sole hope was that the lives of Captain Hutchinson and the two other British in the place might somehow have been preserved. It was obvious that Koi without Hama Agha would become untenable, while there were already rumours in the air that the Surchi and the insurgents from the Rawanduz area proposed to descend upon Arbil.

On the next day, September 1st, in reply to my continued requests for military assistance, I received a promise that aeroplanes would visit Rawanduz the following morning. I talked with Captain Bradshaw at Koi over the telephone, and warned him to be ready for immediate evacuation, despite his assurances that all was still quiet there. Although the Political Officer Sulaimaniyah protested that the safety of his division would be imperilled, the Civil Commisioner had ordered me to take this step in the event of the situation deteriorating, as it was not worth while risking a valuable British life in a remote spot in the present state of the country. We now began more vigorously to despatch personnel, Government property and private kit to Mosul, as we had again been informed that no troops could be spared for us and that we must, if necessary, evacuate Arbil. I was determined to stay myself as long as possible, as I knew the chaos and misery that would ensue on my departure. The town would be looted by the tribes, and untold suffering would be brought upon the poor; my friends, in any case Ahmad Effendi, would have to fly and leave their property to be destroyed. Ainkawa would certainly suffer heavily and there was a possibility of the poor Christians being massacred. All communication with Baghdad was now interrupted except from Mosul, and Arbil was the sole means of communications between that place and Kirkuk. Before the evening news came in that the Kushnao were collecting their men to attack both Arbil and Koi, and I calculated that unless troops arrived a week would be the limit of my endurance.

On September 2nd I held further long conversations with Captain Bradshaw at Koi. The aspect of affairs there was now rapidly changing for the worse. Jamil Agha, who, if he had been a man, could have made himself master of the situation, shrank from the struggle and weakly joined an alliance which had been contracted between Abdulla Agha, Rasul Agha, and Mulla Ahmad Agha i Mam Sulaiman, who belonged to a junior branch of the Ghafuri family. These four formed themselves into a junta for the control of the situation, their only opponents being the other Mulla Ahmad Agha and Mulla Hawaiz, who remained loyal to the Government and kept Captain Bradshaw informed of all developments. They further began to collect their men to resist the rumoured Khushnao attack.

Captain Bradshaw was now living in the barracks on the mound overlooking the town. His rooms were above the gateway which led into a large open courtyard. On the night of September 2nd a party somehow gained access to this courtyard and poured a volley of shots into the A.P.O.'s quarters. He was fortunately uninjured, but the fire returned by the gendarmes at the gate killed one of his ponies. All the notables of Koi immediately hurried to his assistance with their retainers, and a pretence was made of scouring the country. It is my belief that the whole of this affair was organised by Abdulla Agha's party – in fact, one of his nephews appeared the next day with one eyebrow singed off as if by a bullet – the intention being not to injure Captain Bradshaw, but to hasten his departure from the town.

In any case next morning Jamil Agha advised him to leave, and it was arranged that he should entrust Government money and property to the self-constituted committee of four and escape that night with Mulla Hawaiz and a large escort. It was alleged that the Khushnao had sent a message to say that they would certainly attack the town if the A.P.O. were not expelled, and the four promised to take charge of Government interests until an improved outlook should enable him to return. There was nothing to do but accept the situation. The whole plot had undoubtedly been carefully arranged by Abdulla Agha; it is a typical piece of Kurdish cunning, universally adopted in disturbances of this nature, the idea being to obtain possession of as much Government property as possible, with the object of keeping it if the Government goes under, or, if it survives, of returning it, in the expectation of some substantial reward for its preservation.

On the evening of September 3rd Captain Bradshaw handed over the money, amounting to some 30,000 rupees, to Jamil Agha to be distributed in equal portions amongst the four for their safe custody. After saying farewell to all the notables and dining with little Muhammad Ziad in Hama Agha's house he took his departure with Mulla Hawaiz, who, warning him that attempts would be made to intercept him, led him by an obscure route through the worst part of the sandstone hills, bringing him the next morning in safety to Shaikh Maruf's house at Alaja.

On the morning of the 4th I received a call from Koi on the telephone, and, to my surprise, found that the Indian accountant, Mr. Muhammad Sadiq Batt, was still there. He narrated to me the events that took place immediately following Captain Bradshaw's departure. No sooner had he left than Saleh Agha, an unprincipled and reckless young man belonging to the faction of Hama Agha, had galloped into the town with a large following and forcibly seized from the committee of four more than half the money over which they were gloating. General disorders then broke out in the town and the A.P.O.'s house was looted; his servant with his kit was intercepted and compelled to return to Koi, where he found an asylum in Hama Agha's house. Firing continued all night long and several acts of violence were committed; only with daybreak had peace been restored. The committee of four were alarmed by the fiend of disorder which their action had called into being, and Jamil Agha now spoke to me over the telephone, regretting the departure of the A.P.O., and asking for his early return with troops; he suggested that Mr. Batt should be allowed to remain in the town to show that he and his fellow members were acting with the support of Government authority. I gave my assent and appointed Mr. Batt as Government representative in Koi till the A.P.O. should return. He stuck to his post, being provided with a guard by Jamil Agha, and carried out his difficult duties with tact and courage. 'The Bishop'. otherwise Mulla Muhammad

Effendi, who had been so prominent during the last two years, and an account of his haughty and dictatorial manner had made himself very unpopular, on the A.P.O.'s departure decided to withdraw for a time from politics and retire to his village. Leaving Koi, therefore, with a reasonable state of order maintained by the committee of four, and still connected by telephone with Arbil, we will return to events at Rawanduz.

For two days after Captain Littledale's return from Batas I remained in a state of the greatest anxiety as to the fate of Captain Hutchinson and his companions. At length to my great relief I received a message over the telephone from Captain Cook at Darband to the effect that he had received a letter from Shaikh Muhammad Agha stating that Captain Hutchinson, Mr. Turner, Sergeant-Major Shepperd, and Ismail Beg were safe with him in Walash, and that he proposed sending them across the mountains to Rania. Three days later I was able to speak to Captain Hutchinson over the telephone and ascertain the details of what had occurred.

On receiving the news of the Surchi attack on Batas from Yahya Beg on the 27th, just before the line was cut, Ismail Beg, without consulting Captain Hutchinson, had sent out to the two Sulaiman Aghas of Balikian, Mir Muhammad Amin Beg of Dargala, and his relations in the Vale of Akoyan, to mobilise their men for the defence of Rawanduz. They began to stream in that evening, and the following day the town was full of tribesmen clamouring for arms and ammunition.

Meanwhile Captain Hutchinson was in a terrible predicament, being as yet poorly acquainted with the local situation and personalities. He waited in vain for instructions from Arbil, and finally despatched a message which reached Captain Littledale at Sisawa; an answer was sent but never arrived. On the 29th news was received that Nuri and the Surchi were at Kani Wutman making preparations to march on Rawanduz; a scheme of defence was therefore adopted, and picquets from the levies were posted on commanding positions round the town. The tribesmen were also asked to supply men for these duties, but few complied; the majority remained in the town and surrounded the levy barracks, for they had now moved from the camp on the hill into Hajji Nauras' vacated house, making insistent demands for ammunition. Their attitude grew more and more threatening, and it soon became clear that their sole idea was to obtain as much loot as possible before the Surchi arrived. Kurdish tribes are the most dangerous friends in the hour of need unless there are means at hand to keep them under control.

By the 30th the assembled tribesmen were quite out of hand, when fortunately Shaikh Muhammad Agha arrived. To the disappointment of the Government party he was accompanied by only fifty men, and did not appear to be prepared for resistance. Immediately on his entry to the town he summoned all the notables to attend a council of war, as a result of which he informed Captain Hutchinson there was no alternative to evacuation, and that he must leave at once for Walash. Plans were made accordingly. There were now some 150 levies in Rawanduz, of whom seven only, all natives of the place, had deserted since the beginning of the trouble; of the remainder all those whose families were living in the town were allowed to stay behind and arrange for their removal or protection. The party that left with Captain Hutchinson numbered about a hundred, in addition to which Shaikh Muhammad Agha, Abdulla Pasha, and Ismail Beg also accompanied him with their tribal followings. If any of the levies strayed at all on the road he was immediately deprived of his rifle and ammunition by the tribesmen. Leaving the men under their Yuzbashi Sabri Effendi, a native of Koi, at Dargala, to make their way independently to Rania, Captain Hutchinson, with his British companions and Ismail Beg, followed on with Shaikh Muhammad Agha to Walash. Here they were well treated and, after obtaining news from Captain Cook that they could safely make their way to Darband, departed for that place with a tribal escort. After resting there two or three days they proceeded to Kirkuk via Sulaimaniyah, except for Ismail Beg, who remained at Darband.

The levies were entertained at Dargala by Mir Muhammad Amin Beg, and while they were sitting at meat the majority of them were suddenly deprived of their rifles. Doubtless if the Government recovers its authority in this area Mir Muhammad Amin Beg will produce them saying: 'Here are some rifles preserved from the hands of the tribesmen. Please make me head of the district and give me a

'JOY-WHEEL' USED AT KOI

during the 'Id,' 1919

MULLA HAWAIZ AGHA OF KOI

REMAINS OF LOWER TOWN, RAWANDUZ

salary as a reward for my forethought.' Fifty rifles in all were taken, which left only about twenty men still armed. Sabri Effendi marched over the hills to Rania where he arrived some fifty strong; the party made its way thence without much difficulty to Arbil, whither most of those who had stayed behind in Rawanduz or strayed subsequently had already returned. It is noteworthy that hardly any of the men lost their lives, not even the Christians.

The old Pasha, who, I believe, managed to save his money bags, took up his residence for the present with Mir Muhammad Amin Beg at Dargala.

Within an hour or two of the departure of the levies Shaikh Mazo at the head of the Surchi and Nuri with his following entered Rawanduz without opposition. It is reported that Nuri heaved a deep sigh of disappointment when he found that Ismail Beg had escaped his clutches. The whole town was looted with the exception of the property of Hajji Nauras, and all the remaining notables, such as Muhammad Ali Agha, Karim Beg, and Mulla Suayid Effendi, fled. I would mention here that the last-named was the only man in Rawanduz who proved of any assistance to Captain Hutchinson when the crisis came; he further concealed and protected many of the levies who had stayed with their families and enabled them to escape to Arbil. Ahmad Agha of the Shirwan came down with a considerable force to assist the Government, but hearing when he reached the Dasht i Dian that Captain Hutchinson had departed, immediately turned round and made his way back to his own country.

For a few days Shaikh Mazo and the Surchi controlled the destinies of Rawanduz, and it was rumoured that they even sent for their families, proposing to settle there. The presence, however, of an alien body in their midst caused much resentment amongst the surrounding tribes; dissensions broke out and the Surchi withdrew to Batas. Bawil Agha and Nuri alone remained, and they sent for the aged Shaikh, Kaka Amin, and set him up as Governor. They took toll off caravans and made efforts to collect land revenue, spreading reports that a large Turkish force was on its way from Van to assist them, and they had received orders to collect grain ready for its arrival.

Thus we must take our leave of Rawanduz. According to the latest information I have received, at the end of the year Nuri and Bawil Agha were left with only a following of thirty men, and were selling their rifles and ammunition to buy food. All the other inhabitants had fled, so that the little of the town which was spared by the Russians and the Turks is now desolate and falling into ruins. This, then, was the fruit of all my efforts and hopes.

CHAPTER XIX

KHURSHID AGHA KEEPS HIS WORD

KHURSHID AGHA ARRIVED IN Arbil on September 2nd
with a following of eighty men, and for the next twelve days
was the virtual ruler of the town.

Letters now arrived for Mustafa Agha, explaining that
after the failure of the attack on Batas, Qadir Beg had been
unable to control his relations, and against his will had been
compelled to join the insurgents. He was anxious to make his
peace with the Government, but was afraid of the punishment that was likely, to reward his own and his tribe's
treachery. The forces of the Surchi were now concentrated
round Batas, while small gatherings of the Khushnao were
reported from various points in their country.

On the 4th we received news, which proved to be false,
that Qadir Beg was about to make his submission, and that
Shaikh Obaidullah and the Surchi had returned to their own
side of the river. This revived our drooping spirits. In the afternoon Major Longrigg arrived from Kirkuk with Lieut.
Bicknall, the Local Purchase Officer, who had brought a large
convoy of Ford vans to remove as much as he could of the two
lakhs of rupees which were still in my Treasury. This money,
which was all in silver, was a source of considerable anxiety
to me, as it offered a great temptation to the local notables
and chiefs. Its evacuation caused a further fall in Government prestige in the town, as the people thought I was about
to fly; from now onwards my authority as Political Officer
was practically nil, and it was only through the kind offices of
Khurshid Agha and Ahmad Effendi that I was able to exert
any influence. It was a great blessing, however, in the days
that followed that the money had been removed; its presence
would have tempted too far the avarice of men like Saiyid Abdulla Pasha and Ahmad Pasha, who, as it was, were content

to remain neutral until the issue of the struggle should declare itself.

Captain Bradshaw arrived safely about sunset, and we had a champagne dinner to celebrate the gathering. I have rarely passed such a hilarious evening; we somehow felt that ere many hours had passed the clouds which now hung heavy on the horizon would envelop us, and we feasted in the spirit of 'Let us eat, drink, and be merry, for tomorrow we die.' Moreover, with Captain Bradshaw's arrival, a great part of my anxiety vanished; for all the British officers and men who had been in the outstations of Rawanduz and Koi, where I was powerless to take any steps for their protection, were now safe.

On the 5th the sky darkened. News arrived that the Surchi together with the Khushnao and the Girdi of the Koi district had collected their forces and were advancing to attack the town. The notables and assembled chiefs held a hurried conference, and Ali Pasha, hoping to create a situation which would frighten me into flight, asked Khurshid Agha to bring all his tribesmen into the town. Major Longrigg and Lieut. Bicknall departed with the greater part of the treasure; there were, however, some Rs.30,000 still left, and arrangements were made for more cars to be sent from Kirkuk to remove this, should the situation allow.

Captain Bradshaw and Lieut. Bois left for Mosul, while some of the Indian personnel with the confidential records were evacuated to the rail-head at Sherqat. Captain Dickinson from this time onwards did yeoman work driving our car up and down the road to Quwair – for the regular driver happened to be absent on leave to Baghdad. He sometimes performed the journey there and back three times a day, dumping personnel and kit at Quwair to be removed by cars from Mosul. He ran a considerable risk, as he was never attended by more than one gendarme; he several times encountered armed parties on the road, but fortunately no one attempted to interfere with him. He usually spent the night at Quwair, which was guarded by a detachment of gendarmes from Mosul. The old car did marvels; it was bent and battered by the heavy boxes it had to carry and its engines rattled and roared, but it never succumbed.

I now packed up all my private kit and the furniture of
our house; it was a most melancholy proceeding breaking up
the old home, and wandering round the bare carpetless
rooms, and it was still more melancholy to contemplate that
the efforts which I had lavished during the last few months
to promote peace and prosperity in the town now seemed
likely to end in bringing destruction upon her palaces and
death to her people.

In the evening the Dizai began to gather and the town
was full of armed men. My bodyguard attended me closely
wherever I went, and in the familiar places where I had once
wandered free and unattended death now seemed to lurk. I
looked out towards my beloved hills over which I had often
ridden so gaily, and where I had been so hospitably entertained, and it seemed most strange to think that they were
now enemy territory and that if I entered them I should probably never return.

That night was the last for some time that we spent in our
house. Situated right out in the fields half a mile from the
town it was too open to a sudden raid to be pleasant, and we
had decided the next day to move into the gendarme barracks. This was one of the only two occasions during the
trouble on which I suffered from a bad attack of nerves. The
house became a place of terror; unknown perils seemed to
prowl round it in the dark, and the hours passed sleepless
while I listened for the shots which should announce an attack. We were well guarded, with strong points at the four
corners of the roof, where we were sleeping, and a Lewis gun
which Captain Littledale had managed to annex from an
aeroplane that had visited us.

The nest morning we moved into the barracks, a square
building with a spacious courtyard, on the western edge of
the town just beneath the Fort. Here we prepared to hold out
as long as possible, though I proposed to withdraw to Mosul
rather than stand a siege should the tribes attack. Those who
remained with me were Captain Littledale, Sergeant-Major
Kennard, and Mr. Robbins, who was in charge of the town
police. Captain Dickinson, as previously related, was busy
running up and down the Quwair road, while all the other
British personnel had been evacuated. Of the Indian personnel the Treasury Officer, Mr. Duli Chand, and Mr. Baluch,

who was in charge of the Post and Telegraph Office, stayed with me in Arbil, except for the two blackest days, when I sent them down to Quwair. The native telegraph operators remained at their posts, and communication was maintained with both Kirkuk and Mosul throughout the trouble.

Of the levies and gendarmes all who wished were allowed to take their discharge. If the worst came to the worst and we were compelled to fly or fight our way out, we preferred to have with us only a few men whom we could trust rather than a large force the attitude of which was doubtful. We were left with some fifty levies and twenty gendarmes, besides which the town police, some thirty-five in number, remained with us almost to a man; they were devoted to Mr. Robbins, were much more highly trained than the other bodies, and probably feared the results of their unpopularity with the townspeople in the case of trouble. The men who stayed with us, though if they went out into the streets they were insulted by the tribesmen, and though our cause at times appeared almost hopeless, behaved throughout with the greatest courage and endurance; they were always on the alert, and there was never amongst them a hint of treachery, which I feared more than the savagery of the tribes.

The town was now swarming with armed men. The previous evening Khurshid Agha had sent his 'hawar', or call to battle, to all his supporters in the district, including the Tai Arabs, and they flocked into the town to the number of three thousand. I would gladly have averted this, for I feared the wild Kurdish passion to loot. A small spark would cause a conflagration which chiefs like Khurshid Agha, with all the goodwill in the world, would be powerless to extinguish. It was the prospect of loot which brought the men in so readily and influenced even most of the aghas themselves. They were guided now by a wish to serve loyally Khurshid Agha and myself, and now by a desire to terrify me into flight in order that the well-stocked bazaar and the property of the unfortunate townspeople might be at their mercy.

That day at noon I was just coming out of the Telegraph Office, which is situated at the eastern end of the bazaar, when I heard again the 'hooroosh' that had startled me in Rawanduz, the putting up of shutters, the bolting of doors, and the scurrying of many feet. Men, women, and children began pouring out of the bazaar streaming past me and shouting, 'The tribes have come; the tribes have come.' My bodyguard tried to hurry me to the barracks; but I was determined not to join in the panic, and rode back slowly and deliberately. On the way I passed Hussain i Mulla hastening to the scene of the disturbance with his face redder than ever and a big stick in his hand. At the barracks I found Littledale had sounded the alarm and was ready with his Lewis gun; in a few minutes, however, all was quiet, and Ahmad Effendi came and related what had happened. It appears that a tribesman, tired of haggling with a Jewish shopkeeper in the bazaar, had roughly thrown his money down and seized the article he required. The Jew had then started yelling that he was being robbed, and that the tribes were looting the bazaar; a panic followed, and not unnaturally the tribesmen seized the opportunity and began helping themselves. Hussain i Mulla then appeared with his big stick, and by means of curses and drubbing quickly restored order. The Jew who had given the alarm was seized and imprisoned, while such property as had been taken was restored to its owners. The incident served as an example of the nervous apprehension of the townspeople, and the readiness of the tribesmen to seize every opportunity for loot.

For the next eight days Hussain i Mulla took upon himself the policing of the town; and it is a great tribute to his energy and power of command that he was able to control the thousands of wild, greedy, and well-armed tribesmen so thoroughly that not a single crime was committed save for one murder due to an old feud between two of the townspeople. Here, too, the murderer was swiftly arrested and imprisoned. Further, assisted by Khurshid Agha's elder brother, Rahman Agha, Hussain i Mulla undertook the rationing of all these men, who, as they had been called in to assist the Government, had to be fed at Government expense. Though fortunately we had a sufficient store of wheat in the granaries, and were able to purchase the other necessaries, the unruly tribesmen besieged the distributors all day, complaining of the quantity and quality of the food.

My old enemy, Sawar Agha of the Piran, now quite innocently became the source of the greatest trouble to me. As has been related, he was arrested by Captain Barker in the

autumn of 1919 and imprisoned at Baghdad. Subsequently
he had been entrusted to my care at Arbil on a security provided by the Dizai chief Hajii Pir Daud. Fearing that in the
event of any disturbance in the town he might make good his
escape to Rania there to plague the A.P.O., Captain Cook, I
had two or three days previously arrested him and sent him
under escort to Mosul. His wife had then appeared in person
and thrown herself at the feet of Khurshid Agha, begging him
to intercede for her husband. Now for a chief's wife, who is
usually so closely secluded, thus personally to address
another chief, who is a stranger to her family, is amongst the
Kurds the extremest form of supplication, and Khurshid
Agha, much against his will was compelled by tribal
etiquette to grant her request. He therefore came to me and
opened up the matter, and I could only reply that under present conditions nothing could induce me to permit of Sawar
Agha's return. Khurshid Agha is a dogged old man, and once
he gets an idea into his somewhat thick head he will never
give it up; for three days, therefore, he continued to plague
me on this question, but I would not yield.

Alarming rumours were now received from the hills, and
there was no longer any doubt that the combined forces of the
Surchi and the Khushnao were advancing to attack the town.
They mustered probably not more than a thousand rifles, but
on entering the district it was almost certain that they would
be joined by Ahmad Pasha, Hajji Pir Daud of the Dizai, and
Jamil Agha of the Girdi, all of whom I refused to call upon for
the assistance which they treacherously volunteered. Within
the town were the hostile retainers of Hajji Rashid Agha and
Ali Pasha, while I felt sure that the mass of the tribesmen
who had come in at Khurshid Agha's bidding would, with the
Government's prestige at its present low ebb, refuse to fight
their fellow Kurds. On the approach of the hostile force they
would anticipate them in the looting of the town and withdraw. Only the personal following of Khurshid Agha, Mushir,
and Ahmad Effendi could be relied upon to fight for me. I
devoted my efforts to an endeavour to detach Qadir Beg from
the enemy; he had been much alarmed by visits of aeroplanes
to Shaqlawah and Sisawa, and was said to be ready to make
his dakhalat if he could obtain easy terms.

On the afternoon of the 6th I held a long conversation over the telephone with certain of the Koi notables. Karim Agha was now in the town and was about the only man there who acted throughout the crisis with clear-headed loyalty. He informed me that Abdur Rahman Beg with a force of 200 of the Khushnao was at Nazanin, about four hours from the town, and had just sent a letter addressed to all the notables requiring them to invite him and his men as guests to their houses. Failing such invitation he would come by force. I informed Karim Agha that I had already asked for aeroplane assistance and could do nothing more to help him; I advised him to temporise. A few minutes later the wire to Koi was cut.

During the evening a telegram arrived from Baghdad, announcing that the Civil Commissioner, Sir Arnold Wilson, would visit me on the 8th with three aeroplanes. Though somewhat alarmed for his safety I published the news in the town, where it had a reassuring effect. I wired in reply that I might have to evacuate any minute, and that if when the aeroplanes arrived there was no flag on the Serai, it would mean that I had left and it was dangerous for them to land.

This was one of the most anxious nights I passed. About 8 p.m. Ahmad Effendi came in for a talk clothed not as usual in European dress, but in a long blue gown, which Captain Littledale used to call his master mason's costume, saying that it signified that the situation was serious but not hopeless. I supplied him with rifles and ammunition for a party of loyal adherents he had collected in the town, and also for the unfortunate Christians of Ainkawa, who had been pestering me for days.

Unfortunatly we had with us over 100,000 rounds of Turkish ammunition, besides a considerable number of rifles collected from the men who had taken their discharge. A part of the Dizai aghas, not including Khurshid Agha, now visited me, and clamoured for the ammunition with the greatest importunity. Many of their followers forced their way into the barracks and simply became so threatening that I was driven to comply with their demands. Rahman Agha, usually a mild man, was particularly insistent, his face becoming livid with passion. I ordered that 15,000 rounds should be given him, saying I could spare no more, provided he would first expel from the barracks all the tribesmen who had entered it. This he did, but many of them forced their way back again past the levies, who were too unnerved to keep them out, and before I knew what was happening he had entered the magazine himself and removed some 50,000 rounds. My one consolation was that this ammunition had fallen into the hands of Khurshid Agha's faction instead of those of my enemies. They appeared content with their spoil and did not trouble me again on this score.

We passed a most anxious night, fully dressed and with our ponies ready saddled. Ahmad Effendi and two or three of the Dizai aghas were with us. We were prepared to fly at any moment but beyond few odd shots in the town, which caused Captain Littledale and his men to fly to their posts, nothing of an alarming nature occurred. The next day at dawn and for several mornings after many of the townspeople collected round the barracks to discover if I was still with them. Their attitude was most friendly, and they brought provisions for the levies, for whom it was unsafe to enter the bazaar.

The affair of Sawar Agha now reached its climax and it came to this, that I must either bring him back or leave Arbil; his release was to be the price of Khurshid Agha's support. The old man did not say this in so many words, and he was bound by his brother's dying behest to ensure my personal safety; but I knew that if I did not give way he would leave the town taking me with him. Very reluctantly, therefore, I relented, and it was arranged that Sawar Agha should reside at Makhmur, which Khurshid Agha promised he should not leave unless the whole of Kurdistan were evacuated. Sawar Agha was despatched by car from Mosul the following morning; a large party of the Dizai met him at Quwair and triumphantly conducted him to their chief residence, where he remained till the trouble was over.

On my giving my consent the situation became easier, and the assembled chiefs met in conclave and swore a solemn oath 'by the divorce' that they would protect Arbil against all comers for ten days; at the end of that period, if the situation had not improved and troops did not arrive, they would enable us to withdraw from the town in safety. Khurshid Agha, Hussain i Mulla, and all the leaders of the Baiz faction took part in this oath together with Rasul Agha, Sulaiman

Agha, the notorious cousin of Hajji Pir Daud, and Shaikh Muhammad Agha, 'the Villain' of the Koi Girdi. I was much surprised by Sulaiman Agha's behaviour on this occasion; he had been in the town for several days and his attitude throughout appeared loyal and straightforward. I even began to think the leopard had changed his spots, but I discovered later that he spent most of his time in trying to divert the allegiance of the younger aghas of the Baiz faction and in writing letters to the Khushnao urging them to attack the town. 'The Villain' had come in partly to intercede for Sawar Agha, his relation by marriage, and partly for fear of his cousin Aarib Agha, who had ranged himself with the Khushnao against the Government.

I visited the Serai every day but one while I was in the barracks, but naturally there was little business to transact. I usually sat in my office for about an hour and then returned to my quarters, where I passed the time quietly reading novels. In many ways I enjoyed the life; despite the anxiety, it was the first time for many months that I was able to give myself a rest and take things easily.

On the 7th a convoy arrived from Kirkuk and removed all my treasure except a small sum which I kept for emergencies. It was fired on from an enclosure a few miles outside the town.

Early the next morning we prepared the aerodrome for the Civil Commissioner's arrival, and I was much alarmed during the proceedings by a rumour, which proved to be false, that a party of men had entered the Serai and hauled down the flag. The aeroplanes arrived at 7.45 a.m. A strong guard was ready at the aerodrome, but thanks to the efforts of Ahmad Effendi and Khurshid Agha the people and tribesmen were kept within the town. Having seen the Civil Commissioner and the R.A.F. officers with him safely into the cars, I galloped off to the house where breakfast was prepared for them. They did not appear, and after waiting for a few minutes I discovered they had proceeded towards the town. I therefore rode after them and found them driving through the crowded streets accompanied by a swarm of Khurshid Agha's horsemen. We then returned to the house, where after breakfast I explained the state of affairs, insisting that the despatch of a small body of troops to the town would completely restore the situation. The root of the trouble was a general conviction that the Government was about to evacuate the country, and this step alone would be sufficient to allay the fears of our friends and disappoint the hopes of our enemies. We then adjourned to the Serai, where the Civil Commissioner first received the notables, and then the assembled Kurdish chiefs, amongst whom I was surprised to see Ahmad Pasha, Hajji Pir Daud, and Jamil Agha. He made a speech suitable for the occasion to each gathering, to which Mulla Effendi and Khurshid Agha respectively replied, each of them begging him to apply for the immediate despatch of troops to Arbil. After he had seen Khurshid Agha and Ahmad Effendi alone and thanked them for their services to the Government, we returned to our house where lunch had been made ready.

We had chosen the house for the Civil Commissioner's entertainment on account of its proximity to the aerodrome. A fine meal had been prepared, including a roast turkey, which we had been preserving for Christmas. I was now assailed for the second time by a bad attack of nerves. I felt again the house's exposed position, and pictured to myself hordes of mounted tribesmen descending upon us. My anxiety chiefly centred round the Civil Commissioner, for whose safety I was responsible. Mr. Robbins, with the Lewis gun and a large party of police and gendarmes, was above us on the roof. In the middle of the meal a note was brought to Captain Littledale, which caused him to turn pale and rush out. I could not restrain myself from following him. The note proved to be from Mr. Robbins, and in it was written: 'They are coming over the rise, sir.' We rushed up the stairs and anxiously scanned the horizon, to discover to our relief that 'they' were a flock of sheep.

The Civil Commissioner and the other officers left with their aeroplanes at 2 p.m. Khurshid Agha and Ahmad Effendi came to see them off, and informed me that Hussain i Mulla had returned from a visit to the Khushnao, with whom he had been sent to negotiate, bringing a message from Qadir Beg that if all their acts were forgiven and no fine inflicted, he and his relations would make their submission to the Government. They suggested that I should seize the opportunity to ask the Civil Commissioner for permission to accept

these proposals. I told Ahmad Effendi to address Sir Arnold
Wilson himself, which he did, after the latter had already
taken his seat in the aeroplane. The necessary consent was
given, and the machines buzzed off smothering us all in a
cloud of dust. When we could see them again they were well
up in the air, and I felt a heavy load of responsibility lifted off
my shoulders.

I repaired at once to the office of the Rais Baladiyah to
discover the reason for the presence in the town of Ahmad
Pasha and his companions. I found somewhat to my surprise
that they had been invited in by Mulla Effendi, who considered that the whole district should make common cause
against the invader, and that it was much easier to ensure
the loyalty of these chiefs, who had not yet shown open
hostility, if they were under our eyes in the town, than if they
remained in their villages. I had a long talk with them, and,
of course, they protested their fidelity to the Government and
devotion to myself; but I well knew that but for the presence
of Khurshid Agha and his men they would long ere this have
been revealed in their true colours. As it was, I recognised
that however much they might intrigue, they would openly
support me as long as there appeared a possibility of the
Government party winning.

The Surchi were now massed round Dera and along the
Bastura Chai, only twelve miles from Arbil, with Shaikh
Obaidullah at their head. Nuri was also with them and
several contingents from the Rawanduz tribes. The Khushnao gathering was on the near side of the Bastura Chai, some
nine miles from Arbil round the village of Mulla Umr. The
whole body of the insurgents could therefore easily march
upon and attack Arbil between dusk and daybreak.

Khurshid Agha and Mushir paid me a visit after the evening meal. It had become known that Khurshid Agha's son,
Alu, and brother, Muhammad Amin Agha, had told a representative from the Surchi that in the event of an attack upon
Arbil they would withdraw their forces without opposition.
Khurshid Agha now assured me that this was all child's talk,
and I am told he severely rebuked the delinquents. He had,
he said, sent patrols out along all the roads leading towards
the Bastura Chai, and as soon as news arrived that the insurgents were advancing, Mushir would march out to repel

them with his whole force. Whether they were Muhammadans or not, once the Surchi had crossed the stream, blood
would be spilt. He would not hear of our leaving the town; he
had taken the matter in hand and would see it through,
despite the childish babblings of some of the younger aghas.
His firm attitude greatly reassured us, and despite the proximity of the enemy we passed a quiet night. The next morning Khurshid Agha despatched the venerable Saiyid, Shaikh
Maruf, to interview Shaikh Obaidullah and warn him that if
he crossed the Bastura Chai much good Muhammadan blood
would flow.

The day passed quietly until about 1 p.m. when a large
cavalcade was seen approaching the town from the Khushnao
country. There was immediately a scare. The levies stood to,
Captain Littledale rushed to his Lewis gun, and Mushir mobilised his men and covered the barracks. Alu and some
others who were leaving the town with a large number of the
tribesmen, whom it was found difficult to feed, galloped back
post haste. The approaching cavalcade, however, stopped at
Badawa, and we soon learnt that all the Khushnao chiefs had
arrived, and were lodging at the house of Mulla Effendi.
Ahmad Effendi rode out to see them, and on his return reported that they were very truculent, calling him a traitor
and an infidel for the part he had played on our side. It appeared that Mustafa Agha and Khidhr Beg of Balisan, whom
I had so much despised, had throughout the trouble coun-
selled Qadir Beg to remain firm in his loyalty, while all the
other chiefs led by Saleh Beg and Rashid Beg, wishing to
ruin him, had urged him in the opposite direction. He had
wavered from this side to that, and had not yet definitely
made up his mind, but since he had come so far it was probable that he would make his peace, especially as Mulla Effendi was expending much eloquence in an endeavour to
bring him back to a reasonable attitude.

That evening we despatched a large caravan of mules and
donkeys with all the kit and personnel that there remained
to evacuate. We passed a most anxious night ready to fly at
any moment; it was fully possible that the Khushnao chiefs
intended treachery, and Captain Littledale had little reason
to trust Qadir Beg. We were alarmed by some shots, but

nothing further occurred to disturb us, until with daylight we returned to a state of comparative security.

The morning of the tenth passed quietly. About 11 a.m. Ahmad Effendi brought in Saleh Beg to see me. He hypocritically kissed my hand with his heavily moustached mouth and assured me of his eternal devotion to myself. I appealed to my former personal friendship with him and reproached him for his present attitude, while he protested that the Khushnao had never fired on Captain Littledale's party, and that they had only mobilised subsequently because they knew they were suspected and feared punitive action on the part of the Government. It was arranged that Qadir Beg and all the other chiefs should meet me in the Serai that afternoon.

Accordingly at 2 p.m. I proceeded to my office and from the window watched the Khushnao chiefs arrive. A considerable crowd lined the streets, and the Dizai jeered to such an extent at the bad horsemanship of the men from the hills that a fracas nearly ensued. Qadir Beg entered first followed by Khurshid Agha; then came Saleh Beg, Rashid Beg, Mustafa Agha, Khidhr Beg, Aarib Agha of the Girdi, and others of less note. They all sat round the room, Saleh Beg and Rashid Beg looking particularly sullen. It was a strange position; for nearly two years I had been accustomed to give orders to these chiefs, and now the situation was such that they could dictate terms to me. Their attitude, though less subservient than usual, was by no means aggressive. Qadir Beg acted as spokesman, Saleh Beg occasionally interrupting with platitudinous remarks. They agreed to disband their forces, return to their homes, and restore all Government property in their possession, on the condition that I would let bygones be bygones, continue to pay their salaries as official chiefs, and treat them with the same honour and favour as I had shown them before the trouble. I was compelled, indeed I was only too glad, to accept their proposals. To save their faces they added a proviso; for they had sworn a solemn oath to Shaikh Obaidullah that they would pursue the feud against the Government to the bitter end. They asked me in a half-hearted fashion to arrange an armistice with the Surchi on favourable terms. They knew, and I knew, that little would result, but I promised to do all I could. The negotiations

being thus satisfactorily concluded, the meeting was dissolved.

Before I left the office Shaikh Maruf returned and came in
to see me. He had a strange tale to tell. On reaching the Surchi he had been greeted by Shaikh Obaidullah with bitter re-
proaches. 'Why are you, a saiyid, a descendant of the
Prophet, having dealings with these infidels? Join with us
and help to expel this cursed race from our sacred land.' After
continuing in this strain for some minutes the leader of the
insurgents had finally concluded by saying, 'Of course, if the
Government install me as chief of my tribe and pay me a
salary and give me the wherewithal to raise a force of tribal
gendarmes, I will collect and deliver all the revenue that is
due to them and serve them with the utmost fidelity.' In the
course of the conversation a letter arrived from Ali Pasha re-
vealing that gentleman, who had behaved outwardly with the
greatest loyalty, in his true light. It stated that Khurshid
Agha and the Dizai had been compelled by an Arab invasion
to return to their homes, and that Arbil was now defenceless,
and it urged Shaikh Obaidullah to make an immediate attack. Shaikh Maruf stoutly denied the falsehood, and on his
return reported to me that it appeared unlikely that the Surchi would cross the Bastura Chai as long as Khurshid Agha
remained in Arbil.

After their interview the Khushnao chiefs left the town
and spent the night in Banisilawa, about six miles away. In
the evening, to our great joy, a telegram arrived stating that
G.H.Q. had consented to the despatch of troops, and that
columns would leave Mosul and Kirkuk the following morning and reach Arbil early on the 14th; so that if we could hold
out for four more nights all would be well.

This night and the following day, September 11th , passed
quietly. I visited the Serai, and in the afternoon rode out to
choose a camp for the troops; we selected a spot by a kariz-
head between our house and the aerodrome. The next night
was our worst. About 9 p.m. Ahmad Effendi entered with a
woe-begone face, and clad in a big coat, riding breeches, and
gaiters, which Littledale christened his farmer's costume,
saying it betokened that the worst was at hand. He coun-
selled immediate flight to a village a few miles distant on the
Quwair road, saying that the Khushnao chiefs were still at

Banisilawa with a large force, and that he had received certain information that they and the Surchi intended to attack
that night. We put on our belts and revolvers, saddled up our
ponies, and had all our men drawn up ready to march, when
in stalked Khurshid Agha. He turned to Ahmad Effendi in a
rage crying, 'What is all this nonsense? Am not I here? Let
the whole of Kurdistan attack, I will repel them. Why are you
being frightened by a mere rumour? It is through me that
you have been able to stay here all these days and I am not
going to permit you to leave now', and he sat down muttering
and crying, 'Ai-ee. Ai-ee', with a long-drawn note to signify
disgust. He then addressed me saying that his patrols were
out and there was no cause for alarm; his men were ready to
repel any attack, and Mushir with a large body of horsemen
was stationed in a khan close by to assist me should necessity arise. On this I gave up all idea of flight, and old Khurshid Agha insisted on sitting up with us in the barracks all
night.

The morning found us sleepless but reassured. It was true
that the Khushnao had tarried at Banisilawa the previous
day; they had apparently been discussing the situation at
Koi, whither they despatched old Ali Beg, one of Qadir Beg's
uncles, with a small force to control matters in their favour.
Information was now received that they had left for their own
country at dawn.

Captain Dickinson arrived at lunch-time with the news,
which we took care to spread, that the column from Mosul
was already encamped at Quwair. He left soon after the meal
to begin the task of bringing back again some of the personnel and kit which he had evacuated. All the factions in Arbil
sent out their spies to confirm the report of the approach of
the troops. The people at first were inclined to be sceptical of
its truth, but by the evening their attitude began to change.

In the afternoon I rode out to visit Mulla Effendi in his
house at Badawa. He alone seemed to be unaffected by the
general panic. He received me as usual with every sign of affection and respect, and treated me to much pleasant conversation and sound advice. It was he really who inspired all our
supporters and directed public opinion, it was he who dic-
tated Ahmad Effendi's every action, it was he who moderated
Khurshid Agha's wild tribal instincts, it was he who talked

the Khushnao chiefs over to a reasonable attitude. Yet I have
rarely met a more modest man; he would not listen to my ex-
pressions of gratitude, and merely stated that he strove and
always had striven for the good of his country and his people.

But all was not over yet; we had still one more scare to
survive. After the evening meal Khurshid Agha entered the
barracks unusually agitated. He advised us to be ready for
flight, assuring us at the same time that he was determined
to do all he could to prevent such a contingency. With Khurshid Agha adopting this attitude we thought the situation
must indeed be serious. This time it was Ahmad Effendi who
reassured us. It appeared that shortly after dark the arch-
traitor, Saleh Beg, had galloped into the town and hurrying
to where the Dizai chiefs were assembled had cried, 'Fly, fly,
the Surchi are upon you.' A considerable commotion ensued,
and patrols were sent out in all directions. They soon returned with the news that there was no sign of any hostile
force. The Dizai aghas now realised the trick that had been
played upon them, and the younger among them wished to
seize the traitor and hand him over to me. Khurshid Agha,
however, when he heard this, objected, saying it would be
contrary to tribal custom and the laws of hospitality. Saleh
Beg was, therefore, ordered to leave the town, whence he
slunk away dejected, his last bolt shot. Though we did not
know it, the Surchi had already abandoned their project, and
were even now preparing to ford the river at Girdmamik
towards another objective.

With the dawn of the 13th the state of siege in which we
had been living came to an end. The whole spirit of the place
seemed to have changed and the heavy clouds which had so
long darkened the sky rolled away. I drove out in my car with
Rahman Agha to meet the column approaching from Kirkuk,
and prove to him, if proof were needed, that the troops were
really coming. It was a great delight to travel again over the
broad rolling plain and breathe the cool autumn air. We
found the column encamped at Qush Tappeh, and right glad
we were to see them; they, too, had been afraid that they
might be too late, and gave us a warm welcome. The force
consisted of one company of British infantry and two troops
of Indian cavalry. We returned with light hearts to Arbil,

bringing with us a sick corporal whom we accommodated in
the barracks.

That night all the four Dizai chiefs, Khurshid Agha,
Ahmad Pasha, Hajji Pir Daud, and Rasul Agha, together with
Jamil Agha of the Girdi, slept with us unattended as a sign of
their united loyalty. We still feared a possible 'coup' on the
part of Hajji Rashid Agha or others of his party, and remained on our guard, but the night passed quietly.

We rose early on the 14th and rode out with a party of
mounted levies and Mushir Agha to meet the Kirkuk column,
which was due to arrive first. We entered the town with them
about 9.30 a.m., while all the tribesmen and the entire populace joyfully lined the streets, some of the women greeting us
with their strange 'ulu-lu-lu-lu', the cry that is used both at
weddings and funerals. The Mosul column, which consisted of
two guns, a squadron of Indian cavalry, and two platoons of
Indian infantry, arrived at noon, and the whole force encamped on the spot which I had chosen. Here the people
flocked to see them, the hawkers bringing out fruit, biscuits,
and cigarettes, while I conducted Khurshid Agha and Ahmad
Effendi on a tour of inspection round the camp. We now returned to our house and began life once more on the old lines,
although for some time the past hung over us like a shadow.

The first fortnight of September, 1920, will ever remain to
me as an inspiration, and a time to be remembered with
thankfulness; the terror of it has now faded away, and there
lives only in my mind the tense excitement, the wild exhilaration of adventure, and the loyalty and devotion of my
friends. Of these I have already mentioned the wire-puller,
Mulla Effendi, but the two who endured the toil and heat of
the day were Ahmad Effendi and Khurshid Agha. The former
did not sleep for nights on end. He was continually running
to and fro collecting information, scenting out the latest intrigues, encouraging wavering friends, defying declared enemies. He excelled himself in the anxious days when the
question of Sawar Agha threatened to be our ruin; his active
brain was ever devising subterfuges and compromises, while
he alternately implored the Dizai chief and myself to relent
in our purposes. Though devoted to me and a loyal supporter
of the Government his real anxiety was for his beloved Arbil
and its people and the poor Christians of Ainkawa. During

the two years he had held the office of Rais Baladiyah he had devoted his life and soul to the welfare of the town and the protection of the poorer classes from the injustice and rapacity of the aghas. He saw now the people whom he loved, the artisan and shopkeeper, the orphan and the widow, threatened with terror and destruction. While Mulla Effendi was protected by his sanctity and all the other notables safeguarded themselves by professing friendship to both sides, Ahmad Effendi, by his single-hearted devotion to his cause risked his property, his family, and his life.

Khurshid Agha was of an entirely different calibre, and it was not till now that I learnt that in protecting me, he and his family had been obeying the dying behest of Ibrahim Agha. I feel certain that that chief if he had been alive could not have served me with such constancy and singleness of purpose; his superior intellect would have found a compromise whereby he could have saved me without giving offence to his neighbouring Kurdish chiefs. Once Khurshid Agha, however, had conceived the idea that it was his duty to stand by me, nothing whatever could alter or modify his purpose. While his relations wavered, while all the other notables and chiefs plied him with every inducement to betray me, though he was led to believe that the Government was at its last gasp he refused to move an inch from his resolve. Abu Agha managed to find him alone in the mosque one day and offered him £1,000 in gold there and then merely to bring pressure upon me to secure the release of his brother, Hajji Suayid Agha, imprisoned for the murder of Sergeant Methuen, but he vehemently declined the bribe. He was the backbone of our resistance to the elements of disorder, refusing to give way when both Ahmad Effendi and myself were ready to yield. It was his influence and his alone which saved the town from attack; if he had not been with us we should have been compelled to fly at the first news of Shaikh Obaidullah's hostile intentions. In no Kurd have I ever seen such determination and unselfish unity of purpose as Khurshid Agha displayed during the dark days when Arbil was threatened by the tribes.

CHAPTER XX

RECONSTRUCTION

BEFORE PROCEEDING TO THE conclusion of the narrative it will be well to examine briefly the causes of the troubles related in the two previous chapters. I have little hesitation in saying that the mass of the people in the Arbil, Koi, and Khushnao districts were on the side of the Government. They are an industrious race perfectly willing to pay revenue in return for the security and protection from the greedy aghas which an honest administration assures them. During the disturbances not a single case of brigandage occurred in the Arbil district, and no attempt was made to molest officials in the nahiya headquarters or to sever the main telegraph communication with Kirkuk and Mosul. In Koi, but for the death of Hama Agha, all would have been well; it was the attitude of the Khushnao chiefs and a handful of the town aghas that rendered the place untenable. I traversed the Khushnao country three or four days before the disturbances broke out, and was received by all even in the most remote villages with the utmost friendliness. Here, too, it was only Qadir Beg's thickheadedness and his relations' greed and jealousy that led to hostile demonstrations; and it was largely because the chiefs found that their men would not follow them that they repented of their folly.

In the Rawanduz district, however, the case was different. Here the people are wild and ignorant; most of their villages are inaccessible, and the soil is so poor that the cultivator has little to lose through civil disorders. The Surchi of the Aqra district had so long defied the Government with comparative impunity that their brethren of the Dasht i Harir were inspired to follow their example, especially as the disturbances north of the river had necessitated the presence in their midst of a large number of gendarmes, whose extortions and petty tyrannies had exhausted their patience. Further east, too, in the neighbourhood of Rawanduz the tribesmen, though they had little to complain of Government interference, and were only asked to pay an extremely small revenue, had grown tired of peaceful pursuits and welcomed a little excitement and the chance of loot.

At the root of everything was the spirit of unrest which spread upwards from the south, and inspired all who had any grievance to foment trouble, while the Government was involved elsewhere and there were no troops in Arbil. It is a sign of the goodwill of the people as a whole that the most important district, that of Arbil, remained intact, despite the desperate situation, and that it was found possible to restore order without any punitive action throughout the whole of the division with the exception of the Dasht i Harir and Rawanduz.

It is interesting to reflect upon the part played by Nuri in these events. Without his instigation, would the Aqra Surchi have crossed the river and thrown the whole division into confusion? It is a difficult question to answer. Although I was so strongly of the opinion that the presence of the refugees would deter them, there is no doubt that the Surchi had long contemplated a descent on the Dasht i Harir, and it is probable that in the state of embarrassment in which the Government found itself, they would have seized the opportunity, Nuri or no Nuri. But what we may say is, that it was Nuri who finally supplied the fuel which caused the smouldering fires to break into flame.

We must also take account of the cold-blooded murder of Nuri's brothers, which aroused the sympathies of local Kurds and seemed to call down the vengeance of God and man upon the house of Ismail Beg.

Providence alone saved Arbil and maddened the Surchi, so that they left the easy prey that awaited them to pursue another that well-nigh proved their ruin. Shaikh Obaidullah informed Shaikh Maruf on September 10th that his actions depended on Qadir Beg; if that chief told him not to attack Arbil he would refrain. Whether it was due to the action of Qadir Beg or caprice I know not, but on September 12th the Surchi force suddenly abandoned their project and moved towards the ford over the Greater Zab at Girdmamik. The following day they crossed and on the 14th delivered an attack

on the refugee camp at Jujar, which is on the road between
Mosul and Aqra. They were severely repulsed and fled with
considerable loss of life. The refugees pursued them and attacked them while they were recrossing the river higher up
opposite Kandil, where they again suffered heavy loss, many
being reported drowned. These events broke their spirit and
greatly lowered their prestige among the surrounding tribes.

Little of the tale now remains to be told. It had already
been arranged that I should proceed to take up new duties in
India at the end of the year, and when Sir Arnold Wilson visited us on September 8th I had asked for leave to England on
the transference. On September 15th I was much surprised
by a telegram stating that my leave had been granted, and
that I was to hand over immediately to Major C. C. Marshall,
D.S.O., then A.P.O. Aqra. I protested, asking for time to reor-
ganise the division before my departure, and it was arranged
that I should be relieved early in October. I therefore set to
work at once to repair the shattered administrative machine,
my first anxiety being to induce Qadir Beg and his companions again to visit Arbil in order that a proper settlement
might be made of matters outstanding between them and the
Government. This proved more difficult than I expected, for
owing to the machinations of my enemies in Arbil the Khushnao chiefs were led to believe that I intended treachery. It
was not till September 24th that they plucked up the courage
to come in.

With the arrival of the troops in Arbil the prestige of the
Government recovered immediately. Petitions poured in as
before the trouble, while in the sub-districts the officials were
besieged by cultivators bringing the first instalment of their
revenue on the wheat and barley crops. The levies and gendarmes who had taken their discharge applied for re-enlist-
ment, and within a week the old routine was in full swing.
The only innovation was that, at Khurshid Agha's request, I
garrisoned the posts at Mahkmur and Qush Tappeh with
armed tribesmen in the place of the regular gendarmes.

On the afternoon of the 15th, accompanied by Khurshid
Agha and Ahmad Effendi, I paid a visit to Shaikh Mustafa to
thank him for his support during the trouble; for living on
the eastern outskirts of the town and having a large following in the villages near the Bastura Chai he had kept us well

supplied with information. Further, by delivering a religious decree denouncing as impious the proposed attack on Arbil and calling on all good Muhammadans to support the Government, he had been largely instrumental in maintaining the friendly attitude of the non-tribal Kurds in the vicinity of the town.

On the 18th arrived the great Saiyid Taha of Shemsdinan. He held a position in the country north of the Rawanduz district and on both sides of the Persian frontier not unlike that of Shaikh Mahmud in Sulaimaniyah previous to the British occupation. His family had been the dominating factor in that area for several generations; his grandfather had led a formidable revolt against the Turks, aspiring to Kurdish national independence, and his uncle, Shaikh Abdul Qadir, had obtained great favour from Sultan Abdul Hamid, and even now was a prominent personage in Constantinople. In the previous year it had been proposed to set up Saiyid Taha as a hukmdar like Shaikh Mahmud, including the Rawanduz district in his area; owing to his excessive demands, however, negotiations had been abandoned. At the present time his importance was somewhat eclipsed by that of Simko, chief of the Shikak, to whom he had allied himself. He was, however, still a person of great influence, and I had arranged to meet him at Rayat on the frontier in the first week in September for the purpose of discussing with him matters concerning the repatriation of the Christian refugees to Urmia. Hearing on his arrival at the rendezvous of the disturbances which had prevented my meeting him, he had of his own volition performed the difficult journey over the mountains to Rania. Here he found Ismail Beg, whom he brought with him via Koi to Arbil.

He unexpectedly appeared at my house in the company of Mulla Effendi. He was clad in ordinary European riding costume, with a handkerchief fastened over his head in Arab fashion by a rich gold and green scarf. Though only twenty-eight years of age he is of enormous build, being over six feet tall and extremely fleshy: he has a very big head with flabby cheeks and small keen eyes. He has travelled in Russia, in the language of which country he is fluent, and knows French; he possesses tremendous brain power, combining the dialectical faculties of a European politician with the natural cunning of an Oriental potentate.

He stayed four days in Arbil, and on each day I spent several hours in conversation with him, feeling like some in-experienced novice arguing with a Socrates. On the 20th I took him to Quwair to meet Colonel Nalder, when for a brief hour I was relieved of the onus of answering his searching questions. We had invited him to meet us for the purpose of discussing repatriation; he on the other hand had come to see us to obtain British support, i.e. arms and money for an inde-pendent Kurdistan. He displayed much good sense, empha-sising especially our weakness in propaganda; for we had made little or no effort to counteract the lies which the Sheri-fian party and the Turkish nationalists were everywhere dif-fusing among the Kurds. He alleged that in the north at least two important tribal confederations were working for the es-tablishment of independent Kurdish states, and urged us to assist in their establishment in order to provide a barrier against the Bolshevik menace, which he took care greatly to exaggerate. When he had completely overwhelmed me with his ideas on this subject, he began to refer casually to the question of repatriation and to criticise the scheme that was proposed. Unfortunately one day when he was in my house discussing this matter his eye fell on an illustrated paper which happened to be lying on the table. He opened it at the picture of a lady in Oriental dress. 'Ah,' he exclaimed, 'who is this?' I informed him that it was a portrait of Surma Khanum, the first lady ambassador, representing the Syrian Christians in London. 'There you are,' he said, 'these Christi-ans are not returning to their home in peace. They aspire to become a big nation with us Kurds as their subjects, so much so that they have an "ambassador" in London, which is much more than we have. Why, this very lady whom you see por-trayed here, plotted to murder me when I was in Baghdad last year.' I was left speechless. It was with feelings of consid-erable relief that I said good-bye to Saiyid Taha Effendi at Mulla Effendi's house on the morning of the 23rd.

Ismail Beg had become a nervous wreck immediately after hearing of Nuri's escape, and he was now more than ever crushed by the calamities that had fallen upon him. All his own and the Pasha's property were in the hands of his enemies, and he was compelled to live on the charity of his friends. I pitied him extremely, for despite the murders, for which he was wholly or partly responsible, he was an extraordinarily nice boy, and had served me with the utmost fidelity. It was chiefly, too, the situation which I thrust on him at Rawanduz that had brought him to his ruin. I promised to continue his salary for the present and to make every effort to recover his property. After a short stay he left us to join his grandfather, the old Pasha, who had succeeded in making his way from Dargala to the house of his son-in-law, Rashid Beg, at Shaqlawah. I never saw the old man again, though before I left Arbil I received a letter in his shaky handwriting full of regrets for my departure and hopes for the punishment of the Surchi. I have since received news that Qadir Beg has succeeded in re-installing him in his house at Batas, where I can picture the querulous old man detailing the events that led to the fall of Rawanduz and reiterating how all would have been well if only his advice had been followed.

On the 22nd Miss Martin rode in on her white donkey from Shaqlawah, whither she had proceeded a month or two previously to spend the worst part of the hot weather and carry on her missionary work among the Chaldaean Christians. She had remained at her post unperturbed throughout the trouble, and put heart into the terrified people, who hourly expected to be massacred. The Khushnao in accordance with their custom never molested them, for they consider them in the light of valuable slaves; and Qadir Beg throughout treated Miss Martin with the greatest respect, paying her personal visits, undoubtedly with the hope that she would eventually assist in making his peace with the Government. She most humorously reported his panic-stricken return to Shaqlawah after the first appearance of aeroplanes over Sisawa. He was still in a state of nerves, and hesitating to come in for fear of my wrath, now that Government authority was restored in Arbil.

At length, however, he plucked up courage, and on September 24th arrived with Mustafa Agha and Saleh Beg. His attitude was very satisfactory; he agreed at once to return all Government property in his possession, and on his advice I allowed the old system of administration in Shaqlawah to

continue. In a private interview he informed me that Ahmad
Midhat Effendi and Saleh Beg were entirely responsible for
misleading him and persuading the Kushnao to join in the
disturbances; he promised to kill the former, who had fled,
should he ever return to Shaqlawah, while he said that it was
necessary for the present to leave Saleh Beg, whom I should
have liked to strangle there and then, until some more
favourable opportunity presented itself for dealing with him
according to his deserts. I rewarded Mustafa Agha for his
services with a small increase of salary, and gave him the
wherewithal to compensate the men who had been with me in
the Gorge for their losses.

The Khushnao question being now settled I was able to
turn my attention to Koi. The Committee of Four, though
they had been powerless to prevent minor disorders, and a
party of brigands had made nightly raids on the town, had
outwardly maintained an attitude of benevolent neutrality
and, on the whole, had successfully carried out the functions
of Government through a very trying crisis. Mr. Batt had behaved with the greatest acumen, and his presence had been
sufficient to deter possible enemies from demonstrations of
open hostility. I now held long conversations over the telephone and persuaded the entire body of notables with the exception of Rasul Agha and 'the Bishop', who was still living in
retirement, to come into Arbil and discuss the situation. As I
had no force at my disposal and could not punish Abdulla
Agha, I was compelled to placate him. I thought at one time
of appointing him as Governor of the town, for which post he
was undoubtedly the most capable man available; but I
found, somewhat to my surprise, that even his nearest relations objected to him in such a capacity. I therefore relegated
him to the mudirate of Taqtaq, satisfying him with a reasonable salary, and removing from Koi a powerful and
dangerous man. Jamil Agha was reconfirmed as Governor of
the town, and the allegiance of all the lesser notables was
bought by the grant of paid appointments. On September
30th the cavalcade set out again for Koi taking with them
Captain Bradshaw, who was returning for a period to reor-
ganise the district and recover, if possible, the Government
moneys and property which had been dispersed amongst
various of the notables. In the latter task he met with consid-

erable success, for within a few days two-thirds of the treasure that had been left behind was again in his hands.

At the end of September Ahmad Beg of the Zarari, a small tribe living round Dera, made his submission, so that by the time Major Marshall arrived to relieve me the whole of the Koi and Khushnao districts and the Rawanduz district as far as Babachichek had by peaceful means again been brought under Government control.

There remained the Surchi and Rawanduz. Qadir Beg visited me again on October 12th to say good-bye to me, and reported that the Surchi chiefs of the Dasht i Harir desired to make their submission. As they, however, were the originators of the disturbances within the division, it was impossible to let them off so easily as the Khushnao and Zarari chiefs. I have learnt that subsequent to my departure a punitive column visited the Dasht i Harir and occupied Batas, while the levies burnt Mawaran, where the gendarmes had been so treacherously murdered.

On October 2nd Major Marshall arrived and I began to prepare for my departure. On the 5th I toured the Arbil district with my successor and visited all the leading Dizai chiefs. We found Khurshid Agha delighted with the brand new Ford car which had been presented to him by the Civil Commissioner as a reward for his services.

On October 17th Captain Littledale was successful in performing the one act of vengeance which I was determined to effect before my departure. That day a portion of the Mosul column set out on its return journey to its headquarters and reached about noon its camp by Terjan, where resided Hajji Rashid Agha. Captain Littledale, with a party of levies, rode out with the troops. Accompanied by only two men he called at Hajji Rashid Agha's guest-house and asked to see him. The attendants replied that their master had gone out to inspect his rice-fields. 'Oh,' said Captain Littledale, 'that's a pity, because a party of troops is encamped just outside, and they require grain and fodder.' Pricking up his ears at the prospect of obtaining a high price for his goods, old Hajji Rashid Agha appeared all smiles from an inner room. Captain Littledale then turned to one of his men saying, 'Go and tell Darwish Effendi that I shall require the car in five minutes.' The man went out and gave the required signal, on which a party of le-

vies rushed up and surrounded the house. Hajji Rashid Agha
was made prisoner and hurried off to the camp, vigorously
protesting his innocence. The column took him to Mosul,
where he was confined. This arrest caused consternation
amongst the notables of Arbil, and during the next few days
on every possible occasion they begged me to obtain the prisoner's release, some of them because they feared for themselves, others, who really rejoiced to see him go, because it
was the custom for all to unite to protect any one of their
number who fell into the hands of the Government. Amongst
the former class Ali Pasha evinced the greatest anxiety.

On the 12th I entertained my leading officials to lunch,
and formally handed over to Major Marshall my duties as
Political Officer. The following day was occupied in farewell
ceremonies. In the morning I visited all the notables, and
Shaikh Mustafa Effendi, and in the afternoon rode out to see
Mulla Effendi at Badawa; after which I was entertained to a
garden party by the Indian and local officials. The Treasury
Officer, Mr. Duli Chand, delivered a most flattering speech,
to which I made the necessary reply. I also took the opportunity to hand to Ahmad Effendi a gold watch presented by the
Civil Commissioner as a reward for his services. Tears came
into his eyes as I gave it to him. In the course of the proceed-
ings telegrams arrived announcing the award of the M.C. to
Captain Littledale, and of the Military Medal to Saiyid Ali
Effendi for the bravery they had shown in the attack on
Batas. Saiyid Ali joined uproariously in his own applause and
became as excited as a child.

The next morning at 6.30 a.m. Shaikh Mustafa Effendi
paid a private visit to me to say good-bye. He gave me his
blessing and asked me to write to him. At 8 a.m. the entire
body of notables and officials, some sixty in number, arrived
at the house. They all partook of tea and coffee, and the notables begged me for the last time to procure the release of
Hajji Rashid Agha. I shook hands with all and took my seat
in the car, the assembled party gathering round and bidding
me many farewells.

I was accompanied by Khurshid Agha, Ahmad Effendi,
Enver Effendi, the chief Revenue official, and Saiyid Ali Effendi. We halted for two or three hours at Makhmur, where I
partook of my last Kurdish meal, Khurshid Agha and Mushir

producing their very best for me. With great sorrow I said good-bye to them both and watched Makhmur fade into the distance. Ahmad Effendi, Saiyid Ali Effendi, and Khurshid Agha's son Alu came with me to the river and saw me across to the further bank in the ferry. Here I bade them farewell, and my last memory is of Ahmad Effendi standing bowed and dejected on the foreshore.

CHAPTER XXI

CONCLUSION

SO WITH A HEAVY HEART I turned my back on Kurdistan,
wondering if ever again it would be my fate to partake of her
lavish hospitalities or tempt the perils of her dark mountains. For here we have an unspoilt country inhabited by an
unspoilt race; hilly recesses never penetrated by the
European traveller, a primitive people still in its Golden Age
adhering to the simple purity and naive savagery of primeval
mankind. For do not the traditions of a Golden Age common
to so many nations date from a time when all lived much the
same lives as the Kurds live now, it being the fortunate characteristic of the human race to forget all that is unpleasant in
the past and remember what is sweet and wholesome, so that
the rapine and murder of the dark ages lies buried in ob-
livion, and there remains in the memory naught but the rural
simplicity and high morality of the childhood of mankind?

Similarly with the writer, whatsoever of discomfort,
anxiety, or terror was experienced in Kurdistan has faded
away, and there remain only memories of rides over rugged
mountains and flowery valleys, of the delight of observing
strange customs and inquiring into old traditions, of the ancient politeness and hospitality of white-bearded patriarchs,
of the high spirits and joyous companionship of hot-blooded
young chiefs, of the gay-coloured raiments and wild pic-
turesqueness of a primitive Eastern people. I feel at times as
though I could sacrifice my whole future for an evening with
Khurshid Agha at Makhmur or another ride through the
Gorge to Rawanduz.

I made many friends in Kurdistan, and not a few enemies,
but of the latter there is only one whom I feel I can never forgive – and that probably because he is the only one that
really deceived me – namely, Saleh Beg of the Khushnao.
Ahmad Pasha and Hajji Pir Daud were honest enemies; their

protestations of loyalty and fidelity were merely a matter of form which they never expected me to believe. Our personal relations were always quite friendly and their intrigues both amused and interested me. I should love again to hear the Hajji's silvery hypocritical voice and to listen to the extravagant boasts and blatant commercialism of the profiteering Pasha.

But foremost in my mind stands the slight elusive figure of Nuri, a man fired with a purpose other than the avarice which is characteristic of his race, a patriot and a hero whom one would far rather see honourably reconciled than brought to the gallows. Without money or tribal influence, solely by his personality he became a force with which the Government found it hard to cope. A wayward fantastic streak in his character will prevent his ever becoming a ruler of men; if he does not come to an early end he will pass his life as a sort of Robin Hood in honourable defiance of all constituted authority.

Amongst the friends I made in the Arbil Division Ahmad Effendi must always occupy the highest place. As in this narrative extraordinary events have been related, to the neglect of the normal administrative routine, comparatively scant reference has been made to him. But he was ever at my side detailing the previous history of tribes and individuals, quoting legal precedents for cases that I might be trying, keeping me informed of all the latest rumours and gossip in the bazaar, and generally aiding me in a manner conducive to the promotion of Government interests and the people's welfare, which he had so much at heart. In normal times he came to see me when there was trouble afoot, he was continually going to and fro visiting me every two or three hours with fresh information and fresh suggestions. Once or twice a month he would invite me and any other British officers that happened to be in Arbil, to a meal in his house, and there must be several who have vivid memories of their endeavours to struggle through the thirteen or fourteen excellently cooked courses which he would produce. With my other friends the reader is already sufficiently acquainted – the holy men, Mulla Effendi and Shaikh Mustafa Effendi, old Khurshid Agha and young Mushir, Mustafa Agha of Kora, who showed me more disinterested devotion than any save

Ahmad Effendi, 'the Bishop' and Jamil Agha of Koi, the centenarian Abdulla Pasha, and Shaikh Muhammad Agha of the Balik, and finally, 'Henry VIII', or Miran i Qadir Beg of Shaqlawah, for whom, since his temporary defection, I shall never be able to feel quite the same friendship. Even now all these figures, though so far distant, seem present in my imagination with all their peculiarities and quaint ways, and I long to ask each how it has fared with him since I last saw him.

I cannot pass without mentioning the lion-hearted Saiyid Ali Effendi, who, though a Syrian Arab with no stake in the country, and peculiarly open to the influence of Sherifian propaganda, served the Government with the utmost fidelity and on numerous occasions came very near to sacrificing his life on its behalf.

Of the future of Kurdistan it is not within the scope of this book or the province of this writer to discuss; it is impossible, however, to refrain from saying this much, that if all British control is withdrawn without that of the Turks or some similar external Government being substituted in its place, the country will relapse into the extreme of anarchy. Though it is admitted that financial considerations offer little or no alternative to withdrawal, it is a hard thing to think that where we set out to bring relief from the oppressor and the benefits of good government, we shall basely abandon our purpose, leaving shepherdless the people, who have confided in us, to be consumed by the uncontrolled fires of tribal feud and civil disruption.

The writer having set out purely to narrate his personal experiences has been compelled sadly to neglect the admirable exploits of the A.P.O.s who served with him or ruled in neighbouring districts. Little has been said of Captain Kirk's months of anxiety in Rawanduz and Batas, and nothing of his trials in Aqra, when the Surchi invaded and occupied the greater part of the town. It has been impossible also to give any details of Captain Rundle's sound administration of Koi, where he was A.P.O. from May, 1919 to May, 1920, suffering all the time from ill-health, or of the anxieties which he and Captain Barker faced together at the time of the rising of Shaikh Mahmud. Three officers in succession assisted in the administration of Arbil, Lieut. Curtin, Captain Bradshaw, and Captain Dickinson, and it is difficult to pay a sufficient tribute to the energy and good sense which they displayed in the discharge of their duties. Captain Bradshaw relieved Captain Rundle at Koi, where, as has been related, he had to deal with the difficult situation caused by the death of Hama Agha, and the defection of the Khushnao. Of Captain Littledale little more need be said, for his exploits already described should prove a sufficient indication of his worth; he is one of the bravest men the writer has ever known, and was a tower of strength during the days of trouble at Arbil. He was ably assisted in his work with the gendarmes and levies first by Lieut. Barlow, who took over the command of the former when they became a separate force, and subsequently by Captain Hutchinson and Lieut. Bois.

Further, as this book is in no way intended to be an administrative report, no reference has been made to the work done in Arbil by the Medical, Educational, and similar services. Captain Williamson, who arrived as Civil Surgeon in March, 1920, with the assistance of an Arab doctor, introduced great improvements into the already existing hospital; he treated large numbers of the poor free daily, while tribesmen flocked in to him from the neighbouring villages, so that his work, besides bringing relief to the suffering, was of the greatest political value.

The British non-gazetted officials and the Indian personnel, too, did yeoman work. Mr. G. O. Turner spent many trying months endeavouring to organise the Revenue and Customs at Rawanduz, while Mr. C. Brown was chiefly responsible for the running of the Divisional Headquarters office in Arbil, and acquitted himself admirably in his task. Captain Littledale was most ably supported in his work with the levies by Sergeant-Majors Kennard and Shepperd, who worked unremittingly in the face of tremendous difficulties. The Town Police, probably the most efficient locally recruited body in the division, owed their high standard almost entirely to the efforts of Mr. H. C. Robbins, who commanded them practically the whole of the time the writer was at Arbil. Of the Indian officials Mr. Duli Chand, a most capable and indefatigable Treasury Officer, and Mr. Muhammad Sadiq Batt, who stuck to his post at Koi when everything was at its blackest, deserve special mention.

There has been no space to describe the work of Political Officers of the neighbouring divisions, such as Lieut.-Colonel L. F. Nalder, C.I.E., astutely sowing dissensions amongst the powerful Shammar tribe to prevent them attacking the communications between Baghdad and Mosul when the situation was at its worst, and Major S. G. Longrigg, refusing to be driven into hasty action by the seditious speeches of the Kirkuklis and gallantly restoring order in his area with the assistance of a handful of troops, or Major E. B. Soane, C.B.E., who in the entire absence of military support maintained intact the wild mountainous district of Sulaimaniyah.

It has been the object of the writer to provide in these pages a sample from his own experiences of the life of an officer of the Political Department in Mesopotamia ; there must be many members of the Civil Administration of that country who if they set pen to paper could relate far more startling adventures than ever fell to his lot. All, or nearly all, were inspired in their work by the great spirit of Sir Arnold Wilson, who showed towards each of his officers a personal regard and consideration, encouraging them by his example and advice and rarely, if ever, interfering with their initiative. In the darkest days of 1920 no man could complain of his lot, when he thought of his chief still at his post resolute and undaunted, though stricken with grief at the tragic ends of so many whom he loved as his children, and scourged by the savage criticisms of men at home who knew little of Mesopotamia and less of his work there.

More especially is this humble effort intended as a memorial of those British officers and non-gazetted officials serving in a civil capacity in Mesopotamia, and especially in Kurdistan, who gave up their lives in the service of their country and the people committed to their care. Many of their experiences must lie buried with them, and it is the writer's hope that their relations and friends may find in this narrative an echo of their hopes and ambitions, and a reflection of their daily pursuits and adventures.

The first to meet his fate in Kurdistan was Captain C. Pearson, A.P.O. Zakho, who was murdered in April, 1919, while travelling unarmed with missionary zeal amongst lawless and hostile tribes. Early in July, Sergeant Methuen perished in Arbil, as related in the narrative. Later in the month came the rising at Amadia, when Captain D. Willey, newly appointed A.P.O., Captain H. Macdonald, officer-in-charge of gendarmes, and Sergeant R. Troup were attacked while asleep on the roof of their house and foully done to death. At the beginning of November Mr. H. Bill, I.C.S., Political Officer Mosul, a man whose work on the North-West Frontier of India and in the Persian Gulf had earned him a high reputation, and Captain K. Scott, M.C., lately appointed A.P.O. Aqra, were treacherously killed by their Zibari hosts at Bira Kapra. A few weeks later Captain F. R. Walker, M.B.E., probably the most brilliant of the younger officers in the Civil Administration, who had succeeded Captain Scott at Aqra, died at the age of twenty-two of pneumonia, contracted on operations against the tribes who had murdered Mr. Bill and his predecessor. In June, 1920, a force of Arabs led by Sherifian officers attacked Tel Afar, and by means of bombs killed Lieut. B. Stuart, D.S.O., Sergeant A. Walker, and Mr. W. R. Lawler, who had collected to resist them on the roof of the Government offices. The A.P.O., Major J. E. Barlow, D.S.O., M.C., who was visiting the chief of a neighbouring village, was made prisoner by his host, and subsequently shot down as he was attempting to escape. Finally, in August, Captain G. H. Salmon, the A.P.O. Kifri, was captured by a party of Kurdish tribesmen who seized his headquarters, and was subsequently murdered in cold blood in revenge for attempts made by the military to retake the town.

Many, too, perished in the Arab uprisings that took place on the Euphrates and in the Baqubah area. Foremost among them stands Lieut.-Colonel G. E. Leachman, C.I.E., D.S.O., who was Political Officer Mosul from November, 1918, to October, 1919. Early in August he paid a visit to Shaikh Dhari of the Zoba, a tribe living between Baghdad and the Euphrates, in an endeavour to persuade him to maintain his hitherto loyal attitude; after a long conversation he was shot in the back by his host's son, just as he was leaving the tent, an act of treachery almost unparalleled in the blood-stained annals of Mesopotamia. He possessed a remarkable personality, and both in his features and his manner of life resembled a Beduin chief of the desert; though of quick temper and violent tongue he was loved by all who served under him, and there are few who would not have gone through the fires of hell at his bidding.

So commending to the memory and respect of his reader these brave spirits whose mortal remains lie scattered beneath the sands of the Arabian deserts and the flowery turf of the little Kurdish valleys, the writer bids adieu, proud to be of the number of those officers and men who served under Sir Arnold Wilson in Mesopotamia, and can boast, in the words of St. Paul, of their labours in the interests of their country and the communities entrusted to their charge, 'in journeying often, in perils of waters, in perils of robbers, in perils in the city, in perils in the wilderness, in weariness and painfulness, in watchings often, in hunger and thirst, in fastings often, in cold and nakedness.'

APPENDIX A

ADMINISTRATIVE SYSTEM OF THE TURKISH EMPIRE

THE TURKISH EMPIRE IS divided into a number of mutually independent *vilayets* or provinces, each administered by a *Wali* or Lieutenant-Governor directly responsible to Constantinople. Before the war Mesopotamia or *'Iraq* consisted of three such provinces, Mosul, Baghdad, and Basra. The *vilayets* are split up into a number of *liwas*, corresponding to divisions under the British Administration of Mesopotamia. The head of a *liwa* is known as a *Muttessarif*. A *liwa* again is divided into *qazas*, or districts, under *Qaimaqams*. The smallest administrative unit is the *nahiya*, or sub-district, under a *Mudir*, who deals with the people through the tribal chiefs or the village headmen. The *Mudir*, though he possesses magisterial powers, is really little more than a revenue official. The executive authority is vested in the *Qaimaqam*, who corresponds to the A.P.O. under British rule.

It is a curious anomaly that a superior officer performs the duties of inferior officers for his actual headquarters; e.g. the Wali acts as Mutessarif, Quaimaqam, and Mudir for the Liwa, Qaza, and Nahiya in which his headquarters happens to be situated.

Qaimaqams and their superior officers are normally assisted by a council of notables, who in Mesopotamia before the British occupation had little or no say in the government of the country.

Most towns with a population of 3,000 or more possess a *Baladiyah* or Municipality to which special revenues are allotted. A Municipal Council is elected for a period of four years by the people, all male householders with a certain property qualification having the right to vote. The Council is elected *en bloc*, and the head of the poll, with the local governor's approval, automatically becomes *Rais Baladiyah*, or

Mayor, for the whole of the four years. The Governor (i.e. Qaimaqam or superior officer) supervises the affairs and checks
the expenditure of the Municipality.

It is unnecessary to explain the judicial system in detail;
besides Criminal and Civil Courts there are the *Shará* Courts
under the *Qazi* who deals with matters affecting marriage,
divorce, inheritance, etc., in accordance with the Shará or religious law. Where the headquarters town of the qaza
possesses only a small population the Qazi is also vested with
a limited criminal and civil jurisdiction.

Besides a Qazi every qaza headquarters possesses a
Mufti, a religious official whose duty it is to issue decrees re-
garding the interpretation of points in the Muhammadan
Canon Law and to announce the commencement of the month
of fast and the two great festivals.

APPENDIX B

SUMMARY OF THE EVENTS IN MESOPOTAMIA FROM THE ARMISTICE TO THE END OF 1920

1918, *Nov., Dec.* – Occupation of Mosul Town and the whole of the Mosul vilayet under the terms of the Armistice. An endeavour is made to form the liwa of Sulaimaniyah plus the districts of Koi, Rania, and Rawanduz into a Kurdish State with Shaikh Mahmud as ruler.

Dair uz Zur on the Euphrates is occupied and administered. (N.B. Under the Turks Dair uz Zur was the headquarters of an independent liwa corresponding direct with Constantinople. It is not part of 'Iraq.)

1919, *April.* – Murder of Captain Pearson, A.P.O. Zakho, by the Goyan tribe.

May – Shaikh Mahmud imprisons all the British in Sulaimaniyah and declares his complete independence.

June – The Sulaimaniyah rising is suppressed and its author captured and deported.

July – Murder of Captain Willey, A.P.O Amadia, and his companions. Punitive action is taken against his assassins and the Goyan tribe.

Nov. – Murder of Mr. Bill, P.O. Mosul, and Captain Scott, A.P.O. Aqra, by the Zibaris and Barzanis. Operations are undertaken against these tribes.

Dec. – Arab raid on Dair uz Zur. Evacuation of the portion of the Dair uz Zur liwa under British occupation. Operations against the Euphrates tribes west of Hit continue for several months.

1920, *Jan.* – Beginning of the Surchi rising. In April the tribe attack Aqra and operations are undertaken against them.

May – Train on the Baghdad–Sharqat line wrecked by Arabs.

June – Raid on Tel Afar and murder of the A.P.O., Major Barlow, and his companions. The town is recovered by military action.

July – Commencement of the great Arab rising on the Euphrates. The Diwaniyah Division and Karbala are evacuated, and Kufa and Samawah, with their Political Officers and garrisons, are invested by the tribes. Hillah is attacked and large portions of the Basra–Baghdad railway are destroyed.

Aug. – The trouble spreads east of the Tigris and Baqubah and Kifri are captured by the tribes. Murder of Lieut.-Colonel Leachman.

Sept. – Order restored east of the Tigris.

Lieut.-Colonel Sir A. T. Wilson, who since 1917 has been acting as Civil Commissioner, leaves Baghdad, and Sir Percy Cox arrives in Mesopotamia as High Commissioner.

Sept. to Dec. – Operations against the Euphrates tribes Kufa and Samawah are relieved and the rising suppressed.

Nov. – An Arab Government is formed in Baghdad.

www.ingramcontent.com/pod-product-compliance
Lightning Source LLC
Chambersburg PA
CBHW062047270326
41931CB00013B/2972